Elvis, Hank, and Me

Horace Logan

WITH Bill Sloan

Elvis, Hank, and Me

Making Musical History on the Louisiana Hayride

ST. MARTIN'S PRESS ※ NEW YORK

Design by Maureen Troy

Library of Congress Cataloging-in-Publication Data

Logan, Horace.
    Elvis, Hank, and me : making musical history on the Louisiana hayride / Horace Logan with Bill Sloan
      p. cm.
    ISBN 0-312-18573-1
    1. Country music — Louisiana — History and criticism.   2. Presley, Elvis, 1935-1977.   3. Williams, Hank, 1923-1953.   4. Logan, Horace. 5. Louisiana hayride (Radio program)   I. Sloan, Bill.   II. Title.
ML3524.L64   1998
781.642'09763 — dc21   98-9795
                                                        CIP
                                                        MN

First Edition: June 1998
10 9 8 7 6 5 4 3 2 1

Contents

Foreword

The Louisiana Hayride holds a special place in the history of American popular music. It also holds a special place in my heart. I was born in Shreveport while my daddy and the Hayride were helping each other gain national prominence.

When it first started out in the spring of 1948, nobody expected the *Hayride* to be anything more than just another Saturday night country music show, like any number of others across the southern United States. But it turned out to be a whole lot more. Between the late forties and the late fifties, it became an innovative force that changed the style and sound of country music and its impact on the American listening public.

The *Hayride* was a star maker. It built hundreds of careers in country music—more than any other show of its kind. All told, it produced about two dozen of the century's premier country music artists. My daddy was the first of these, but there were many more to follow: Webb Pierce, Slim Whitman, Jim Reeves, Johnny Horton, Faron Young, Floyd Cramer, Kitty Wells, Johnny Cash, George Jones, and others. Even Elvis Presley used the *Hayride* stage in Shreveport's Municipal Auditorium as his launching pad to musical immortality.

At the same time, the show provided steady work for lots of people who never became major stars but who wanted the opportunity to make a living doing what they loved best—playing music.

The *Hayride* never displaced the *Grand Ole Opry* as the "promised land of country music," and the majority of stars developed on the *Hayride* moved on to Nashville within a relatively short time. But if the *Opry* was the promised land, the *Hayride* was heaven's gate. It never saw itself as a mere stepping-stone to the *Opry*, or advertised itself that way. It had its own role and it played that role proudly and with class. It had a fun-loving spirit and was never afraid to try something different.

It more than earned its title as "The Cradle of the Stars."

The *Hayride* also did a lot to refine and redefine what was then called "hillbilly" music and make it a respected part of America's musical culture. It helped make it possible for country artists like my daddy to break out of the narrow "hillbilly" category and cross over into the mainstream of popular music.

I'm personally grateful for the opportunity the *Hayride* gave my daddy. And if he changed the *Hayride*, it changed him, too. The Shreveport days represented a fresh start for him, and he did some of his best and most creative work in the ten months he was there before moving on to the *Opry*. In a sense, though, he never really left. In his farewell *Hayride* performance, he told his friends in Louisiana he'd be back, and sure enough, three years later, he did return.

As producer of the *Hayride*, Horace "Hoss" Logan was the "big daddy" of all the stars who played there. But he was more than just the boss—more even than the guy who made the final decision on who went on the show and who didn't. He was also a good friend to many of his performers, my daddy included, and he never stood in the way of an artist's success or tried to hold somebody back for selfish reasons.

Horace's book on the *Louisiana Hayride* is long overdue, and it brings the old show back to life. It's an important addition to the musical history of America. The *Hayride* was a fast-moving stream that fed the big river of country music. It lives on in the music of the people who played there and in the hearts of the folks who listened and yelled for more.

This book will help keep the legend alive for generations to come. My daddy would've loved it. Thanks, Hoss!

—HANK WILLIAMS JR.

Introduction

When I was first invited to appear on the <u>Louisiana Hayride</u>, very few people outside the Memphis, Tennessee, area had ever heard of Johnny Cash, much less heard me sing. I'll never forget how excited I was as I stepped up to the microphone on the stage of Shreveport's Municipal Auditorium that Saturday night in 1955. Besides the live audience of thirty-eight hundred people out beyond the footlights, I knew that thousands of radio listeners across the whole country were about to hear my voice for the first time.

It made this old Arkansas farmboy mighty nervous, I can tell you. The biggest audience I'd played for up to then had been maybe two or three hundred folks, and the idea of performing for so many people all at once filled my stomach with butterflies.

But when I finished my first number and heard the cheers and applause from the crowd out front, it made those butterflies go away and gave me the greatest feeling anybody could imagine. I've had many unforgettable moments in my career since then, but that first night on the *Louisiana Hayride* has always been in a class by itself.

The man responsible for giving me my big chance that night was Horace Logan, the *Hayride's* producer. He invited me to sing on the *Hayride*—which ran a close second to the *Grand Ole Opry* in those days as America's favorite country music radio show—at a time when I probably couldn't have gotten a shot at a national audience anywhere else.

Just a few months earlier, I'd finally talked Sam Phillips at Sun Records into recording and releasing a couple of my songs. That first single—with "Hey Porter" on one side and "Cry, Cry, Cry" on the other—had sold fairly well in Memphis. But the rest of the country didn't know me from Adam, and I'd never done but a handful of public appearances when Hoss Logan heard my record and put me on the *Hayride*. At the time, I still had to work a Monday-through-Friday job as a door-to-door salesman to feed my family.

But Hoss and the *Hayride* had made stars out of long shots and unknowns before—not once but lots of times. And when he gave me a job as a regular member of the cast, it changed my life forever. The nationwide exposure I got on the *Hayride*, via the CBS Radio Network, was the key factor in making my early records successful. Within a year, my name and voice were familiar to country music fans from coast to coast. The *Hayride* gave me the boost every successful recording artist has to have, just as it had with Hank Williams, Kitty Wells, Webb Pierce, Faron Young, Slim Whitman, Jim Reeves, and Elvis Presley before me.

The *Hayride* was also a place where I made some of the deepest, most meaningful friendships of my life—with Elvis, Johnny Horton, Merle Kilgore, and many others. One of the longest-lasting friendships that grew out of those days was with Hoss Logan.

I've waited almost forty years for the chance to mention these things about Hoss and the *Louisiana Hayride* and say how much they meant to a struggling young singer named Johnny Cash.

Actually, I did express my gratitude publicly once before. It was in an ad I ran in *Billboard* magazine after my final appearance on the *Hayride*, in which I thanked Hoss and the show for all they'd done to further my career. But that message was aimed primarily at my fellow show business professionals. Now I finally have an opportunity to express my appreciation in a permanent way to everybody who loves country music.

If that includes you, this is your kind of book. If you're a country music fan, I don't think you'll read a more fascinating book this year. *Elvis, Hank and Me* is the complete inside story of the *Hayride* and the people who made it what it was—as only the man who created and produced the *Hayride* could capture it.

If you weren't fortunate enough to be at the *Hayride* in person like I was, this book is the next best thing. And if you *were* there, you'll like it even more.

—JOHNNY CASH

The Shy Kid
From
Memphis

When the phone rang at my house that fall afternoon, I was tempted at first not to answer it. It was a little past lunchtime on Saturday, October 9, 1954 — still three or four hours before I had to report to the Municipal Auditorium near downtown Shreveport to get ready for that week's edition of the Louisiana Hayride — and I was trying to relax.

I was program director for radio station KWKH, one of a handful of powerful 50,000-watt broadcasting "giants" scattered across the southern United States. I was also the *Hayride*'s producer, emcee, talent boss, and chief architect. From the time the show went on the air at 8 P.M. until long after it signed off at midnight, it would demand my undivided attention and every ounce of energy I could muster. But right now I was enjoying some quiet time at home with my family, and the last thing I wanted to do was get stuck in some long-winded telephone conversation.

Finally, though, I picked up the receiver, muttered a not-too-friendly "Hello" into the mouthpiece, and heard a husky male voice coming back to me over the line.

I recognized the voice immediately. It was the kid from Memphis, the one who was scheduled to make his first appearance on the *Hayride* that night. He sounded nervous as hell.

"I-I sure hate to bother you, Mr. Logan," he said hesitantly, "but we just got to town, and I was wonderin' if maybe there was some way me and the boys could get into the auditorium early. I'd like to get a feel for the place, you know. I mean before everybody gets there."

It was an unusual request—one I rarely heard from a first-time performer. The last time I could remember anybody insisting on an advance visit to the auditorium had been several years earlier when Gene Autry was doing a guest appearance on the *Hayride* and wanted to let his horse, Champion, get familiar with the place before he was brought out on the stage during the show.

"Well, right now it's just a big old empty building, son," I told him. "There's really nothing very unusual about it." I was half hoping I could talk him out of the idea, but his next words made me realize that was a lost cause.

"Yes, sir," he said, "but I never . . . I mean, me and the boys ain't used to playin' for this many folks at one time, and I'd feel a lot better if we could just kinda check things out ahead of time."

I smiled in spite of myself. The auditorium seated thirty-eight hundred people, and our show usually came close to filling the place. In addition, countless thousands of other listeners in Louisiana, Arkansas, Texas, and other states would be tuned into the show on KWKH. When you were accustomed to playing in front of cozy crowds of a couple of hundred, the *Hayride* atmosphere could be pretty awesome. Consequently, in nearly six and a half years of overseeing the show—and watching it develop a national audience on the CBS Radio Network and grow into one of America's most popular country music shows—I'd soothed the stage fright of dozens of young singers and musicians. By this time, I'd spent over twenty years in radio and show business, but I also hadn't forgotten the butterflies that fluttered in my own stomach when I was starting out.

The kid and his two sidemen had to be dead tired after their six-hour drive from Memphis. If they'd been more seasoned performers, they probably would've checked into a motel and gotten some rest instead of worrying about the auditorium. But I could tell the kid was too keyed up to rest anywhere. Besides, until they got paid for the show tonight, I doubted if the three of them put together could scrape up enough money for a room at the cheapest dump in Bossier City.

"Okay," I said, "I understand. The auditorium's on the edge of downtown and just off Texas Street, which is the same thing as Highway 80, the road you drove in on. I'll bring my key and meet you down there in about twenty minutes."

"Thanks, Mr. Logan," the kid said. "I sure appreciate it."

When I drove up, the three young guys were waiting for me in an old faded blue sedan—a Plymouth, to the best of my recollection—with the doors hanging open and the radio playing. I didn't have any trouble picking out the leader of the group. He was also clearly the youngest of the three. He'd told me he was nineteen. The other guys looked to be in their early to middle twenties.

The kid was sitting in the front seat on the passenger side of the car. I later learned that his sidemen rarely let him drive, especially on long trips; they said they couldn't relax when he was behind the steering wheel. His baby face made him look even younger than his years. He wore white pants, a pink shirt, bushy sideburns, slicked-back hair, and an uneasy smile. I was surprised at how boyish and clean-cut he was, considering what I'd heard of his music. A couple of weeks earlier, when my friend Tillman Franks, a local freelance talent manager, had first given me one of the kid's records, I'd had to ask a pointed question: "Is this a black boy or a white boy, Tillman? I can't tell."

"Oh, he's white, all right," Franks had assured me. "He's just got a different sound, that's all."

The sound *was* different—different from anything I'd ever heard before—and I was relieved to learn the kid was white. He had the distinctiveness of style and sound that we were always looking for on the *Hayride*. There was something more, too—something wild and contagious about his music. But in spite of all that, I don't think I would've dared put him on if he was black. After all, this was the Deep South in the mid-1950s, and I didn't think the region's country music fans were quite ready for a black performer.

"So you're the Hillbilly Cat from Memphis," I said, sticking out my hand. "I'm Horace Logan. Most everybody calls me Hoss."

"Pleasure to meet you, sir. Thanks for havin' us on the show."

He clearly wasn't comfortable with first-name familiarity—in fact, he didn't seem comfortable about much of anything—and I was struck by how polite he was. Most young people were polite in those days, but politeness was deeply ingrained in this kid. I knew right away he'd had "good manners" and "respect for his elders" drummed into his head by someone, probably his mother, from the time he was in diapers.

"We're much obliged to you for lettin' us mess up your Saturday afternoon, Mr. Logan," he said as we shook hands. Then he turned to the two other young men lounging against the side of the car. "This here's Scotty Moore and Bill Black. Scotty plays the guitar and Bill handles the bass."

After the two sidemen and I exchanged handshakes, they got their instruments out of the car and I led them around to the back door of the auditorium and unlocked it. Scotty had a pretty nice looking guitar, but Bill's bass was old and battered. The kid's guitar was undersized like—well, like a *kid's* guitar.

"The place is all yours for the next couple of hours," I told them, "so make yourselves at home."

As show time approached and other performers and staff people started drifting in, you could see the tension mounting in the kid. He didn't seem able to stand still for more than a minute or two. He alternated between pacing the length and breadth of the Municipal Auditorium, pausing to tune his guitar, and whispering and laughing with his sidemen.

I left them there for a while to get acquainted with the place on their own. When I came back, the kid approached me and asked shyly, "What do you think I ought to do tonight, Mr. Logan?"

I shrugged. "Just do whatever you do best," I said. "Just be yourself."

"Well, I think my best song's the one called 'That's All Right, Mama.' You heard it on my record. You think it'll be okay?"

"Sure, if that's the one you want to do."

"And I only get to do one song on the part of the show that's bein' taped for the CBS network, right?"

"That's right," I said. We limited everybody to just one number on the CBS segment because we wanted to showcase as many artists as we could. "Later on, you can do a couple of numbers for our live audience — or more if you get an encore."

I explained again to him about the system we followed on the *Hayride.* If the audience applauded loudly enough after an artist finished his two numbers on the later segments, he could come back for one or more encores. The artists who encored regularly were obviously the audience's favorites, and they were the ones we tried to sign to long-term contracts with the show. The ones who didn't encore usually moved on after a short time.

I also made sure he understood the way our payment system worked. Our performers were paid union scale — eighteen dollars per Saturday night for a soloist, twelve dollars for backup musicians like Scotty and Bill, and twenty-four dollars for a bandleader with at least five musicians in his group. This sounds like pocket change today, but back in the fall of fifty-four, many young guys were putting in a week's worth of long hours and hard physical labor for wages of thirty to thirty-five dollars or even less, so it wasn't bad pay for three or four hours' work.

"Sounds good to me," the kid said. "I can buy lots of hamburgers for eighteen bucks. And if I get a contract I'll get that much every week, right?"

"That's the way it works," I said. "And you'll have the other six nights a week free to sing wherever you want to."

"You think my music's gonna fit in on the *Hayride,* Mr. Logan?" The uneasiness was back in his voice again.

My response was the same one I'd given to at least half a hundred other aspiring young artists over the years: "Sure, son, you'll do just fine."

I wanted to cross my fingers as I said it, but I didn't. The truth was, a lot of regular *Hayride* fans weren't going to know what to make of this kid's music, and some were probably even going to hate it. It clearly wasn't the kind of "pure country" our audiences were used to, but I was willing to take a gamble on the kid because his style was so striking and unusual.

I knew one reason why the kid was so tense and worried right now. News traveled fast in our business, even in those days, and I'd heard how, just a week ago, the kid had gone to Nashville to audition for the *Grand Ole Opry,* and it had turned into a real disaster—one of the worst experiences of his life. He hadn't been allowed on the portion of the *Opry* that was broadcast every week on the NBC Radio Network, and by the time he'd finally gotten onstage it was the tag end of the evening, so much of the crowd at the Ryman Auditorium had already left. The kid had gone ahead and sung his two allotted songs, but the crowd had just sat there, and Jim Denny, the producer of the *Opry,* had ridiculed his music and made him feel like a fool.

"If I were you," Denny had told him, "I'd just go back to driving a truck and forget about trying to be a singer!"

Understandably, the kid was crushed. For two years, he'd been pounding the pavement, bucking the establishment, trying to get somebody to listen to him, and hoping to sing his way out of the housing projects where his parents lived. But except for one record on a label almost nobody ever heard of and a few hundred young fans in Memphis, he didn't have a cotton-picking thing to show for it. Now he'd seen his biggest chance yet go down the drain. He was deeply disappointed and depressed. Even worse, he was also angry and humiliated.

"He cried all the way back to Memphis," Scotty Moore told me at one point that afternoon while the kid was prowling around the auditorium out of earshot. "If he doesn't do better here, he just might take Denny's advice and forget the whole thing."

A little later, I listened while the kid and his two sidemen ran through the song they planned to do for the CBS taping. I'd liked it on the record, but it sounded even better in person. There was a quality to the kid's voice that was hard to describe. It had a current of electricity flowing through it, and it grabbed at your emotions.

For two weeks, I'd had a strong feeling about this kid and his music. I'd gotten pretty good at predicting which artists would be warmly received by our audience, but what I was feeling now was more than that. It was an intuitive sensation that I'd never felt this strongly more than a few times in my whole life. On an August night in 1948, I'd had almost the same feeling about another un-known singer — a young man named Hank Williams — as he walked out onto the *Hayride* stage for the first time. Tonight the feeling may have been even more overwhelming, if that were possible.

"I want to do something to make my mama proud of me, Mr. Logan," the kid confided during a break. "I sure hope I'll make her proud tonight."

"I've got a feeling you will, son," I said.

At two minutes until eight o'clock, there were close to thirty-five hundred eager, restless people packed into the auditorium as I started warming them up for a typically uproarious opening to the network portion of our show.

I asked how many people were there from Arkansas and drew a burst of cheers from the Arkansans in attendance. I asked the same question about Louisiana and got an even louder response. Then, with the second hand on my watch only a few ticks from the hour and the entire cast of tonight's show massed along the front of the stage to my right and left, I shouted a question that I knew from long experience would cause a thunderous explosion of sound.

Since we were only thirty miles from the "hillbilly havens" just across the state line in East Texas, there were always hundreds of Texans in the audience, and they always enjoyed making noise.

"And how many people are here from the great state of Texas?" I yelled.

The answering outburst made the old auditorium's rafters ring, just as one of our staff bands swung into the *Hayride* theme song:

> *Come along, ever'body, come along,*
> *Come while the moon is shinin' bright.*
> *We're gonna have a wonderful time*
> *At the* Louisiana Hayride *tonight!*

The CBS portion of the show would be broadcast live over KWKH but also taped for delayed broadcast the following Saturday night over nearly two hundred CBS stations from coast to coast, and during this half-hour, things moved fast, as always.

There was just enough time on the network segment for six numbers, and I'd placed the kid near the middle of that night's lineup. We always led off with a strong act, like the Browns or Red Sovine, and closed with one of our top stars, like Slim Whitman or Johnny Horton, the "Singing Fisherman"—all of whom had risen from obscurity to national prominence on the *Hayride*. The kid wasn't big enough for that yet, but I had a feeling it wouldn't take him long to get there.

Soon it was the kid's turn. I could plainly see his knees shaking as he stepped to the microphone. He was still wearing the same white trousers and pink shirt he'd had on when I first saw him that afternoon. The only thing he'd added was a sportcoat that was neat and clean but somehow looked secondhand. I knew he was scared to death, and I wanted to say something reassuring to him, but there wasn't time.

Instead, I leaned toward my own microphone and spoke the following words: "Ladies and gentlemen, you've never heard of this young man before, but one day you'll be able to tell your children and grandchildren you heard musical history made tonight."

I smiled and held out my hand toward the shy kid from Memphis as polite welcoming applause swelled up in the auditorium.

I had just introduced Elvis Presley to America.

2

Birth of an Entertainment Legend

Elvis changed everything. He changed the way popular music sounded, the way it looked, the way it acted — everything about it. I don't mean just country music or rock music, but all popular music, and not just in the United States, but all around the globe. It lit the fuse for the most meteoric rise to stardom in the annals of show business. It happened with such amazing speed that even those of us who witnessed it at close range still have a hard time believing it. And it all started that October night in 1954 when the Louisiana Hayride gave Elvis his first chance to sing for a nationwide audience.

Elvis wasn't the first performer to soar to sudden stardom from the stage of the *Louisiana Hayride,* and he wouldn't be the last. But his dramatic ascent to the pinnacle of the entertainment world over the next eighteen months unquestionably brought the *Hayride* its greatest moments of glory. For me, it was a breathtaking, almost magical experience — one I'll cherish as long as I live.

Surely, one of the most incredible parts of the Elvis phenomenon was where it all started — not in New York, Hollywood, Las Vegas, or even Nashville. It happened in a small, fairly obscure southern city that no one had ever accused of being a capital of the entertainment industry. Today's Shreveport has a population of more than two hundred thousand and its economy got a recent shot in the arm when gambling was legalized in Louisiana and new casinos, hotels, and related businesses started moving in. But in the

Hayride's heyday, it was a quiet, comfortable, slow-paced community a little more than half that size. It was a town with no particular destination in mind and in no great hurry to get there.

But Shreveport did have one asset that many other cities its size lacked. It had a clear-channel 50,000-watt radio station that could be heard at night all the way to the Pacific Ocean. Owned by the same wealthy family that owned two of Louisiana's largest daily newspapers, the *Shreveport Times* and the *Monroe Morning World,* KWKH was one of only two 50,000-watt stations in the whole state (the other being WWL in New Orleans), and even weaker radio stations weren't all that plentiful. Right after World War II, there were only about nine hundred radio stations in the whole country (as compared to more than twelve thousand today), and only a few dozen had an operating capacity of 50,000 watts.

Television was just getting started in those days, and the major radio networks — CBS, NBC, ABC, and Mutual — still claimed a huge national audience. As the area's only CBS affiliate, KWKH was the dominant radio voice in the "Ark-La-Tex," a growing region encompassing northeast Texas, northwest Louisiana, and southwest Arkansas.

If it hadn't been for the presence in Shreveport of this powerful electronic link with the rest of the nation, I almost certainly wouldn't have been able to become one of the youngest major-station radio announcers in America's history, or rub shoulders with some of the greatest entertainers of all time, or enjoy a show business career spanning more than half a century.

And, of course, I would never have had the opportunity to know Elvis, Hank Williams, Johnny Cash, Johnny Horton, Jim Reeves, or any of the other two dozen rising young artists I was able to help along the road to stardom — much less to form deep, lasting friendships with many of them, as I did.

On the contrary, if my early employment experiences are any indication, I might well have ended up spending my life selling root beer or delivering ice door-to-door.

I'm forever grateful that it didn't work out that way.

Birth of an Entertainment Legend

I was ten years old when my parents separated and I moved with my mother and brother Bobby from Monroe, Louisiana, to Shreveport. We rented a small house and I enrolled in the fifth grade at Creswell Elementary School. The Great Depression was still a year or so away, but times were far from easy for a woman trying to make it on her own with two small sons, and not long after my eleventh birthday, I had to go to work part-time to help us make ends meet.

My first job was at the Triple X Root Beer stand on King's Highway, where I went each afternoon straight from school. I worked a full eight-hour shift from 4 P.M. until midnight and earned fifty cents a day plus tips. There weren't many of those. If customers left a few pennies on their tray, it was a cause for celebration. People didn't believe in throwing money around in those days.

It took me months and months to save up enough to buy a bicycle to ride to work. In the meantime, there was nothing to do but walk the five or six miles back and forth every day.

By the time I enrolled at Byrd High School, the depression was at its worst point. The economy had hit rock-bottom, and we were having a tougher and tougher time surviving. After my second year at Byrd, I had to drop out of school and try to make more money. I got a job with an ice company, working on a truck and delivering fifty-pound blocks of ice to homes and businesses. It was back-breaking labor, but at least it helped me stay cool in the summer.

After a year, I managed to go back to school but continued working part-time at the ice company. Up until then, I'd been a fairly nonassertive sort of youngster, one who didn't much like calling attention to himself and who would just as soon leave the limelight to others. But a series of events that were definitely not of my own making were about to change all that and lead me, indirectly, into a life on stage in front of a microphone.

The first thing that happened was that a friend of mine "volunteered" me to try out for the position of drum major with our high

{ 11 }

school band. This friend made up a cock-and-bull story about how much "experience" I had at this sort of thing, and almost before I realized what was happening, I was picked for the most high-profile assignment of my young life. Suddenly, I was expected to put on one of those tall, fluffy hats, fling a baton into the air and lead the band as it marched up and down the field during halftime ceremonies at football games.

In reality, my only experience consisted of living next door to the drum major from Centenary College and watching him practice occasionally. The truth was, I'd never had a baton in my hand in my life, much less ever performed in public, and when I found out I was the new drum major, I was scared to death.

I practiced frantically during the few days I had before I had to go out and make a spectacle of myself, and I made a little progress, but it wasn't nearly enough. The only thing that saved me from total panic on the day of the first game was that my friend snitched a bottle of homemade wine from his parents' house and he and I hid under the bleachers and drank the whole thing. I was half drunk and staggering slightly when I started marching, but I somehow managed to keep the baton in the air the full length of the field, and everybody thought I did okay.

I've never been much of a drinker, and I've never repeated that experience. And I definitely don't recommend that anyone look for courage inside a bottle of booze. But I've thought back on that long-ago episode hundreds of times, and it's helped me realize how some entertainers can let themselves become so dependent on alcohol or drugs that they can't perform sober. That memory made me a more tolerant person on those countless nights when I had to roust out some of my artists from the beer joint across from the Municipal Auditorium, where they'd gone between performances to "sharpen their skills" with a few drinks.

After a lot of hard, time-consuming work, I finally did become a pretty good drum major. I did so well at it, in fact, that when I eventually graduated from high school, I succeeded my next-door neighbor as drum major for Centenary College — and that was one of the most enjoyable, exciting adventures of my life.

Centenary was and still is a small, four-year Methodist school located on the south side of Shreveport. It had an enrollment of only about six hundred students at that time, but the year I served as drum major for the college band, our football team, the Centenary Gentlemen, went undefeated against some of the top teams in the nation. As unbelievable as it seems — especially with only seventeen players in uniform — we played such powerhouses as Arkansas, Texas A&M, LSU, Tulane, Rice, Ole Miss, Baylor, and SMU, and we beat every one of them.

It was a real thrill to be there to see that happen, but it was something more than just a thrill. It made me realize that you don't necessarily have to be the biggest to be the best, and that a modest beginning doesn't mean you can't make it to the top.

But actually, I'm getting a little ahead of myself. I was still in high school when I stumbled into an announcing job at KWKH. As it turned out, it was the biggest turning point in my life, one that thrust me into a broadcasting career and allowed me to escape from the ice truck forever. It was also a pure accident. Or maybe "quirk of fate" would be a better term.

Another high school friend of mine, Bernard Segal, had heard about a contest being sponsored by the radio station and a local coffee company to select a young man from the Shreveport area to take over a new position on the KWKH announcing staff. The job paid fifteen dollars a week. That was a very attractive salary in those deep depression days, particularly for someone still in his teens, so it was quite a prize. Bernard was determined to take a shot at it, and the day he was scheduled for his tryout, he asked me to go along, strictly for moral support.

Bernard was one of five contestants, and just before the contest started, one of the other boys suddenly became ill. I think it was probably just a bad case of stage fright, but when the guy started throwing up and his face turned a pale shade of green, it was obvious he wasn't able to go on.

I was just sitting there, minding my own business and waiting for Bernard to get through, when some station officials came out and grabbed me.

"We've got to have a fifth contestant in order to pick a winner," they said, "and since you're the only person around, you're it."

I shrugged and went with them. I didn't have a bottle of wine to fortify me this time, but I figured talking into a microphone in front of a handful of people couldn't possibly be as scary as twirling a baton and leading a band in front of a stadium filled with football fans. I read an announcement about "Half Past Seven Coffee," and listeners sent in their votes.

I couldn't believe it when I actually won. I kept pinching myself to make sure I wasn't dreaming. At the tender age of sixteen, I was an announcer for a major radio station—certainly one of the youngest individuals in the whole country to hold such an impressive job. And just as important at the moment, I was actually going to be paid a living wage. The year was 1932, and Franklin Roosevelt was about to tell Americans that "the only thing we have to fear is fear itself."

I decided maybe FDR was right.

I enjoyed radio from the very beginning, but my job was definitely no picnic. The broadcast day began at 5 A.M. Monday through Saturday on the theory that our rural listeners out on the farms liked to tune in early. As the junior member of the staff, I got the "honor" of being the sign-on announcer seven days a week. But I got a break on Sunday, when we didn't go on the air until 6 A.M.. That extra hour almost made me feel like I was on vacation.

Nobody complained about working seven days a week back then. People felt so lucky to have a job that they would've worked eight days a week if that had been possible.

For several years, I managed to hold down my announcing job and continue in school. I'm not sure when I slept, but somehow I got by. Finally, after a year at Centenary College, I left school for good and went into broadcasting full-time. It was a decision I made with some regret, but I was soon promoted to chief announcer and that made me feel better.

I also did newscasts and worked extensively with the station's news department. In March 1937, I was one of the first newsmen to reach the scene when a gas leak caused a horrifying explosion at a crowded schoolhouse in the small town of New London, Texas. It was the worst school-related disaster in the nation's history. More than two hundred persons, most of them children, were killed.

The KWKH studios were just across the street from the Shreveport office of a major oil company, which was notified of the explosion almost instantly by personnel at the oil company installation located adjacent to the New London school. Within minutes, the station learned what had happened, and Jack Jones, the studio engineer, and I were on our way to New London.

When we got there, we paid the owner of a house near the school a hundred dollars for exclusive use of her telephone for the next couple of days and ran a line to where I was setting up to do my broadcasts. For several hours, I was the only radio reporter at the scene. Because of this, I was the first broadcaster in America — at least as far as I know — to be carried live by all three major radio networks (CBS, NBC, and Mutual) simultaneously.

About a year before the New London disaster, the management of KWKH first began to discuss the idea of starting a regular Saturday night country music show. It wasn't an original idea — far from it. The *Grand Ole Opry* had made its debut on WSM in Nashville in 1927 and had already been a Saturday night fixture on NBC for nearly a decade. The *National Barn Dance,* which originated from WLS in Chicago, was also heard across the nation on network radio.

Meanwhile, several other stations had already followed the *Opry*'s lead and established Saturday night shows of their own, so our idea for a show at KWKH was just a natural reaction to a national trend. Country music was the lifeblood of most radio stations in the South and Southwest, and virtually every station of any

size in the region had several fifteen-minute morning shows featuring live country bands and singers. KWKH was no exception,
and the performers on these morning shows provided the station
with a nucleus of talent to build a show around.

We named our show the *KWKH Saturday Night Roundup,* and it
went on the air in late 1936. It drew a good audience and was reasonably successful, but to be perfectly honest, it was also very ordinary. The talent was good for the most part, but it was never
great. We had occasional guest artists, but we didn't have the budget to bring in the few really big-name stars of country music at the
time, and we didn't have much luck developing our homegrown
artists beyond the local or regional level. There weren't a lot of
touring groups in those days. Traveling across country by car was
still slow and uncomfortable, and most performers were too broke
to venture very far from home anyway.

Some of our regulars on the *Saturday Night Roundup* included
Bob and Joe Shelton, who called themselves The Sunshine Boys; a
female quartet known as the Arizona Ranch Girls; Hoke and Paul
Rice, and the Mercer Brothers. The show was on the air for three
hours, 8 to 11 P.M., and was presented in the Municipal Auditorium, just as the *Hayride* would be later.

I was the only master of ceremonies the *Saturday Night Roundup*
ever had. B. G. Robertson was the producer, and for five years, I em-
ceed every minute of the show. I enjoyed it, but by mid-1941,
preparations for World War II were already putting a serious dent
in our talent pool, as more and more young men reported for the
military draft. Even before the Japanese attack on Pearl Harbor, it
was apparent that the show would have to be shut down because
so many of our musicians were trading their guitars for army rifles.

Early in 1942, I received my own induction notice — although as
a married man with a young son, I was supposedly exempt from the
draft — and I reported for active duty. When I came home on leave
a few months later as a staff sergeant in the United States Army, I
remember picking up a copy of the *Shreveport Times* and reading a

headline that said, "Fathers May Be Drafted Soon, Selective Service Says."

I had news for the Selective Service. At least one father had already been drafted.

I didn't really mind my three-and-a-half-year stint in army ordnance, though. I knew that every able-bodied man was needed in the war effort, and my military service provided me with some memorable experiences. It also enabled me to learn a great deal about guns of all kinds — knowledge that I'd put to much practical use in later life.

After a year and a half as an enlisted man, I enrolled in officer candidate school and emerged as a second lieutenant. I tested weapons at Aberdeen Proving Ground and made a total of thirteen trips overseas during the war — to North Africa, Anzio, England, France, and elsewhere — collecting and studying captured enemy weapons and looking for ways to convert them to our own use. I discovered that the Germans, in particular, were far ahead of us in some types of weapons development. The bazooka, for example, named for an outlandish musical instrument played by a popular Arkansas entertainer named Bob Burns, originated in Germany, but it was "adopted" by the U.S. Army, and our troops were armed with bazookas by the thousands by the end of the war.

After being discharged as a first lieutenant, I came home to Shreveport in late 1945. There was a job waiting for me at KWKH, but I decided I wanted to try my hand at something outside of broadcasting, at least for a while. I used some of the skills I'd learned in the Army and opened a gun repair shop, along with a partner. The shop did well, but radio was still in my blood, and when I got an offer, early in 1947, to return to KWKH as program director, I laid my guns aside and went back to my first love. When I accepted the offer, the idea of reestablishing a Saturday night country music show was already kicking around in my head.

I was convinced that the timing and atmosphere were perfect for such a venture. The dark days of the Depression and the anxiety of

World War II were behind us now. For the first time in a long time, people were feeling really optimistic. They were in the mood to celebrate and in a hurry to make up for lost time. They wanted to be entertained and have fun, and they were willing to pay for it. People were buying new cars as fast as the assembly lines in Detroit could crank them out, and gasoline was plentiful again, so I felt certain that country music fans from miles around would flock to Shreveport for a good time on Saturday night.

The more I thought about it, the more excited I got about producing a major new musical variety show. With the right kind of package, we might even be able to interest one of the networks in picking up the show and running it in a prime-time slot. But for a new show to succeed in the environment of the late forties, it would have to be more than just good. It would have to be fresh, fast-paced, and different. It would have to have a variety of outstanding talent.

In other words, it would have to be something truly special.

Directing bands as a drum major and my several years working with musicians as the announcer for the *Saturday Night Roundup* had helped me develop an acute sense of what was good and what was only average. I started campaigning for the new show a few weeks after I officially assumed my duties as program director. But I encountered more resistance than I'd expected.

The problem — as was often the case with the ownership and management of KWKH — was a matter of money. The station was owned by John Ewing, whose family holdings included three daily newspapers and another 50,000-watt station in Hot Springs, Arkansas. The Ewings had made a fortune in the media business, but John was never interested in investing a dollar in anything unless he believed he could make at least two dollars in return. He didn't give a damn about setting trends or capturing national attention or developing fine, young talent. His main concern was the bottom line, and his annual goal was seeing each of his properties produce a bigger profit this year than it had last year.

Ewing didn't take a direct hand in managing his newspapers or radio stations, but he made sure the people he put in charge understood his rules about making and spending money—even if some of them didn't know diddly about the business they were supposed to be running. Unfortunately, the newly hired station manager at KWKH fit this description to a T.

The station manager was a young navy veteran named Henry Clay (no relation to the famous nineteenth-century lawmaker, as far as I know), and he was a reasonably bright, reasonably personable young man. But Henry's total radio experience consisted of three months as an advertising salesman for a small station in Muscle Shoals, Alabama. His sole qualification for his new job was the fact that he had recently married John Ewing's daughter. That made him part of the family and entitled him to a position befitting his exalted new status.

Fortunately for Clay, he had some capable people on the staff, because whatever he eventually discovered about running a radio station would be through a slow and sometimes painful on-the-job learning process.

Henry did understand one important thing going in, though. He knew he was expected to keep a tight rein on the station's purse strings. Sometimes I got the feeling he'd made up his mind to be even more tightfisted than John Ewing himself. But if I ever expected to get the new country music show off the ground, Clay was the man I was going to have to convince.

"I like the idea, but it sounds like we could be getting into some pretty heavy expenses there," Henry said. "Let me think about it."

Several months passed while Henry thought. Finally, one day in the fall of 1947, he called me into his office and told me he'd come up with a plan. What we were going to have to do, he said, was put the show together without any start-up investment by the station.

"Instead of putting up a bunch of money out front and risking losing a bunch more if we draw bad audiences," he said, "everybody who participates in the show will get shares in it and receive a percentage of the profits—if there *are* any."

I raised an eyebrow and smiled wryly. "And who's supposed

to talk our morning performers into going for this deal?" I asked.

Henry smiled back at me. "You're the program director, and you're going to be producer of the show — if there is a show — so I guess that's your job. Look, it's simple. Each soloist, bandleader, and announcer gets two shares apiece, and each sideman gets one share. We deduct expenses from the gate receipts after each performance and divide up what's left among the shareholders. What could be fairer?"

I was pretty sure I could persuade most of our morning performers to go along with Henry's idea. But I also knew that this type of arrangement wasn't going to work for very long — not if we wanted to attract the kind of talent I was hoping for. But I told myself that once the show was on the air and sustaining itself financially, I could probably talk Henry into a more secure payment plan for performers.

"I'll see what I can do," I said.

It took me until late January 1948 to get all our regular performers to agree to Henry's terms, and once that was accomplished, planning for the new show hit full stride.

It's worth noting, by the way, that I was right about the share setup being extremely short-lived. From the very first show, the *Hayride* drew impressive crowds to the Municipal Auditorium and became instantly profitable — so much so that Clay soon decided it would be much more to the station's advantage to pay straight union scale to all the performers and keep the profits from gate receipts "in the family." Within a few weeks after the *Hayride*'s birth, the share system was permanently scrapped.

Despite his penny-pinching and the maddeningly slow pace at which he sometimes moved, Henry developed an increasingly active interest in the idea of such a show as the weeks passed, which was gratifying and reassuring to me. In taking on a project of this size, it was always nice to have the boss on your side.

Henry didn't know his butt from a bass fiddle about country music, but his level of interest really picked up after he talked to some people at CBS about the possibility of getting the show on the network and received an encouraging response. Various officials at CBS could see possibilities in offering their affiliates a network Saturday night country music show to compete with the *Opry* on rival NBC. CBS stations in the North and East might not get overly excited about this kind of show, but we felt many in the South and Southwest — even some in the Far West — would react positively.

"Well, if we're going to be on CBS," I said, "we're going to have to come up with a whole lot better name than the *KWKH Saturday Night Roundup*. You have any suggestions?"

"That's your department," Henry said. "I'm sure you'll think of something. Just make it good."

I spent the next week or two wracking my brain in search of a name that would be descriptive and appealing to listeners. Whatever name we eventually used needed to say something both about our state and about country music. It also needed to project a feeling of casual fun and excitement. Whenever I thought of a potential name, I scribbled it down on a piece of paper. Before long, I had compiled a list of six or eight possibilities.

The one I liked most was *Louisiana Hayride*.

It seemed to say everything that needed to be said in two words, and it had a nice ring to it. The only big problem was that it wasn't original. As a matter of fact, it had been used several times in the past. There was, for example, a book about Huey P. Long, the late, flamboyant governor of Louisiana, entitled *Louisiana Hayride*. (I happen to own a copy of it autographed by its author, Harnett Kane.) There had also been a Broadway production by the same name.

There were no legal restrictions, however, on "borrowing" the name for a radio show, so that's exactly what we ended up doing. In early 1948, we made the first official use of *Louisiana Hayride* as our show title in a series of promotional articles in *Billboard, Cashbox,* and other music industry publications, outlining our plans for the show and announcing a search for talent.

Within a few days, we started receiving reel-to-reel tapes by the dozens from all over the United States. It was my job to listen to them, then try to decide which ones among this conglomeration of artists and would-be artists would best complement the cadre of regular talent we already had working at the station. It was extremely time-consuming work, and the tapes were mostly from singers and musicians I'd never heard of, performers who were unknown outside their own localities. But the longer I listened, the more I realized that these tapes represented a tremendous reservoir of untapped talent.

One day Henry Clay called me into his office and told me about a singer who had called long distance from Alabama to inquire about the songs he'd sent to us. The singer asked for the station manager and ended up talking to Henry, who described him as "hell-bent" to land a spot on the *Hayride.*

"This guy's really persistent," Henry said. "I wish you'd get him off my back."

After I left Henry's office, I went back and dug out the tape from the Alabama singer. It had been sent to KWKH by Fred Rose of Acuff-Rose Music in Nashville, who had bought several songs from this same young artist.

I'd already heard through the grapevine about this singer-songwriter from Alabama. I knew he'd made several records — including one that he'd probably paid for out of his own pocket on a totally unheard-of label called Ponchartrain. The two songs on the record were tunes he'd written himself, "Pan American" and "On the Banks of the Old Ponchartrain." He'd also had a religious number on the Sterling label called "When God Comes and Gathers His Jewels." A few months ago, he'd even done some songs for MGM, which was one of the nation's top record companies. But none of his stuff had ever done much of anything in the marketplace.

When I played the tape, I liked him immediately. There was a rich, arresting quality about the Alabama singer's voice that I thought our listeners would like, too. It was the kind of voice that, once you heard it, you'd be apt to recognize instantly when you heard it again. The note accompanying the tape said the singer was currently doing a daily radio show on WSFA, a 3,000-watt station in Montgomery.

It was a day or two later when Henry asked me matter-of-factly if I'd had a chance to listen to the guy's music.

"Yeah, I have," I said, "and I think he's good. In fact, I think he's damned good. But I've heard some talk going around about him that bothers me and makes me think hiring him might be a big mistake. This guy's only about twenty-four years old, but he's already got himself a reputation for hitting the bottle pretty hard. The word's out that he's not only a drunk, but sometimes a mean drunk."

"Nothing much new about that," Henry said. "The music business is full of boozers. What do you think we ought to do about hiring him? Is it worth taking the risk?"

I shook my head. "I don't know," I said. "We sure as hell don't need any drunks or troublemakers messing up our new show, but he seems to want the job pretty bad. Maybe we could just lay it on the line with him. You know, tell him he's got to stay sober for a certain period of time before we let him come on."

"Sure, why not? We've got plenty of performers knocking on our door, so there's no hurry about signing this one, even if Acuff-Rose is pushing him," Henry said. "Just tell him, 'Look here, uh . . . ' What was the guy's name again? I can't remember."

"It's Williams," I said. "Hank Williams."

It was a day in mid-February 1948 when I phoned the young singer with my proposition. He seemed surprisingly cooperative and eager to please. Given the same circumstances, plenty of guys would've cussed and blustered and tried to deny the truth when I brought up the drinking. He didn't do any of that.

"No use lyin' about it, I've had some problems," he said, "but it ain't nothin' I can't handle. I can stay sober as long as I need to. I can do whatever it takes to get on the *Hayride*, 'cause I really want the job. You don't have to take my word for it, though. I'll call you up every day and let you talk to my station manager if you want me to. He'll tell you if I'm showin' up on time and stayin' outta trouble or not."

"Okay, Hank," I said, "I'll tell you what I'll do. I'll give you a chance to prove you can do what you say. You stay sober and behave yourself for six months, starting now, and at the end of that time, I'll put you on the *Hayride* as a regular every Saturday night."

To be perfectly honest, from the scuttlebutt I'd heard about him, I frankly doubted if he could do what I was asking.

"But I hear the show's supposed to start in April," he said, "and I sure would like to get in on the ground floor. Do I have to wait six whole months before I go on?"

"That's the deal, Hank," I told him. "I admire your talent, but that's the best offer I can make you right now. I guess you'll just have to take it or leave it."

"Well, in that case, I'll take it, Hoss," he said. "And you don't have to lose no sleep over it. I won't let you down."

There was a stark sincerity in his words that suggested two things to me about this young man: (1) He'd most likely let people down pretty often during his short lifetime, but (2) he truly believed what he was saying was the God's truth—at least for right now.

From the first time I'd heard his voice, I'd had a feeling that Hank Williams was going to get people's attention in the field of country music. Sooner or later, I figured he'd have at least one or two hit records—records he didn't have to pay for himself. But I didn't realize until much later what a legendary giant he was destined to become. It never crossed my mind that I was "discovering" one of the greatest talents in American musical history.

Likewise, I had no way of knowing what triumph and turmoil lay ahead for Hank and the *Hayride* and me. As I look back on it now, from a half-century later, I think it was probably best that I didn't know.

If I'd understood then what a fateful chain of events my arrangement with Hank was about to set in motion, I just might have called the whole thing off.

The Louisiana Hayride had its premiere performance on April 3, 1948. The Municipal Auditorium curtain went up at 8 P.M. and the show lasted for three hours. It featured a large cast, including the Bailes Brothers, a gospel quartet; Johnny and Jack and the Tennessee Mountain Boys, with Miss Kitty Wells; the Four Deacons; Curley Kinsey and the Tennessee Ridge Runners; Harmie Smith and the Ozark Mountaineers; Pappy Covington's band; the Mercer Brothers (the only holdover act from the *Saturday Night Roundup*), and Tex Grimsley and the Texas Playboys. I served as emcee and was assisted by Ray Bartlett, one of the station's regular announcers.

As I noted in writing a brochure on the *Hayride* some years later, "It was a good show, loud and long with lots of mistakes which nobody seemed to mind, and the audience loved it." There had been no agreement yet on a network spot for the show. We were still talking to CBS about it, but they were taking a wait-and-see attitude.

Notably missing from the first night's cast was Hank Williams. I hadn't budged on the six-month trial period while Hank walked the straight and narrow, and I didn't intend to. But I realized from the start that, for the show to achieve long-term survival, much less long-term success, it had to have a steady stream of top-notch talent presented in a well-planned, well-staged performance. Eventually, I hoped Hank would become a vital part of this stream, and I was eager for his "probation" to pass. But in the meantime, I had to keep priming the pump. Building and maintaining a high-caliber cast would be a tough, tedious, and unending job.

Over the next few months, we added several new acts. Curley Williams and his Georgia Peach Pickers came and stayed for more than a year, and Wayne Rainey joined the Mercer Brothers as a soloist. But by early summer, almost everybody on the show had heard about the agreement between Hank and me, and an attitude of curious waiting had started to develop.

Hank continued to call me regularly to assure me he was staying sober, showing up on time for work each day, and generally toeing the line. Rumors would circulate later that he was less than 100 percent reformed during this time. In fact, Hank's wife, Audrey, filed a divorce action against him in April 1948 in which she accused him of being drunk "most of the time." Three or four weeks later, though, they had reconciled. Once I got acquainted with Audrey, I knew she wasn't above stretching the facts a little whenever it was to her advantage.

Personally, I still believe Hank was telling me the truth about staying on the wagon. I can't prove he never took a single drink for that whole six months, but I know he wasn't boozing regularly. There wasn't a week that passed when he didn't call me at least once or twice, and he often insisted on putting the station manager on the line to confirm what he was saying. As I learned later, it didn't take much to set Hank off on a binge, but I remain convinced to this day that Henry Clay's assessment of Hank was right: He was "hell-bent" to get on the *Hayride,* and he wasn't about to do anything to seriously jeopardize his chances.

Anyway, by the end of July, I decided Hank had fulfilled his end of the bargain. Now it was time to fulfill mine. I called him and told him to come on to Shreveport.

"I've got a spot for you on the *Hayride* next Saturday if you want it," I said.

"You mean it, Hoss?" he asked.

"Sure, I mean it. A deal's a deal. But just don't go out tonight and start celebrating, if you know what I mean. Staying sober for those folks in Montgomery's one thing. Now I want you to stay sober for me."

"Don't worry, I will," he promised. "See you in a few days."

We continued to call the show the *Hayride* after that momentous week. But for most of the year following Hank's debut performance on August 7, 1948, the speed of events more closely resembled a runaway train.

Until Elvis exploded on the scene six years later, the entertainment world had never witnessed a sight like Hank Williams bursting out of nowhere to become the king of hillbilly music.

The first few months were often beautiful to watch. But after that, everything started turning uglier and uglier.

3

Hank Williams I—

A Ticket to

Immortality

Nobody could've looked less like a budding star than Hank Williams did the day he arrived in Shreveport for his first scheduled Hayride appearance. Along with his wife, Audrey, and seven-year-old stepdaughter, Lycrecia, Hank had made the five-hundred-mile drive from Montgomery in a road-worn old Chrysler sedan. The car was so loaded down with their worldly possessions that there was barely room for the three of them to sit, and they had their mattress and box springs tied on top. They reminded me a little of those Okies in *The Grapes of Wrath*.

I'll never forget how Hank looked when he walked into my office that day — tall, dark, long-legged, and handsome, but with a kind of drawn look about him, too. He was wearing a wrinkled, light-colored suit, a black tie, and a wide-brimmed western hat.

"I'm Hank Williams," he said with a tight smile, "and I'm ready to go on the *Hayride*."

He stuck out his hand, and I stood up and shook it. "I'm Hoss Logan. Glad to see you," I said. "Welcome aboard."

I wondered if Hank planned to keep working at the station in Montgomery, despite the considerable distance involved, and just commute to Shreveport on weekends for the show. I had no idea what the Montgomery job paid. Maybe it was more than the twenty-four dollars a Saturday Hank was going to draw from the *Hayride* — and then again, maybe not. Small stations like the one in Montgomery often thought the exposure they offered was payment enough for unknown artists struggling to make a name for themselves. (Hank had left all the members of his original Drifting Cowboys band behind in Alabama, but we arranged to let him use some members of our staff bands as sidemen, which allowed him to qualify for the higher bandleader salary scale of twenty-four dollars. Otherwise, his pay as a *Hayride* soloist would've been just eighteen dollars—the same as Elvis got when he started on the show six years later.)

When I walked outside with him, though, one look at Hank's family and that overloaded car told me they wouldn't be going back to Montgomery anytime soon. He said he'd quit his other job the week before, and I'm sure that station manager who'd regularly vouched for Hank's good behavior over the past six months had to be upset. Anyway, Hank left no doubt that he was here to stay. I assumed he'd managed to save a few dollars to tide the family over until he could line up some local personal appearances, but Hank left no doubt that, as of right now, the Williamses were full-time residents of the Shreveport area.

"We're stayin' in a motel in Bossier City for a few days," he said, "just till we can find us a place to rent. I'm in this for the long haul, Hoss, and it feels good just to finally be here. You won't be sorry for givin' me this chance."

I said hello to the little girl and introduced myself to Audrey, who gave me a wide smile and shook my hand warmly. Hank's wife was blonde, well-built, and attractive, but there was a kind of hardness about her features that told me she could be tough as nails when she wanted to be.

"Thanks for puttin' Hank on the *Hayride*, Mr. Logan," she said. "This is just like a brand new start for Hank and me. It's the break we been hopin' for, and we're mighty grateful to you."

"Well, I hope you like it here," I said. "I think Hank's going to be a real hit on our show."

"I sing and play, too," Audrey volunteered. "Maybe Hank and me can do some duets for you sometime."

"We'll see how it goes," I said.

Hank gave his wife a withering stare, but she didn't seem to notice. It was easy to see her comment had struck a raw nerve of some kind. (Later I'd find out just how determined Audrey was to be a singer in her own right—and how god-awful bad she was.) Finally, he sighed and pulled a crumpled pack of Camels out of his pocket. He jammed a cigarette into the corner of his mouth and lit it with a Zippo.

"Well, I guess we better be goin'," he said. "Thanks, Hoss."

Even then, as young as he was, the marks of a hard life showed plainly on Hank's thin face. He could have passed for a man a dozen years older than he actually was. He didn't smile much, and there was something in his eyes . . . like a fire burning deep inside.

In the months and years that lay ahead, I honestly think I became one of the closest friends Hank Williams had on the face of this earth—at times maybe *the* closest. I still don't know why it happened, but I do know Hank didn't trust most people, and he developed only a handful of real friendships in his whole life. I was only a few years older than he was, but maybe I represented a father figure for him, or just a steadying influence when he needed one.

Whatever the reason was, I feel honored to have been Hank's friend. But I'd never claim to understand everything that went on inside this troubled man. I don't think anyone else could claim to, either. If that kind of understanding had been possible, somebody might have been able to keep Hank from destroying himself—and clearly nobody was. But as our friendship deepened and Hank's wild roller-coaster ride ran its inevitable course, I gradually did come to realize what fueled that dark fire inside him.

It was, I think, a unique mixture of pure genius and utter madness.

Hank's opening song on the *Hayride* that night, after I introduced him for the first of many times to come, was "Move It on Over," an original composition he'd recorded for MGM some months earlier. It was also one of his livelier, more lighthearted tunes and a far cry from the sorrowful ballads that helped immortalize him later on.

Almost none of the fans in the auditorium had ever heard Hank sing in person before, and nobody had known beforehand he'd be there. We didn't advertise our cast ahead of time for any given show, and although our regular performers were familiar to a large percentage of the audience, newcomers were always unknown quantities. They could be instant sensations or resounding flops, depending on the audience's reaction.

But in anticipation of his arrival, we'd been playing Hank's records on KWKH for weeks, and many in that first audience had heard him on the air. As I'd expected, the thousands in the auditorium took an immediate liking to Hank. They gave him a lusty round of applause after that first number, and when he followed it up with "On the Banks of the Old Ponchartrain," he got an ovation that merited an encore with plenty of room to spare.

It was the first of hundreds he'd receive on the *Hayride* stage en route to becoming the show's all-time champion for encores.

As he sang, hunched over toward the microphone and doing a little shuffle with his hips, I looked out into the audience and marveled at the reaction I saw among the fans in the first few rows—especially the women. Hank's hip movements were nowhere near as suggestive as Elvis's pelvic gyrations were a few years later, but at that time, they were something you just didn't see performers doing. And although Hank's distinctive voice came across with forceful impact on his records, you didn't realize what a magnetic personality he was until you saw and heard him in the flesh.

When he made eye contact with a woman, she could be totally mesmerized by him. There was something deeply personal and almost sensuous about his delivery—a quality that made every female in the audience feel as if he was singing directly to her. He projected an aura of sexiness that no male country singer ever had before. But at the same time, he also managed to come across as a man's man. Older guys admired him and young guys didn't resent him the way they later resented Elvis. Hank had already been playing in dives and honky-tonks for close to ten years, and he'd been in his share of brawls. Despite his frail build, there was a tough, nononsense look about him, but there was more to his masculine appeal than that.

For a long time, I wasn't sure just what it was, but I gradually came to understand. Hank sang about the kind of romantic heartbreak that almost every young guy had experienced, and the "villain" was always some beguiling, unfaithful woman. Every man could identify with that situation, so even while Hank was dazzling the ladies, he was simultaneously allying himself with their husbands and boyfriends.

They'd slap their knees and nudge each other and say, "That rascal sure can sing—and he knows what he's talkin' about, too."

All I really knew about Hank when he first came to Shreveport was that (a) I liked his music and (b) he supposedly had a bad habit of getting drunk. As long as I knew him, he never talked much about his background or things that happened when he was growing up. But I've picked up enough information over the years from mutual acquaintances and other sources to know that Hank's early life was about as rough as it could get. His boyhood and mine had certain similarities, but when it came to poverty and hard knocks, Hank had me beat by a mile.

He was born September 17, 1923, in a cabin in a little rural community near Georgiana, Alabama. His mother, Lilly, named him Hiram, but he always hated the name and started calling himself "Hank" when he was eleven or twelve years old. His father, Elonzo "Lonnie" Williams, was a World War I veteran who lost his job at a lumber mill and became a full-time drunk when Hank was about five. A couple of years later, Lonnie left his family, and his son never saw him again until he was grown. The only thing Hank inherited from his part-Choctaw daddy was his dark brown eyes, his high cheekbones, and his taste for alcohol.

Lilly Williams, a strong, domineering woman who weighed over two hundred pounds, supported Hiram and his older sister, Irene, by selling strawberries and other homegrown produce. Every Sunday she took little Hiram with her to the Mount Olive Baptist Church, where she made him sit on the bench with her while she played the organ. When Hank was about seven, the family's house burned to the ground and they lost everything but their nightclothes. After that, they moved to the town of Greenville, and Hank went to work selling peanuts and seed packets and shining shoes.

For his twelfth birthday, his mother gave him a secondhand guitar. He didn't get a chance to play it right away, because later that same day a cow knocked him down and broke his arm. But as soon as the arm healed, he took his guitar out on the streets and started playing for nickels and dimes. He started skipping school and hanging out with a black blues singer named Rufus Payne, who went by the nickname "Tee Tot." He also developed a taste for cigarettes and beer, and most of what he earned went for these "necessities," but sometimes he'd have a little money left to take home.

Hank learned a lot from Tee Tot about entertaining people, and although he and his mother fought and argued constantly about Hank's developing bad habits, late hours, and unsavory company, he soon moved beyond her control. Within the space of a year or two, music—and drinking—became his whole life.

In the summer of 1937, when Hank was going on fourteen, the family moved to Montgomery, where Lilly opened a boarding house on Perry Street. That December, Hank won the fifteen-dollar first prize in a talent contest at the Empire Theatre in downtown Montgomery by playing a song he had written himself entitled "WPA Blues." At about that same time, Hank put together his first band and called it the Drifting Cowboys. It included his boyhood friends, Smith "Hezzy" Adair on bass and Freddie Beech on fiddle, and Hank's sister, Irene, as a vocalist. The personnel of the band would change often in years to come—several times with mass firings and restructurings—but the name would remain the same throughout his career.

He met another aspiring young hillbilly singer named Braxton Schuffert, who earned a living by driving a meat truck but who also performed on WSFA from time to time. The two of them struck up a friendship and started traveling around the area in Schuffert's '35 Ford to book shows at country schoolhouses, backwoods dancehalls, and occasional theaters. In February 1941, at the age of seventeen, Hank landed his first radio singing job on WSFA, but lost it a year and a half later on account of his drinking. It would be more than six years later — in April 1947, to be exact — before he landed another regular job at the Montgomery station.

After getting fired at WSFA, he quit school for good in September 1942. He was nineteen years old and still in the ninth grade, so it was pretty clear that formal education wasn't one of his major priorities. He tried to join the navy but flunked the physical because of a congenital abnormality in his spine — one that would cause him untold misery in years to come and hasten his addiction to drugs.

He drifted to the West Coast with the idea of going to work for a shipyard in Oregon, but he ended up hanging around honkytonks and playing for drinks and loose change. Broke and homesick after a few weeks, he called his mother and begged her to wire him enough money to get home on. She did exactly that, sending just what it took for train fare and not a penny more, probably figuring he'd spend any extra money on booze. Hank almost starved to death on the five-day return trip.

He went back to doing the only thing he knew how to do — picking and singing. By this time, his mother had given up on making him quit the life of an itinerant musician and realized that if she expected to get her hands on any of Hank's earnings, she'd have to keep a closer eye on him. So she started going with him to his engagements, collecting the gate receipts, and sometimes helping him fight off rowdy drunks.

I don't think Hank was joking when he remarked, as he often did, "There's nobody I'd rather have beside me in a fight than my mama with a broken beer bottle in her hand."

He was traveling with a medicine show in rural Pike County, Alabama, when he met a good-looking blonde girl named Audrey Mae Sheppard Guy. The fact that she was married to a soldier serving overseas and had a two-year-old daughter didn't keep Hank from falling in love with her — and falling hard. Pretty soon, Hank was leaving his mother at home in favor of a new traveling companion.

Audrey went on the road with Hank, sometimes playing bass with his band, cooking for him and the other band members, and assuming Lilly's job of collecting admissions at the door on show nights. In December 1944, after Audrey's divorce was final and she'd been living with Hank for a year or more, Hank finally persuaded her to marry him. The ceremony was performed by a justice of the peace who ran a filling station in Andalusia, Alabama.

Audrey later confided that she'd been afraid to marry Hank because of his drinking. "I'd never been around anybody who drank like that," she said, "but he'd been doing real good lately. He hadn't been drinking at all, and I was real proud of him. So when he asked me all of a sudden, I said yes."

It turned out, of course, that Audrey had good reason to be apprehensive about their marriage. As I found out soon after they moved to Shreveport, she and Hank had been fighting like cats and dogs ever since.

Like the drugs and alcohol that came to rule his life and eventually destroyed him, Audrey was an unbreakable addiction for Hank — maybe the most powerful one of all. As the saying goes, he couldn't live with her, and he couldn't live without her. He could never stand being away from her for very long, but they seldom spent a full day together without having a knock-down, drag-out fight.

In certain ways and at certain times, I think Audrey was a genuine asset to Hank's career. For one thing, as I learned later, she was an important factor in Hank's decision to move to Shreveport. Being a domineering woman herself, Hank's wife didn't get along very well with Hank's mother, who was married by this time to a subdued little man named W. W. Stone and was still more or less managing Hank's career, or at least trying to. Lilly and Audrey clashed frequently, and Audrey was eager to get Hank away from Montgomery and his mother's influence. She also recognized that Hank had extraordinary talent but was maybe a little short on drive and ambition. And regardless of what else may have motivated her in addition to wifely concern, she truly wanted to see him reach the top.

On the negative side, Audrey struck me as an extremely selfish person. Her vain, unrealistic insistence that she be allowed to sing on the same stage with Hank delayed his success and even damaged his career early on. Then, when Hank did hit the big time, she spent his money like it was going out of style. She kept him under constant pressure to make more and more, and this contributed to the stresses that finally caused him to unravel completely.

But there's one thing I know for sure. Beyond the slightest doubt, Audrey was the inspiration for many of Hank's greatest songs. The emotional torment embodied in such tunes as "Cold, Cold Heart," "You Win Again," and "Your Cheatin' Heart" was distilled from real life—the direct by-product of his relationship with Audrey. If she'd been a more amiable person, those songs might never have been written.

Part of the time, I know Hank really loved her, at least by his own definition. But God knows, he hated her sometimes, too.

Hank had an obsession with guns. After he became a major star, he kept a suitcase full of them in the trunk of his car, and throughout his career he often carried one or more pistols on his person. He was a terrible shot, though, even when he was sober, and when he was drunk, he couldn't hit the broad side of a barn.

Audrey was lucky that Hank was such a poor marksman. If he hadn't been, I'm pretty sure he would've killed her.

A few days after his first appearance on the *Hayride*, Hank signed a one-year contract with KWKH that made him a regular on the show. Within a few weeks, he was firmly established as one of the favorites of our live audience, but his fan base was spreading far beyond the Ark-La-Tex. We still hadn't struck a deal with CBS, but a few months after Hank joined our show, a regional network of twenty-five stations in the South and Southwest began carrying the *Hayride*. At its peak, this network grew to nearly seventy stations. And KWKH's powerful clear-channel signal alone put Hank's voice within reach of country music fans in twenty-eight states.

He and Audrey and Lycrecia moved into a small but comfortable garage apartment in Bossier City, and Hank settled into what I believe was one of the most peaceful, productive periods of his career. It also may have been the longest period of continued sobriety of his entire adult life. As the weeks passed without any of the unpleasant incidents that had seemed to follow Hank around like a black cloud—incidents I kept half-expecting to erupt at any moment—I allowed myself to relax a little.

Hank had been right. At that point in his life, he *could* stay sober, just like he'd said. I think he realized he'd finally gotten the break he'd been waiting for all his life, and he knew if he could keep a tight rein on himself, there were even bigger things within his reach. Meanwhile, he was working hard to supplement his income from the *Hayride* in any way possible.

Although we allowed our artists to take occasional Saturday nights off, the bulk of their personal appearances had to be scheduled on weeknights. Hank lost no time in organizing a new Louisiana-based version of the Drifting Cowboys, and with the help of local booking agent Tillman Franks, he and his band quickly lined up a series of bookings in the three-state area. Some of these early dates were at nightclubs that paid fairly well. Many others were small-town performances at high school auditoriums and American Legion dances, the kind of places where our artists sometimes actually ended up in the red. But if a five-piece band could clear even twenty-five or thirty dollars after expenses for an evening's work, it was considered worth the effort.

Meanwhile, three or four months before moving to Shreveport,

Hank had signed an agreement with Acuff-Rose that guaranteed him fifty dollars a month against future royalties and ensured publication of at least six of his original songs per year. Hank was always jotting down potential lyrics or song titles on scraps of paper that he carried in his pockets, and I think he came up with the ideas for some of his best numbers during this period. Nobody who knew Hank would've described him as a deep thinker—he was relatively uneducated and seldom read anything more intellectually stimulating than a comic book. He was controlled by his emotions to a great extent, yet he *was* capable of deep, creative thought. His mind was agile and always searching for ideas.

With Hank and the Drifting Cowboys playing at least two or three of these grassroots engagements each week, he was soon making enough money to put the decrepit old Chrysler out to pasture and buy the first really nice car he'd ever owned. It was a sleek, black '48 Packard sedan equipped with a matching trailer for the band's instruments and dual loudspeakers mounted on the roof so that Hank could announce his own arrival as he drove into a town. The Packard wasn't brand-new when he got it—Hank took up payments on the car from a gospel singer named Billy Byrd when Byrd's quartet broke up—but Hank couldn't have been prouder if it'd been a Rolls Royce.

"I don't even mind goin' out on the road in this little jewel," he said the first day he brought it by the studios to show it off. "I been a car nut all my life, and I ain't never gonna drive another damn old beat-up wreck again."

He didn't, either.

Just a couple of months after inviting Hank to join the *Hayride,* I was able to give him another piece of good news. In the fall of 1948, the Shreveport-based Johnny Fair Syrup Company had started negotiating with KWKH about sponsoring a new program on the station. The company had been losing market share and decided to spend five thousand dollars—a sizable chunk of money at the time—on a special promotion in the form of a daily country music show. The program would air at 7:15 A.M. Monday through Friday, just as many of our listeners were having breakfast.

Although there were several other possibilities, Hank was my first choice for the job. It would pay seventy-five dollars a week—a sum that a family could live quite comfortably on in those days. It would give Hank some semipermanent financial security and still leave him free to book as many weeknight shows as he wanted to. But before I made any offers, I knew I needed to sit down privately with him and make 100 percent sure he could handle the extra responsibility with no problems. I called him into my office for a talk.

"It's only fifteen minutes," I said, "but it means you've got to be in the studio by about seven every morning. You've got to be fresh and ready to sing and handle the commercials, even if you were out on the road till one or two o'clock the night before. Think you can do it?"

"I done it before in Montgomery, Hoss," Hank said. "Ain't no reason I can't do it again."

"Well, do you want the job?"

"Damn right I do, and I sure thank you for the offer. I reckon Audrey can find *somethin'* to do with the money." He smiled that tight smile of his and seemed completely at ease as he lit up a Camel.

I felt tremendously relieved. I respected Hank's talent, but more than that, I genuinely liked him. So far, he'd lived up to all my expectations and then some. He was obviously doing fine, and I hoped he always would.

The Johnny Fair Syrup Program started in December, and except for the early hour, it was a piece of cake for Hank. Since he played it solo, there was nobody to split the money with, and there was only time for two or three numbers. One of them was always a theme song that went like this:

When I die, just bury me deep
With a bucket of Johnny Fair at my head and feet.
Put a cold biscuit in each of my hands,
And I'll sop my way to the promised land!

That little ditty never showed up on any of the charts, I'm afraid, but it apparently served the purpose for which it was intended very well. For a while, Hank became known around the station as the "Old Syrup Sopper." After he left and moved on to Nashville, I hired Red Sovine to take over the show, and I have to admit that Red may have made a better "Sopper" than Hank. He never had as many big hit records as Hank did, but he sold a helluva lot more syrup—which may be one reason Johnny Fair is still alive and flourishing today.

I don't recall the exact date when Hank first sang "Lovesick Blues," the tune that would rocket him straight to the top of the country music world, on the *Hayride*. But I know it was sometime in the fall of 1948, probably a month or two before he recorded the song for MGM, and I remember as if it were yesterday the way the fans in the Municipal Auditorium reacted.

The crowd went crazy over that song from the very first time they heard it, and this was just a foretaste of the reception it started receiving across the country a few weeks later. I'd never seen an audience respond with such enthusiasm to a song they'd never heard before. They were so excited and gave Hank so many encores I could barely get the commercials in. I had to plead with them to quiet down, but I never could get them to be still. It was absolutely incredible.

I remember a guitar player named Bob McNett summing it up like this: "My God, they won't let Hank off the stage!"

It went on like that every Saturday night for weeks, as Hank sang his new song for overflow audiences. Tickets to the *Hayride* were quite a bargain—just sixty cents for adults and thirty cents for children, or about the same as the price of a first-run movie. There was never an empty seat in the auditorium during this period, and we were having to turn people away by the hundreds.

As the *Shreveport Times* noted on January 9, 1949, a good six weeks before MGM released the record: "Capacity crowds at the 'Louisiana Hayride' nearly 'tear the house down' for encores of 'Lovesick Blues.' This, among other reasons, necessitated the advance sale of tickets to the Saturday night KWKH songfest."

Hank and Audrey had driven to Cincinnati just before Christmas for Hank's first recording session in over a year, and "Lovesick Blues" had been one of four numbers he recorded for MGM. The others were "Never Again," a tune Hank had originally done on the Sterling label, which was on the flip side of "Lovesick Blues," and two duets with screechy-voiced Audrey called "Lost on the River" and "I Heard My Mother Praying for Me." I don't know if the duets were ever even released. If they were, they were totally lost in the clamor over "Lovesick Blues."

It's always been a little hard for me to understand what caused this particular song to gain such instant, fantastic popularity. Most of Hank's fans were under the impression that "Lovesick Blues" was one of his own original compositions—and many undoubtedly still are—but nothing could actually be further from the truth. The fact is, the song had been around for more than a quarter of a century by the time MGM brought out Hank's version of it. It was an old Tin Pan Alley tune written by Cliff Friend and Irving Mills and copyrighted way back in 1922. It had been recorded three or four times before, most recently on Decca in 1939 by an Alabama singer named Rex Griffin, whose version Hank had undoubtedly heard somewhere and liked. He'd been singing it for years at his shows in and around Montgomery, but it was only after he'd come to Shreveport that he got the style and delivery just the way he wanted it.

My own feeling is that the song itself wasn't all that great. It was good, but Hank wrote and recorded a lot of better numbers in his career. I think what made "Lovesick Blues" one of the biggest hits in the history of country music was the way Hank sang it—with a yodel, a sob, and an emotional outpouring that people had never heard before.

He also did a sort of shuffling, twisting little dance as he sang it that captivated live audiences. As Hank himself once remarked after a show to steel guitarist Felton Pruett: "I don't know if people really like the song that much or if they just like to see me tie myself in knots tryin' to sing it."

Fred Rose also had reservations about "Lovesick Blues." He didn't actually want Hank to do it at the recording session in December 1948, and part of his reason was purely monetary: Since Acuff-Rose didn't own the music, they wouldn't collect a cent in royalties on it. But I also think Fred had serious doubts about the song's appeal. When Hank insisted, Fred gave in, but he was convinced that "Never Again" would be the big seller and that "Lovesick Blues" would be remembered only as the song on its flip side. But as it turned out, of course, the exact opposite happened.

When MGM released "Lovesick Blues" on February 25, 1949, it headed straight for the top of the country music charts, passing some very good songs, like Eddy Arnold's "Don't Rob Another Man's Castle" and George Morgan's "Candy Kisses," on the way. Within a few weeks, it was the number-one folk tune in the nation in record sales and ranked only slightly lower in the number of plays on jukeboxes. Altogether, it stayed on the charts for almost ten straight months.

Acuff-Rose and MGM knew a good thing when they saw one. On March 2, less than a week after "Lovesick Blues" hit the stores, Hank was in Nashville to cut a total of eight sides in one major session. Two of the songs were totally forgettable gospel duets with Audrey, but the other six—"Lost Highway," "May You Never Be Alone," "Honky-Tonk Blues," "Mind Your Own Business," "My Son Calls Another Man Daddy" and "You're Gonna Change (Or I'm Gonna Leave)"—became major follow-up hits.

Just three weeks later, Hank flew back to Nashville—his very first airplane trip—for another recording session. MGM could see this guy was hot as a firecracker, and they knew they'd better jump on the wagon quick. This time, the songs were "Wedding Bells" and "I Just Told Mama Good-bye."

Each of these songs had been introduced recently on the Hayride, so people all over the country were already hearing them and an almost insatiable public demand was building for more of Hank Williams.

A day or two before he first did it on the show, Hank had sung "Wedding Bells" in the KWKH studios for an audience of one—which happened to be yours truly. It gave me a brief but revealing glimpse at the emotions that boiled just beneath Hank's surface.

It was early one morning when he motioned me into the studio where he'd just finished the Johnny Fair program. He was sitting there in his shirtsleeves with a stubble of beard on his face and a cigarette in the corner of his mouth. As always, indoors or out, he had his hat on. As young as he was, Hank was starting to lose his hair, and he never went anywhere bareheaded.

"This is gonna be my next big 'un, Hoss," he said. "Wanta hear it? It's called 'Wedding Bells.'"

"Well, sure," I said. "I'd be honored to be the first person in America to hear Hank Williams's newest hit."

He strummed the strings of his Martin guitar and starting singing very softly, the words flowing out around his smouldering cigarette.

Halfway through the song, I was amazed to see tears streaming down Hank's cheeks. But he was so deeply engrossed in the sorrowful cadence of the melody and the heartbreak of the lyrics that he never seemed to notice he was crying like a baby. I saw Hank moved to tears numerous times after that, but this was when I first began to comprehend what a deeply sentimental person he was.

Hank didn't just sing songs—he lived them. That was what drew people to his music, whether they knew it or not.

During those pivotal months, while Hank Williams was rewriting the record charts and changing from an unknown singer into the hottest name in show business, there was also a whole lot happening in his personal life.

At about the same time Hank began singing "Lovesick Blues" on the *Hayride*, Audrey discovered she was pregnant. Hank was unprepared for this development, and the prospect of being a real father for the first time was unsettling to him in a way. With constant travel expenses he still wasn't making much money, and he fretted about finding a bigger house that he could afford. After he had a chance to adjust to the idea of having a child of his own, he got really excited about it, but the responsibility still worried him some.

"You got kids, Hoss, and you seem to like it okay," he said one day, "but I ain't sure I'm cut out for this."

"You'll do fine," I assured him. "There's nothing better in the world than hearing your own kid call you 'Daddy.' "

He nodded gravely. "Yeah," he said softly, "I think I'm gonna like that."

Audrey was sick a lot during her pregnancy, or at least she said she was. But in one way, the fact that Audrey often didn't feel like getting out of bed, much less traveling or appearing on stage, actually came as something of a relief for Hank. Most of the time, she stayed at home when he and the Drifting Cowboys performed, and pretty soon, those cowgirl outfits she wore for shows wouldn't fit her anymore, anyway. Against my better judgment, I'd let her sing a few times on the *Hayride*—Lord knows, I hadn't wanted to. The woman's voice had all the soft sweetness of a power saw hitting a ten-penny nail, but I had no choice. She badgered Hank constantly until I did.

"I know how she sounds, Hoss," Hank would say, shaking his head apologetically. "Believe me, I *know*. But, dammit, she thinks she's a good singer, and she gives me hell if she don't get a chance to do a song in public once in a while."

Whenever possible, I put her on a separate mike so we could cut the volume down. At least the screeching wasn't quite so nerve-wracking that way, but she got wise to this trick pretty soon, and started making sure she was on the same mike with Hank.

Mercifully, this pregnancy pretty much brought Audrey's performing days to an end during Hank's lifetime. They had some serious fights about it later on, but once Hank was established as a major star, even Audrey could see that she couldn't share the limelight.

In mid-March 1949, about three weeks after "Lovesick Blues" started its fast climb up the charts, Hank signed the papers on a new house for his growing family. It was on Modica Street in a new subdivision in Bossier City, just a little three-bedroom frame cottage—a far cry from the mansion he later bought for Audrey on Franklin Road in Nashville—but it was the first home Hank had ever owned, and he was mighty proud of it.

By Easter time, the Williamses had moved into their new place. Audrey was only six or seven weeks from her due date, and she was uncomfortable and hard as the devil himself to get along with. Hank did the best he could. He bought her an easy chair and a big console phonograph to try to help her relax, but I don't think it did much to pacify her.

On Easter Sunday, Johnny Wright of the Johnny and Jack group; his wife, Kitty Wells; Jack Anglin, Johnny's partner; Jack's wife, Louise; the three Bailes Brothers and several other regulars on the show decided to put on a big Easter egg hunt and picnic for the whole *Hayride* cast. It was to be a family-style outing at Caddo Lake, and the idea was simply for kids and adults alike to have a good time.

But some of the guys brought along a bunch of beer iced down in a washtub. It was a warm afternoon, and pretty soon most of the men—and quite a few of the women, too—were enjoying a few cold ones. Audrey was there with Lycrecia, and she wasn't among the beer drinkers. Even today, if I close my eyes I can see the expression on her face when somebody offered Hank a beer—and he accepted it.

In their own defense, many of the folks who attended the picnic weren't even aware of Hank's drinking problem. He'd been so well-behaved ever since coming to Shreveport that someone who hadn't known him earlier might never have guessed the terrible truth. I'd even started wondering myself if some of those wild stories I'd heard were gross exaggerations.

But Audrey knew better. She'd seen what happened too many times before when Hank decided to "have a few."

At the moment, nobody was getting drunk. In fact, I doubt that anyone, including Hank, had more than two or three beers at the picnic. But when Audrey saw Hank drinking for the first time in months and cutting up a little with the other guys, she got pretty upset. She knew that, once Hank started, there was no way to know where he'd stop. And when it was decided to continue the party at Johnnie Bailes's house, and Hank insisted on going along, she took Lycrecia and went home.

I still shudder when I think about that pleasant spring Sunday. What happened is etched forever in my mind.

By the time he got home that night, he was roaring drunk, and Audrey was furious. When she started yelling at him, he went out and got in the Packard, intending to drive off so he wouldn't have to listen to her, but she'd punched holes in the tires with an ice-pick so he couldn't leave. It was probably a good thing he couldn't, but Hank didn't see it that way. He got so mad he tore up half the furniture in the house and threw part of it out in the yard.

According to Johnny Wright, Audrey called Kitty Wells in a panic and asked her to come over. When Kitty and Johnny got there, Hank was passed out, and Audrey told them he'd swallowed a bunch of the sleeping pills her doctor had prescribed for her. There were no pills left in the bottle, and Audrey didn't know how many he'd taken. They were afraid Hank had overdosed and might never wake up, but when they called a doctor to the house, he checked Hank over and said he was okay.

He was wrong, of course. Hank *wasn't* okay. From that Sunday on, I don't think he was ever really okay again.

The Easter fiasco sent Hank off on a terrible binge. For the next few weeks, he was either drunk or hungover the biggest part of the time. It was as if a dam had burst inside him, washing away every ounce of self-control and common sense he'd ever had. He seemed to be trying to make up for all that lost time he'd spent staying sober by drinking harder and heavier than ever before. It was scary to watch.

Somehow he always managed to make it to the studio for his morning shows, but lots of times he seemed more dead than alive when he got there. It was a good thing he was on radio and not television. Most of his listeners probably would've choked on their breakfast if they'd had to look at Hank while they were eating.

"I feel like hell," he groaned one morning just after he went off the air.

"You've got to get hold of yourself, Hank," I told him. "You can't go on like this. You've got to slow down."

"If I could just quit hurtin' I'd be all right," he said.

"Where do you hurt?"

"All over," he said. "Where I don't hurt ain't been invented yet."

As I watched, he pulled a box of aspirin out of his pocket, opened it with shaking fingers and promptly swallowed all twelve of the tablets inside, washing them down with some kind of cloudy, whitish-looking liquid in a Coke bottle.

"My God, Hank, you shouldn't take all those aspirins at once like that. You'll poison yourself."

He took another swig of the stuff in the bottle and belched. "Naw, it's okay, Hoss. I take 'em like this all the time. It takes that many to make the pain go away."

"What's that stuff you're drinking?" I asked. I hoped it was milk, but I somehow doubted it.

"Aw, I just poured a little ammonia in this here Coke," he said matter-of-factly. "Somebody told me it'll getcha movin' when you're feelin' low."

"For Christ sake, Hank," I said, "are you trying to kill yourself?"

He laughed sourly. "Naw, I've savin' that job for Audrey," he said.

More than once during those weeks, I'm sure Audrey really *wanted* to kill him—and under the circumstances, it was hard to blame her.

When Hank was sober, he was as sweet and gentle and caring a person as you'd ever want to meet. When he was drinking, his personality underwent a drastic change, and it often happened with breathtaking suddenness. In the space of ten or fifteen minutes, alcohol could transform Hank into someone totally—and frighteningly—different. Toward the end, as he mixed more and more drugs with the alcohol, this other personality grew stronger and stronger, until you sometimes wondered if the real Hank was still there at all.

The other Hank could swing his guitar like a club at hecklers, lunge with a broken bottle at someone who teased him about how much ketchup he poured on his eggs, or whip out a pistol and start shooting with no apparent provocation. I've heard enough accounts from reliable sources to know that many such incidents actually happened, and I witnessed some of them myself. Hank never once directed a hostile act or threatening gesture toward me. And although I couldn't swear that he never struck Audrey during their violent confrontations, I know he more often vented his anger on inanimate objects. It was Audrey who usually resorted to physical violence.

It was only a few days after the ammonia-and-Coke episode that Hank showed up at the studio with a gash on his head and blood streaking his face. He was staggering a little, but this time I didn't think it was only from drinking. His eyes were kind of glassy, and he seemed dazed.

"What happened?" I said. "Did you have a car wreck?"

"I had a feelin' Audrey was gonna throw that damn lamp at me," he said vaguely. "Then when she *did* throw it, I didn't duck in time."

There was a deep laceration over an inch long in Hank's scalp, and it was still oozing blood. "That's a pretty bad cut," I said. "Come on, I'll take you someplace and get it stitched up."

"Aw, I don't wantcha to do that, Hoss," he protested. "I don't need no doctor stickin' no needle in my head. I'll just put a damn Band-aid on it an' it'll be all right." Hank feared and distrusted doctors about as much as a person possibly could. He always said they made him feel worse instead of better.

"Like hell you will," I said. "I can't have the star of the *Louisiana Hayride* looking like something the cat dragged in. Now come on."

I went to the restroom and got Hank a wad of tissue to put on his head. Then I helped him out to my car and drove to a small clinic several blocks away where he could be treated quickly and discreetly. If Hank Williams were to show up at a hospital emergency room, I was afraid word might leak out pretty fast. If it did, a bunch of newspaper reporters would be there in no time, all of them asking nosy questions.

As I pulled into the street, Hank laid his head back against the car seat and fumbled for a cigarette.

"Y'know, I love that woman," he muttered, "but, Lord God, she can be a bitch sometimes. It'll be a damn miracle if we don't end up killin' each other."

After the doctor finished with him, I drove Hank out to his house, and I guess it was a good thing I did. If he'd gone home alone, he might have ended up in the ICU — or maybe the morgue. Audrey was waiting for him, and she was still in a dangerous mood.

He was walking through the carport when the back door of the house flew open and I saw Audrey in the doorway with a plate in her hand.

"I told you not to come back here, you sonofabitch!" she howled and threw the plate at Hank. It missed him by several feet, but she followed it up with a bowl and couple of saucers. One of them shattered at his feet.

He raised an arm to shield himself and ducked behind a post. "Damn it, Audrey," he yelled, "we ain't gonna have no dishes left to eat out of if you don't cut that out."

"You can eat off the floor, you pig!" Another plate crashed on the concrete.

"Take it easy, Audrey," I said. "Hank's already got a busted head."

Up until that instant, I don't think she'd realized I was there. She jerked her head toward me and froze with another piece of china in her hand. Then the anger on her face dissolved into tears, and she ducked back into the house, slamming the door behind her. After a few seconds, Hank looked at me and shrugged. Then he followed her inside.

I held my breath and listened, expecting the sounds of battle to resume, but there was only silence from the house. After a few minutes, I decided the crisis was over for the moment, and I got back in my car and left.

I finally talked Hank into going to the Highland Sanitarium, a private facility in Shreveport, and spending a few days getting himself dried out. It would be his first of several stays in the same sanitarium for the same purpose. Hank obviously didn't want to go, but he didn't put up as much resistance as I'd expected, and he was at the point where nothing else was likely to do any good.

Hank never would've admitted needing this kind of treatment, but by then, I think even he realized he was completely out of control and no longer able to cope with his problem. He'd mangled one whole side of his new Packard driving home from a show one night blind drunk. Both fenders had to be replaced, and he'd been lucky not to wind up in jail. He'd also missed a few show dates entirely, and three or four times he'd even been staggering noticeably on late segments of the *Hayride*. And, of course, the fights with Audrey just went on and on.

But one of Hank's biggest motivations for getting straightened up was some news he'd received that spring from Fred Rose, who told him conditions were growing increasingly favorable for getting him on the *Grand Ole Opry*. Being on the *Opry* was still the epitome of success for a country music artist, and although Hank was the biggest name in the field right now, he wouldn't be fully recognized as one of the elite until the *Opry* accepted him. For several months, I'd been feeling it was just a matter of time until he got the call from Nashville, and I used the situation as leverage to get him to agree to go to the sanitarium.

"If an offer does come through from the *Opry,* I won't stand in your way, Hank," I told him. "Bad as I hate to lose you, I'll release you from your Hayride contract and let you go. But you'll never make it on the *Opry* the way you are now. You need medical help, and unless you get it, you'll just go over there and fall flat on your face. And if you do that, you may never get a second chance."

He stared moodily at me for a moment. "Okay, Hoss," he said finally, "ole Hank'll go take the cure if it'll make you happy."

"You're not doing it for me, Hank," I said. "Hell, if it was the *Hayride* and me I was thinking about, we'd be better off keeping you here dog-drunk than getting you sobered up so you can go off somewhere else. But you've got a chance to be one of the great ones if you'll just act like you've got a few brains and do something for yourself for a change."

He held up his hands in mock surrender. "Awright," he said, "I'm ready to go."

It probably didn't take Hank long to change his mind, once he was going through the detoxification process, but by then there was nothing he could do about it. When he was released from the sanitarium, after about four days, he was totally sober for the first time in weeks. I didn't kid myself into thinking it was a permanent cure, but it was good to see how much better he looked and acted, no matter how temporary it might be.

On the night of Thursday, May 26, 1949, I sat with Hank outside a hospital delivery room in Bossier City while he waited for the birth of his child. It was going on 9 P.M. when I got there, and Hank was looking pretty frazzled. He didn't like hospitals in the first place, and he'd been there for quite a while. He was chain-smoking like a blast furnace and having a hard time keeping still, but as near as I could tell, he hadn't had a drop to drink.

"I brought Audrey up here two or three times before, but it was always false alarms," he said. "This time I think it's the real thing. She's sure been yellin' an' carryin' on a lot if it ain't. I keep hangin' around the door, but they won't let me in to see her."

I grinned. "Believe me, it's just as well," I said. "You'd probably just get in there and faint or something."

He stubbed out one Camel and immediately lit another one. "Audrey's sure it's gonna be a boy, and the doctor says she's probably right on account of how big she's gotten. I figger it better be a boy, 'cause she didn't buy nothing' but blue baby clothes."

"How do you feel about it?" I asked. "Are you hoping for a boy?"

"Aw, I dunno. It don't really matter. I'm just hopin' . . . " He paused for a second, then shook his head. "I just wanna get it over with and have ever'thing be okay. But, yeah, it'd be kinda nice to have a son, I guess."

"Well, you ought to know before long."

Hank stared at the floor for a long time. "I'll tell you one thing, Hoss," he said finally, raising his eyes to me. "Whether it turns out to be a boy or a girl, I'm gonna try to be the best daddy I can to this young'un."

"I'm sure you will," I said.

"When I was little, I never even knew my own daddy," he said softly, "and I don't want it to be like that with no kid of mine. I want my kid to have a daddy he can count on—one that'll be there when he needs him."

When I looked at him again, I saw that Hank's high cheeks were wet with tears.

An hour or so later, Randall Hank Williams—Hank Jr., as he would be known from that day forward—came kicking and screaming his way into this world. He weighed a whopping ten pounds and three ounces at birth, and Audrey joked to friends later that he "almost killed us both." He was the biggest baby in the hospital nursery, and his father was the proudest hillbilly singer in seven states.

Hank Jr. was exactly sixteen days old when Nashville rolled out its red carpet and welcomed Hank Sr. to the *Opry*.

4

Hank Williams II—

The Loneliest

Man Alive

Hank made his farewell appearances on the Hayride on June 3, 1949, before a standing-room-only crowd of thirty-eight hundred. By the time they arrived at the auditorium that night, many people in the audience knew they were about to witness the end of an era, not only for our show and Hank but for themselves. Most of them realized this would be their last chance to see Hank in person in Shreveport for a long time—maybe even forever—and their mood was a mixture of excitement and something fairly close to grief.

I didn't think they were ever going to let him stop singing "Lovesick Blues" that night. The tune that had made Hank famous and become his ticket to the *Grand Ole Opry* was now tearing him away from his Louisiana, Texas, and Arkansas fans, but they still loved every word and note of it. Their applause called Hank back for encore after encore—seven of them in all—and there's no doubt in my mind they would have kept him singing all night if they could have.

After the seventh and final encore, everyone in the auditorium stood and gave Hank a deafening ovation. It was a record for encores that no *Hayride* artist before or since ever matched, and the only reason it ended there was because we were completely out of time. Hank waved at the crowd, then bowed his head. He was clearly touched.

"Thank you," he said, when the din finally died down enough for him to be heard. "I want to thank y'all from the bottom of my heart, and I'm makin' you a promise right now. One of these days, I'll be back. I guarantee it."

The crowd applauded some more, and as Hank walked slowly past me on his way off the stage, I could see how deeply moved he was by the audience's reaction. He made no effort to hide the tears streaming down his face.

My own feelings at that moment were pretty much the same as everyone else's, I guess. In the ten months since I'd first introduced him in this building, Hank had put the *Louisiana Hayride* on the national map. It had been a great experience, but now it was over. My head told me there'd be other stars, but my heart couldn't quite believe there'd ever be another one like Hank Williams.

Under the terms of our contract, we could've held onto Hank for a few more weeks. But once the invitation to join the *Opry* had been formally extended by WSM General Manager Harry Stone and the *Opry's* artists' service director, Jim Denny, I'd convinced the management at KWKH not to try to tie Hank up in legal red tape. After all, what was the point? Regardless of what we did, he would be gone in a short time, anyway, I told them. So instead of clinging desperately to the first true national star the *Hayride* had produced, what we needed to do was start seeking out and grooming future stars to fill the void his loss was creating.

At the same time, I felt that loss as keenly as anyone alive. I wasn't just losing a performer. I was also losing an artist with unique musical talents—and I was saying good-bye to a close friend.

I was worried about Hank, too. Those of us in Shreveport who cared about him had established a kind of support system to help him over the rough spots as much as possible, and he wasn't going to have anything like that in Nashville. I'd seen with my own eyes how easily he could lose his grip on stability and go plunging off the deep end. Hank saw Nashville and the *Opry* as the two goals he'd been striving for all his life, but I knew they could also become a deadly trap for him.

Generally, he'd behaved himself pretty well since his release from Highland Sanitarium, and that was encouraging. Still, there'd been occasional slipups and relapses. I hadn't seen him seriously drunk—not the way he stayed most of the time in the weeks after that Easter picnic, and not enough to noticeably affect his performances—but I knew he hadn't been staying sober all the time, either.

One Saturday night, for example, after winding up his second appearance on the *Hayride* stage with no apparent problems, Hank told guitarist Bob McNett he wished he didn't have to sign autographs after the show.

"I just hate for these people to smell my breath," he said.

After a couple of drinks—before his personality underwent that dark change and his behavior turned utterly unpredictable and self-destructive—Hank sometimes went through a silly stage. He had a keen sense of humor, although he kept it under wraps a lot of the time, and he occasionally joked around with the other guys, even when he wasn't drinking. The difference was, after a few snorts, his humor got kind of insensitive and sometimes downright crude. I noticed this on several of the bus trips we made for out-of-town productions of the *Hayride*.

Time could get pretty heavy on hand on those trips, especially on a long haul to someplace like central Texas. It was boring and confining inside the bus, and the scenery outside was drab and uninteresting. Guys passed the time the best way they could—napping, reading, playing cards, tuning their instruments, shooting the breeze, and occasionally getting into some pretty rough horseplay. During one scuffle, Hank accidentally banged Felton Pruett, his steel player at the time, in the face with his knee and blackened Pruett's eye. Hank looked for a minute like he was going to cry when he saw Felton was hurt. He apologized all over the place and kept asking Felton if he was okay for the next hundred miles.

Some of the younger guys had a bad habit of sneaking booze onto the bus, and they thought they were doing Hank a favor by sharing it with him. I think maybe they just liked to see Hank laugh and cut up. On one of the last of these trips we made before Hank left the *Hayride*, I remember him sprawling out in a seat across the aisle from me. His hat was pulled low over his eyes, and he was chuckling to himself as he picked out a little tune on his guitar.

"Listen to this 'un, Hoss," he said. "See if you think I oughta play it on the show tonight."

"What's the name of it?" I asked.

"It's called 'The Dirty Drawers That Maggie Wore,'" he said, and immediately started singing:

> *Oh, they was tore an' they was split,*
> *An' you could see where she had—*

"No, I don't think so, Hank," I said, cutting him off before any of the ladies on the bus had a chance to get offended. "I don't think that one'll ever make it with MGM or Acuff-Rose, either."

Hank was cold sober and dead serious when he came in to tell me good-bye after that farewell show. It was our last face-to-face conversation before he hit the road for Nashville.

"I want you to know I sure hate to leave here, Hoss," he said. "Comin' over to Shreveport's been the best thing that ever happened to me. I just hope I ain't makin' a mistake."

"Well, I'm sorry to see you go, too," I said, "but you've earned yourself a spot on the *Opry* if anybody ever did. I know you'll rattle the roof over there, and I wish you all the luck in the world. Just remember, if you ever get tired of it and decide you want a change, you'll always be welcome here."

"I 'preciate it, Hoss," he said solemnly. "I 'preciate ever'thing. Wasn't for you and the *Hayride*, none of this might ever've happened. You done a lot for me, in more ways than one, and I ain't likely to forget it."

"You take care of yourself," I said, "and stay in touch. Let me know how you're doing."

Hank went alone to Nashville for his *Opry* debut on June 11, 1949. For the second time in less than a year, he'd disbanded the Drifting Cowboys at the end of May, planning to put a new group together after the move, so he had no musicians to travel with him. Meanwhile, Audrey was still recovering from Hank Jr.'s birth, and the baby was too small to be hauled off on a trip like that, anyway. Hank left his family behind at the modest house on Modica Street in Bossier City, where they stayed until late summer.

It was one of the ironies of those pretelevision days that nobody recognized Hank as he wandered around Nashville that first Saturday, not even when he strolled along the street outside the Ryman Auditorium. He had become an instantly recognizable celebrity to many people in and around Shreveport, and this new sense of anonymity must've felt pretty strange to Hank. It was also ironic that, on the brink of his biggest career triumph so far, he was reduced to the status of a solitary nobody and utterly cut off from friends, family, fans, and familiar faces.

In one way, though, it was fitting for him to be so lonely and isolated at that memorable moment in his life. It was almost like an omen of what lay ahead for Hank. The more famous and successful he became, the lonelier he grew, and the deeper he sank into alcohol and drug addiction.

When I think back today about Hank being there in the Capital of Country Music in the big middle of all those celebrities he'd always looked up to, I feel a little sad. Even surrounded by people that admired him, Hank could feel totally alone, and I think he must have felt that way that first weekend in Nashville. Imagining what it was like for him reminds me of another incident that happened a few months earlier.

The first week "Lovesick Blues" hit number one on the record sales charts, Tillman Franks had handed Hank a copy of *Billboard* magazine that showed the rankings and carried an account of the song's meteoric rise.

Hank just sat there for a long time, staring speechlessly at the printed page, as if he couldn't comprehend what he was reading. I think he was just totally overwhelmed when he realized all this was happening to a poor, uneducated country boy like him. I think he was shaken and scared a little by it, too. I can almost hear him asking himself if he really deserved all this acclaim he was getting or if it was just some kind of fluke.

If he'd had these doubts and negative feelings then, I could only wonder how he was going to feel in the weeks and months ahead.

Once he stepped to the microphone on the Ryman Auditorium stage and sang the first line of "Lovesick Blues," Hank was a stranger in Nashville no more. After he was introduced by Cousin Louie Buck, the *Opry* announcer, Hank drew a solid round of applause, but when he wrapped his lanky frame around the mike and started singing, the Ryman audience responded to his debut exactly the same as the fans at the Municipal Auditorium in Shreveport had responded to his farewell—with wild cheers and uproarious applause.

In all the twenty-two years since its founding, the *Opry* had never experienced anything like it. Hank Williams encored six times, something no previous performer on the show, much less a rank newcomer, had ever done. I'm sure those who had shunned Hank for so long were stunned. At least I hope they were.

(It was interesting to me, as an admittedly biased observer, to learn later that the "live" audience that night at the Ryman was actually a little smaller—by a couple of hundred—than Hank's last audience in Shreveport had been. The official paid attendance that night was 3,575, and the *Opry* admission prices were exactly the same as those for the *Hayride*. If anything, the Ryman's hard wooden benches and notoriously poor ventilation system made it considerably less comfortable for fans than our auditorium in Shreveport. Performers on the *Opry* were also paid the same union scale as we paid on the *Hayride*. Yet the *Opry* could call itself "The

Greatest Country Music Show on Earth," and pretend the *Hayride* wasn't even in the same league. It didn't seem fair—still doesn't—but that's show business, I guess.)

Hank had reached the point where the power structure at WSM could no longer ignore him, but it was also obvious they still didn't trust him. The whole idea of Hank Williams made them nervous. As tremendous as his performance and reception were that first night, and as wildly popular as "Lovesick Blues" was, his initial appearance was carefully excluded from the network portion of the *Opry*. It wasn't until a week later, on June 18, that Hank was first heard on NBC.

From that point on, things started happening so fast it was next to impossible for those of us he'd left behind in Shreveport to keep track of them all.

Before the end of August, he was back in Cincinnati for another MGM recording session, and I was surprised to get a long-distance call from him late one night. Well, actually, it was more like early one morning. It was the first time I'd heard from him in a month or more. He was pretty drunk, and he seemed depressed.

"Why don't you come up here to Cincinnati, Hoss?" he said. "I gotta have somebody to talk to."

"I don't think I better, Hank. My wife and kids might not like it if I went off like that."

"Well, bring your wife and kids along then," he said. "I'll pay for the plane fare and hotel and everything. Hell, I'll never miss the money, but I sure miss you an' the rest of that bunch down there in Shreveport."

"We miss you, too, Hank. What're you doing in Cincinnati, making more records?"

"Yeah, I recorded the saddest song today I ever wrote in my life," he said.

"Sadder than 'Wedding Bells'?" I still remembered the time he'd sung it for me and wept the whole time he was doing it.

"Aw, yeah, it's a lot sadder'n that. It's called 'I'm So Lonesome I Could Cry,' and I'm tellin' you, it's gonna tear people up when they hear it. If it don't make you cry in your beer, nothin' will. You sure you can't come up here just for a day or two, Hoss?"

"I'm sorry, Hank, I really can't make it."

"Well, you take it easy. Tell ever'body I said hello."

The Opry was relentless in capitalizing on Hank's exploding fame. The next thing I knew, he was off on a two-week overseas tour that took him and other major *Opry* stars to U.S. military bases in Germany, Austria, Britain, the Azores, and Bermuda. Just before leaving, he'd recorded a series of fifteen-minute programs sponsored by Hadacol, a popular patent medicine that had enough alcohol in it to make almost anybody feel better temporarily.

No sooner was he back in the States than he was booked on a week-long package show at the Hippodrome Theatre in Baltimore. It was the second week in December 1949. Hank had been gone from the *Hayride* almost exactly six months, and he was about to have his first serious problems with booze since becoming a superstar.

Oscar Davis, the promoter of the Baltimore show, noticed pretty quick that Hank was drinking heavily. Davis first asked Elton Britt, the famous yodeler, who was also on the show, to ride herd on Hank and try to keep him in line. When that didn't work, Davis put in an emergency call to Audrey, who flew up from Nashville and took charge of the situation. I don't know what she did—and I'm not sure I want to know—but Hank got through the engagement somehow.

"If Audrey had to come draggin' up here, she could've at least brought along Bocephus," Hank told me on the phone the night before he left Baltimore. "Seems like I never get to see him no more."

As usual, it was well after midnight when Hank called. Between my grogginess and his slurring, I wasn't sure at first what he was talking about. Then I remembered that Bocephus was the nickname he'd given Hank Jr.—one he'd borrowed from the puppet that *Opry* comedian Rod Brasfield used in his act. Hank liked nicknames and used them a lot. Lycrecia was "Jughead," Fred Rose was "Pappy," Don Helms, his new steel guitarist with the Drifting Cowboys, was "Shag." Little Jimmy Dickens, his fellow star on the *Opry,* was "Tater," and so on.

"How's that boy doing?" I asked. "I bet he's big as the side of a house."

"Hell, I don't know how he's doin'," he said disgustedly. "I ain't seen ol' Bocephus in so long, I doubt I'd even recognize him. I don't remember the last time I was home more'n six, eight hours at a stretch. Here it is almost Christmas, and I'll be lucky to spend one or two nights at my house during the holidays. What kind of a damn life is that?"

"An awful hard one, it sounds like. You need to slow down, Hank. You're pushing yourself too hard."

"They won't let me slow down, Hoss. Lord, I'm already booked up solid all the way through May. Besides, I'm scared to take time off. I gotta make it while I can." He paused to laugh, and I could tell he'd just taken a swig of something—something stronger than ammonia-and-Coke, I suspected. "Hell, the way Audrey's spendin' money, I gotta work seven days a week just to keep up with her."

"Tomorrow's another day. You got to remember that, Hank."

"Yeah, I know," he said, sighing, "but tomorrow I got to be someplace in North Carolina."

For close to three years—from the time he and the *Hayride* parted company until he came limping back to Shreveport with his health wrecked and his life a shambles—I never saw Hank Williams in person a single time. Yet we never stopped being friends, and during that whole painful spectacle of Hank's rise and fall, he called me on the phone at least every week or two.

Almost always, the calls dragged me out of a sound sleep long after I'd gone to bed. But whenever the telephone rang in the wee hours of the morning, I always answered it—mostly because I was pretty sure whose voice I'd hear on the other end of the line. He'd be sitting all alone in a hotel room somewhere, trying to wind down and ease the hurting in his back after a hard drive, a handful of bennies, and a long night on stage.

It happened so many times that it became a standing joke between us:

"Hope I didn't wake you up, Hoss."

"Nah, I had to get up to answer this damn phone, anyway."

The year 1950 must've been nothing but a blur for Hank. He did personal appearance tours all over the United States and Canada and cranked out some of his biggest hit records, including "They'll Never Take Her Love From Me," "Moanin' the Blues," "Nobody's Lonesome for Me," and "Cold, Cold Heart." Every Saturday, he was back in Nashville long enough to do an afternoon program on WSM for Duckhead overalls and appear on the *Opry* that night. Then, as soon as the *Opry* ended at midnight, he'd head straight to the airport to start another long cross-country haul.

An article in *Billboard* in April of that year claimed Hank's gross earnings for the past eight months had topped 400,000 dollars. That's probably the equivalent of four million today, and it was easy for some people who knew him "back when" to envy him. But I couldn't help wondering how much of that money Hank had actually seen himself—and how much of it he had left.

I never knew where he'd be calling from next, but I knew it would be somewhere far from home.

"Hey, Hoss, you oughta come on up to St. Louis. I got me a lady wrestler here, and she's showin' me some new holds."

"How's it goin', Hoss? Man, I just drew one helluva crowd up here in Toledo. Over thirteen thousand folks for one show—ain't that somethin'?"

"I'm gonna send you some cuff links I bought here in Oklahoma City, Hoss. They got little .45 revolvers on 'em. I thought you'd like that."

"Hoss, I been on this Hadacol Caravan train so damn long I don't know *where* I am anymore. Wherever it is, it's lonesome as hell, though."

Many people had expected Hank's departure to have a disastrous effect on the *Louisiana Hayride*. Basically, they thought the only reason the *Hayride* had become such a success was because of Hank's popularity, and we were frankly a little worried about what was going to happen. The doomsayers were dead wrong, however. The large cast, the fast pace, and the emergence of other rising young artists kept the show going strong. For the first few weeks after Hank left, attendance sagged a little, but not nearly as much as we'd feared it might.

By this time, I'd realized that the *Hayride* cast was going to be in a constant state of change and that, in fact, this was one of the show's strengths. The continuous introduction of new acts was one big factor in keeping the crowds coming. We filled Hank's spot on both the *Hayride* and the Johnny Fair Syrup program by bringing back Red Sovine, who'd been a regular on the show earlier. In August 1949, the Bailes Brothers also moved on, and we added several other new acts, including Smiley Wilson and Kitty Carson, Boots Woodall and his band, Clyde Baum and the Bayou Boys, Zeb Turner and Sammy Barnhart. And in early 1950, T. Texas Tyler and Leon Payne, two artists who were already pretty well established, joined our regular cast.

But the two young performers who did more than anyone else to take up the slack in the immediate post–Hank Williams period—and turned out to be our next major stars-in-the-making—were Slim Whitman and Webb Pierce. Slim's first *Hayride* performance was on April 7, 1950, and Webb made his debut just one week later. A few months after that, Webb discovered another young singer named Faron Young, who joined the cast that October. All three of these performers were destined to make big names for themselves and become mainstays of our show. None of them ever caused as much of a public sensation as Hank did, but they gave the *Hayride* an even more solid lineup of talented artists than it had ever had before.

Hank's career hit its peak during the summer of 1951. His records were dominating jukeboxes all across the country, and "Cold, Cold Heart" was the most popular song in America, although the biggest selling version of it was by pop singer Tony Bennett, not Hank. The very fact that Hank's songs were able to cross over into the pop market was amazing. That had never happened before. Frankie Laine, Jo Stafford, Tennessee Ernie Ford, and Helen O'Connell had all recorded "Hey, Good Lookin' " on different labels. Guy Mitchell had done "I Can't Help It" for Columbia, Polly Bergen and Teresa Brewer had both released their own versions of "Honky-Tonkin'," and Kay Starr had made "Lovesick Blues" for Capitol. "Hank Williams has blossomed out as a full-fledged pop writer," *Billboard* reported after all these pop singers grabbed up his songs.

On July 15, Hank's hometown of Montgomery, Alabama, staged a big "Hank Williams Homecoming Day" celebration at its new Cow Coliseum, and more than nine thousand people came to see Hank and other stars including Hank Snow, the Carter Family, and Chet Atkins.

In August, Hank joined what can only be described as the biggest, most extravagant traveling medicine show in history—the Hadacol Caravan. It was supposed to make forty stops in eighteen states with an entourage of 150 entertainers and crew members. It had everything—musical acts, comedians, dancers, acrobats, beauty queens, circus daredevils, and fireworks displays. It was a million-dollar promotional stunt aimed at boosting sales of the patent medicine Hadacol. The admission price was two Hadacol boxtops for adults and one boxtop for children.

For the Caravan's appearance in Louisville, Kentucky, Bob Hope was flown in as a guest star. Unfortunately, he had the job of closing the show in a baseball stadium packed with thirty thousand country music fans immediately after Hank sang. The crowd was so loud it was impossible for the emcee to even announce the world's most famous comedian. When the din finally subsided a little, Hope put on a cowboy hat, walked out on stage and introduced himself as "Hank Hope." From then on, nobody closed a Caravan show but the real Hank.

In September, the Caravan ended its run in Dallas ahead of schedule and in deep financial trouble. Most of the checks given to Hank and other performers bounced, and the company that owned Hadacol eventually went bankrupt. From what Hank said on the phone, he was just glad the whole thing was over.

"All these famous people think they're better'n ol' Hank," he told me, referring to his fellow Caravan performers, "but we all got screwed just alike. To hell with 'em, Hoss. I'm goin' home."

Just a few days after the Caravan folded, Hank signed a five-year movie contract with MGM Studios, where producer Joe Pasternak had apparently picked up on the epidemic of Hank Williams fever sweeping the country. *Billboard* reported that MGM planned to cast Hank in both "straight dramatic and singing roles" in feature-length productions at a salary of up to 5,000 dollars a week.

None of it ever happened, of course.

By the time Hank became the first hillbilly singer to be featured on the *Perry Como Show* on CBS-TV that November, it looked as if he had the world by the tail. But behind the scenes, everything was already starting to fall apart. Hank's star had risen as far as it was going to go, and its descent would be steep and sudden.

For one thing, the back problems that plagued Hank all his life had grown steadily worse. I know he was born with a congenital defect called spina bifida, which affected several of the discs in his lower back. The pain from this condition was more or less constant, but it was worse at certain times than it was at others. Hank almost never talked about it unless the pain became unbearable.

He'd unquestionably aggravated this condition over the years in various accidents—many of them related to alcohol. I know, for example, that he fell off a stage at least once. But the accident that took the heaviest toll happened sometime in the fall of 1951. Back in Shreveport, we heard rumors about Hank falling or being thrown by one of the several horses he owned. Another report said he fell into a creek while he was hunting with Jerry Rivers, the fiddle player in his band. Whatever happened, he got to the point where he could hardly move. To dull the pain, he drank more than ever.

When Hank and the Drifting Cowboys got back from a long trip on the road, he was often dead drunk. Instead of taking him home, where he and Audrey were certain to get into another fight over his drinking, some of the band members would take him straight to the Madison Sanitarium outside Nashville and leave him there for a few days to dry out.

He also gulped painkillers and sedatives by the handful. As he'd shown years before by swallowing a whole box of aspirin at one time, Hank had a distorted philosophy where medication was concerned. He figured if taking one pill every four hours did some good, then taking four pills every hour ought to make things even better. The difference was, he wasn't taking over-the-counter stuff like aspirin anymore. Now he was taking strong prescription drugs—as many of them as he could get.

In mid-December 1951, Hank had back surgery at Vanderbilt Hospital in Nashville. The doctors claimed the operation was a success, but if anything, I think the pain only got worse. From then on, it was strictly downhill for Hank.

While he was still convalescing from the surgery, the strain of his constant drinking, drugging, and hurting finally brought his marriage to Audrey to an end. By early January, he'd moved out of the big house on Franklin Road and into a downtown hotel.

"It don't look like we're gonna be able to patch it up this time, Hoss," he said when he called me a day or two later. "The last thing Audrey said to me was, 'I won't never live another day with you,

Hank.' Hell, I don't know what to do. I guess I'll go to Montgomery and see my mama. Sometimes I think about comin' back to Shreveport, too. How'd you feel about that, Hoss?"

The question surprised me a little, but I tried not to show it.

"I told you before, Hank. You're always welcome here."

I knew Jim Denny, my counterpart at the *Opry,* fairly well, and I knew he was starting to lose patience with Hank's drinking and missing shows, even before the back surgery sidelined him and forced him to cancel a big engagement in Baltimore. But this was the first time the possibility of Hank returning to Shreveport had been mentioned since his last night on the *Hayride.* And I have to tell you, even as low sick and bad off as he was, it definitely got my attention.

For one thing, I was vain enough to think if we could ever get him off the road for a while and settled down into a less stressful routine, he might get straightened out and be all right. After all, I told myself, he was still a young man. Even the breakup with Audrey might turn out to be a blessing in disguise, I thought, because it would release him from so much tension and pressure. Under the right circumstances, there was no reason he couldn't turn his life around.

It never occurred to me at the time, of course, that in less than a year, Hank Williams would be dead.

The next six months consisted of one disaster after another for Hank. Audrey filed for divorce on January 10, 1952, charging Hank with "cruel and inhuman treatment." She also filed writs of injunction against every one of Hank's assets, present and future, specifically naming their home on Franklin Road in Nashville and its furnishings, a farm near Franklin, Tennessee, that Hank had paid down on, three Cadillacs, a shop called Hank and Audrey's Corral, bank accounts and income from song and record royalties, personal appearances, and radio shows.

What this meant was that all Hank's assets were frozen until the divorce was final and a formal division of property was decided by the court. If he expected to have any money at all to live on, Hank had to get back on the road as quick as he could.

In order to have a roof over his head, he moved into a house that was already being rented by an upcoming young singer from Texas named Ray Price. Ray and Hank had worked together a number of times and even had written a song together. Ray admired Hank and didn't ask a lot of questions, but after two or three months of wild all-night parties and rowdy crowds that left the house a wreck, he quietly moved out and turned the whole place over to Hank.

Hank's first big show after his surgery was in Richmond, Virginia, in late January, and it was a total catastrophe. His back was still killing him, and he was so full of pills and booze that he couldn't remember the words to his own songs. The crowd booed and jeered at him, and a writer for the *Richmond Times-Dispatch* gave him a scorching review. The next night, he stormed to the microphone at Richmond's Mosque Theatre and dedicated his first song—"Mind Your Own Business"—to a "certain lady writer that you all know." It earned him a laugh and got the crowd off his back. At least Hank still had a sense of humor.

It didn't get any better, though. By the time his divorce from Audrey was final in late May 1952, Hank had been on a continuous binge for close to five months. The *Opry* kept right on pushing him to do more personal appearances, although at least half the time he was too sick or drunk or stoned to perform. Jim Denny assigned an ex-cop named Charlie Sanders to watch Hank constantly while he was on the road and keep him away from alcohol, but Hank always seemed to find a way to smuggle some in.

Every few days, a new story about Hank's latest misadventures was circulating on the show business grapevine. One I heard repeated many times, and one that touched me deeply, was the story about what Hank said to Minnie Pearl while they were in San Diego on a tour for the *Opry*.

Hank was so bad off he almost collapsed on stage after singing a couple of songs, and Minnie and the promoter's wife got him into a car and took him for a drive to try to sober him up and keep him from drinking any more. He was so jumpy and restless that Minnie suggested singing songs to calm him down a little, and Hank started to sing "I Saw The Light." But then, after a few lines, he stopped and started to cry.

"I don't wanta sing that song no more, Minnie, 'cause I *don't* see no light. Oh, God, Minnie, there ain't no light for me."

Sometimes, when he sobered up, Hank knew he was getting himself in deeper and deeper trouble with the brass at WSM. But at this point, I don't think there was really very much he could do about it. All the things he cared deeply about—Audrey and their home and his little boy—had been taken away from him. Audrey wouldn't talk to him and wouldn't let him anywhere near Hank Jr. None of the rest of it mattered.

"Jim Denny come out to my house and laid the law down the other day," Hank muttered to me over the phone one night. "He said management was puttin' pressure on him to suspend me from the *Opry* unless I straightened up. I told him, hell, I'll do whatever I'm gonna do, but if those sonofabitches keep on messin' with me I won't guarantee what that'll be."

"I know you don't want to hear this, Hank," I said, "but you need to get yourself into a sanitarium and stay there till you can think things through. You've got too much going for you to throw it all away."

"You really think so, huh?"

"Yes, I do."

"Well, that's funny," he said, " 'cause I don't feel like I got nothin'."

He sounded like the loneliest man in the world.

On Monday, August 11, 1952, the axe finally fell. Denny called Hank at home to break the news. The previous week, Hank had been ordered to "show up or else" for a program on WSM called *Friday Night Frolics*. When Hank shrugged off the order and stayed away, a "corporate decision" had been made to fire him. Denny told him if he squared up and behaved himself for a year, they'd consider taking him back. Hank told Denny he couldn't fire him because he'd already quit.

Years later, Ernest Tubb mentioned to me that he'd been in Denny's office at the time he made the call to Hank. Ernest said he'd seen Denny wipe away a tear as he hung up the phone. "I told Jim I knew he'd done it to try to straighten Hank out," Ernest said, "but I also reminded him I'd told him months before he ought to take Hank off the road and give him a rest."

From all reports, the firing sent Hank into a real tailspin. He disbanded the Drifting Cowboys again and stayed blind drunk for several days. Johnny Wright had to pick up Hank's last check for him because he was too weak to walk into the WSM studios. Then Johnny drove him to his mother's house in Montgomery. On the way, Johnny recalled Hank mumbling: "It just busted my heart when Audrey left me. It's just too damn hard to take."

Just a week later, on August 18, when he should have been singing on the Ryman Auditorium stage, a brief press dispatch told of him being arrested and thrown in jail on a drunk and disorderly charge in Alexander City, Alabama.

Hank was fuming when he called me the following week, but he seemed to have himself back under control. "I've left the *Opry*, Hoss. I got hit records all over the charts—looks like 'Jambalaya' 's headed for number one—and they say I've sold ten million of 'em since I started out. But I guess ol' Hank just ain't good enough for the fat cats in Nashville anymore. Just tell me straight out—can I come back to the *Hayride* or not?"

"Well, hell yes, you can," I said. "I've always told you you'd be welcome back anytime."

"I'm still at my mama's place, tryin' to rest up a little, and I got some show dates I gotta do over in Texas. Can I start about the middle of September?"

"That's fine with me," I said. "Whenever you're ready, just come on."

I admit I was torn at that moment by mixed emotions of my own.

As far as I was concerned, the brass at the *Opry* Acuff-Rose, and MGM records had milked Hank dry without any regard for him as a person. Because of that, I honestly believed the best thing he could do was get away from Nashville's influences and atmosphere, maybe not permanently, but at least for a while. Part of me selfishly wanted him back on the *Hayride*, but I also thought the change would be for his own good, too. Back in Shreveport, away from the pressure of the *Opry*, the pain of the divorce, and the swarm of drunks, freeloaders, and chippies that buzzed around him like flies, maybe Hank could pick up the pieces and start over. Maybe.

There'd be no twenty-four-dollars-a-night fees on this go-round, either. I already had clearance from KWKH to sign Hank to a long-term contract if I got the opportunity. It wouldn't pay a fortune, but it would give Hank a base salary of 200 dollars a week for a couple of hours work on Saturday night. That was the equivalent of nearly 100,000 dollars annually in today's money, and with his royalties, he could live comfortably without having to grind out personal-appearance tours every week of the year.

Of course, the ownership of KWKH wasn't going to obligate itself to this kind of financial arrangement without some proof that Hank could hold up his end of the bargain. Before the contract was offered, I wanted to be sure he'd show up and perform. After all, if he'd been a no-show at the *Opry*, he could be a no-show at the *Hayride*, too.

Would he really come? Would he really keep his word? Could we keep him in line once he got here? I asked myself those questions over and over during the next few weeks. I knew Hank wouldn't purposely lie to me, but in the shape he was in, the only thing I could do now was wait and see.

I also worried about him as a human being. Getting fired from the *Opry* could be the jolt that set him straight, or it could totally wreck him mentally and physically. Everybody who'd been around him said he was in extremely fragile condition, but I had no idea how far he'd actually declined until I saw him face-to-face for the first time in three years.

It was a little before noon on Saturday, September 20, when Hank phoned me at my office. The excitement in his voice was contagious. It got me excited, too.

"Hey, Hoss, I'm at Tony Sansone's restaurant over on Spring Street," he said. "Come on down here and let's have some lunch. I wantcha to meet somebody."

I didn't have any idea who he was talking about until I walked into Tony's place about fifteen minutes later and saw Hank sitting at a corner table with his arm around a very attractive girl. I recognized her instantly, but I was a little confused. The last time I'd seen her, she'd been with Faron Young. In fact, the last thing I'd heard about her was that she'd quit her job in Shreveport and moved to Nashville to be close to Faron. I knew her as Billie Jean Jones, the daughter of a police officer in Bossier City.

"This here's my French girl, Hoss," Hank said. "We gonna get married here 'fore long. Ain't she the purtiest thing you ever seen?"

"She's a mighty attractive lady," I said, then grinned at the girl. She really *was* beautiful. She had long red hair, large liquid eyes, and a spectacular figure. She was nineteen years old, if I remembered correctly. "Hello, Billie Jean," I said. "What's this about you being French?"

She giggled. "Oh, Hank just says that, Mr. Logan." She turned and kissed Hank on the cheek. "I don't have the faintest notion why."

"I didn't know y'all were acquainted," Hank said, giving Billie Jean a squeeze. "I love this gal, Hoss, and soon as we get settled in here, we gonna have ourselves a weddin' like you never seen."

As strange as it seems, Billie Jean had lived just a few doors from Hank and Audrey when they had their small house on Modica Street in 1949. Hank never paid any attention to her back then, but Billie Jean had often watched him climb into his big Packard and drive off to do a show. Several times she supposedly told her mother, "I'm gonna marry that handsome cowboy one of these days." Later on, though, she ended up marrying somebody else and had a baby by him. At this point, I assumed she was divorced, and I had no idea where her child was.

"Well, congratulations," I said. "Can we have something to eat first? You look like you could use some of Tony's spaghetti, Hank."

He laughed and reached across the table to shake my hand. "Same ol' Hoss," he said. "Sure good to see you again."

"Welcome home, Hank. It's been a long time."

He laughed again. "Yeah, lots of water under the bridge—and a whole buncha other stuff, too."

His appearance shocked me—there's no other way to say it. He had his hat on like always, and its wide brim accentuated the thinness of his face. He was wearing an expensive western suit that hung like a sack on his bony frame. He looked like he'd lost at least twenty-five or thirty pounds since the last time I'd seen him—and he hadn't had it to lose. One of Sansone's famous Italian salads sat untouched in front of him. Next to it was an empty Jax beer bottle. His face was pale, and his long fingers were stained with nicotine. They shook a little as he reached for a cigarette.

"You think the folks'll be surprised tonight?" he asked. "You think they'll be glad to see ol' Hank?"

"Yeah," I said, "I think they'll go nuts."

They did, too. It was a tremendous homecoming. When he sang "Jambalaya" and "Settin' The Woods on Fire," the whole auditorium vibrated with cheers and applause.

Hank held himself together pretty well for a few weeks. Sometimes he had to use a cane to get around, but he made every show and didn't cause any problems. Just a few days after rejoining the *Hayride,* he had to go back to Nashville for another recording session. He cut several of his biggest hits for MGM on that trip—songs that would help immortalize his talent—including "Your Cheatin' Heart," "Kawliga" and "Take These Chains From My Heart."

When he got back, he never mentioned the fact that he'd had to lie down and rest between songs. Nobody ever guessed it was the last recording session of his life.

On September 24, 1952, I signed Hank to a three-year contract at 200 dollars a Saturday night, and for a while, his health seemed to improve slightly. He scheduled only a few out-of-town appearances, and his color got better and he seemed a little more relaxed. But in reality time was rapidly running out.

In early October, he put together yet another version of the Drifting Cowboys and played several dates in Oklahoma, Kansas, and Missouri. It was on this trip, I heard later, that Hank ran into a guy who called himself a doctor, and this guy gave Hank a shot of something that made him feel good for the first time in months. The guy was really an ex-convict named Toby Marshall, and he was no more a doctor than I was, but Hank thought he was some kind of miracle worker. I've got no way of knowing how much of how many different drugs Marshall gave Hank over the next couple of months, but I'm convinced in my own mind that they were a major cause of his death.

Hank was never really himself again after that trip. He seemed to get more and more out of touch with reality. Half the time he didn't even recognize people he'd known for years. Most of his anger and bitterness may have been toward Audrey, but he got to the point where he took it out on everybody.

I was in my second-floor office at the radio station early one afternoon when I heard a commotion in the street outside and rushed to the window to see a very unnerving sight. About a quarter of a block away, a small crowd was gathering in front of the Columbia Restaurant on Market Street. Across the street from them stood Hank. He was holding a gun in each hand and aiming them very deliberately at each car that passed.

He didn't seem to have the vaguest idea where he was, but he looked as if he might start blazing away at any second.

I flew down the stairs about six steps at a time, and it didn't take me more than thirty seconds to reach the street. But by then, a uniformed policeman had seen what was going on, and he was moving warily toward Hank with his own pistol drawn.

Hank was standing there on the sidewalk with a glazed look in his eyes. He was sort of wavering and looking like a stiff breeze might blow him over. He had a .357 Magnum revolver in one hand—and a .45 automatic in the other. He was holding them both out at arm's length and taking a bead on every moving vehicle that came within range.

"For God's sake, don't shoot," I yelled at the cop from a few yards away. "Just let me talk to him. I can handle it."

The cop glanced warily toward me. "You know this guy?" he demanded.

"Yeah, I know him. It's Hank Williams."

"Well, I'll be damned, it sure is," the cop said. "What's wrong with him? Has he gone crazy or somethin'?"

"I don't know," I said. "Maybe he has."

I walked very slowly up to where Hank was standing. He turned and stared at me, but I don't think he recognized me at first.

"Give me the guns, Hank," I said sternly. "Give them to me right now—both of them."

He glanced down at the two guns in his hands as if he'd never seen them before. Then he lowered his arms and his fingers went kind of limp as I took them from him with no resistance at all. He took a couple of stumbling steps toward me, and I'm pretty sure he would've sprawled on the sidewalk if I hadn't been there to steady him. He seemed totally confused, but at least he finally recognized me.

"Are you mad at me, Hoss?" he asked sheepishly.

My heart was pounding so hard I could barely answer him. "No, Hank," I said. "I'm not, but I think the law is. And you just scared the hell out of a bunch of people."

A half-hour later, Hank was back in the Highland Sanitarium, and I was facing some of the toughest questions of my life. I'd talked the cop into letting Hank go without any charges, but he'd warned me to keep a sharp eye on him and not let anything like this happen again.

There was something about Hank that policemen instinctively liked. He made friends with the cops in practically every town where he played. They were the ones who often tipped him off about where he could buy rare guns at the right price. But clearly that wasn't going to help Hank with the cops if he kept pulling stunts like this. The truth was, the greatest country singer in America had become a danger to himself and others. Was he cracking up completely? Did I dare let him run around loose under the circumstances?

After he got out of the sanitarium, I could tell Hank was avoiding me. The only time I had any contact with him during the next week or two was just before and during our Saturday night shows. I don't know if it was because he was embarrassed or maybe just miffed at me. It could have been a little bit of both. He was there when he had to be, and he sang his songs with no big problems, but everybody in the cast knew by this time he was drinking heavily every day.

His weddings to Billie Jean—there were three of them in all—took place on October 18 and 19, 1952. The first ceremony was performed late on a Saturday night before a justice of the peace in Minden, Louisiana. The other two were held on the stage of the Municipal Auditorium in New Orleans as the highlight of a big show Hank was putting on the next day. The first ceremony was at 3 P.M. and the second at 7 P.M. I received a fancy printed invitation from the bride and groom, but I was busy with family matters that Sunday and didn't get to attend. From all accounts and the pictures I saw, it was quite a spectacle. By the time his third wedding was over, Hank was so drunk he couldn't tell if he was in New Orleans or New Zealand.

He'd appeared on the early portion of the *Hayride* the night before, but I agreed to let him skip his late performance so that he and Billie Jean and their witnesses could drive over to Minden. The reason for the quickie ceremony that Saturday night was that they were afraid Hank's mother would try to stop the wedding. Mrs. Stone was again trying to manage his career, and she was dead set against him marrying Billie Jean. She liked Hank's new wife even less than she liked Audrey.

From that weekend on, what was left of Hank's life turned into one pathetic mess after another. By early November, he'd reached the point where he was too incoherent to perform on the *Hayride* or anywhere else. He'd start to sing a song and just keep repeating the first line over and over, or he'd wander away from the microphone and not seem to know where he was.

One night, he refused to come out on stage when I introduced him as "the great Hank Williams."

"That ain't my name," he said. "I never heard of nobody by that name."

"Well, if you'll just come out here and sing, Hank, I'll call you anything you want me to," I said. "Just tell me what you want me to say."

"I'm Herman P. Willis, damn it—and don't you forget it, neither."

I shrugged. "Ladies and gentlemen," I said, "let's give a big hand to the great, uh, Herman P. Willis."

At least he did finally come out and sing.

It was heartbreaking to see such a great talent reduced to the level of a slobbering drunk. Even the fans who'd loved Hank the longest got justifiably fed up with him. But it made me mad as hell when the *Hayride* crowd started booing and jeering at him one night when he was too far gone to stand up by himself, let alone sing. And I told them so in no uncertain terms.

"You folks have been entertained by this man for hours and weeks and years," I said. "You've seen and felt his genius and ability. He needs our help and sympathy now, not our hypocrisy. When he's straight you all know how great he is. But when he's having problems, I won't stand for you laughing at this man."

There was dead silence in the auditorium for several seconds. Then, as I led Hank off the stage, the applause started and gradually grew into a real ovation. I like to think it was because the fans still had some respect for Hank and not solely because of the chewing-out I'd given them, but I'm not sure.

In October and November, Hank was in and out of Highland Sanitarium three or four times, and the diagnosis was always the same: acute alcoholism. They gave him Demerol and B_{12} injections and sodium amytal and chloral hydrate and God knows what else, but nothing seemed to do any good. Within an hour after he got out, he was soused again.

He could no longer control his bowels or bladder. He soiled some of his expensive stage outfits so badly they had to be thrown away. He wet the bed whenever he passed out, which was often two or three times a day. I frankly can't imagine how Billie Jean put up with him, but even as young as she was, I guess she had more patience than Audrey. I'm sure she woke up many a night in a saturated bed, and she and Hank were kicked off a commercial flight once after he dirtied his pants while they were waiting to take off.

Sometimes he'd bloat up like a balloon for a day or two, then go back to looking like a walking skeleton. A doctor at the sanitarium noted that Hank had a constant cough and cold-like symptoms. He complained of chest pains and said they got worse when he took deep breaths.

All his life he'd feared and hated doctors and hospitals, and that much hadn't changed. On the afternoon of December 11, he ripped an IV out of his arm and walked out of the sanitarium. An hour or so later, a policeman responded to a drunk call and confronted Hank downtown. This time, I wasn't there to intervene when the cop found a loaded .38 under Hank's coat. The cop handcuffed him and hauled him to jail, but when the police figured out what had happened, they took him back to the sanitarium that night.

I called Mrs. Stone in Montgomery and told her the situation was completely out of hand. "Hank's going to kill somebody or get killed himself," I said. "He needs to come home for a while and just rest. He needs to eat and stay in bed and not drink anything. I'll give him a leave of absence from the *Hayride* until he gets better."

His mother came over to Shreveport and more or less read him the riot act. By this time, I think he was too tired and worn out to put up much of an argument. After a day or two, Hank and Billie Jean left for Montgomery in a baby blue 1952 Cadillac convertible that Hank had bought a month or so after his divorce from Audrey had become final.

I never saw him alive again. Less than two weeks later, early on the morning of New Year's Day 1953, he died in the back seat of that same car somewhere in West Virginia. He was on his way to the last of three shows he'd signed to do when his teenage driver tried to wake him up and couldn't.

Although it was a holiday, I was at the radio station that morning cleaning up some odds and ends of work. I was looking through the dispatches on the Associated Press wire machine and getting ready to do an hourly newscast when I learned of Hank's death.

I had to catch the wall for support when the meaning of what I was reading sank in.

Oak Hill, W. Va., Jan. 1 (AP)–Hank Williams, singer and composer who was called the "king of the hillbillies" by his followers, died Thursday in his automobile on his way to fill an engagement in Ohio.

I couldn't believe it was true. As sick as he'd been, I was completely stunned. According to the AP dispatch, the cause of death wasn't yet known, but within a few hours an autopsy would supposedly determine Hank had died of heart failure. I didn't believe that either. Deep down inside, I knew what really happened.

It had been an overdose that killed him—an overdose of Hank.

As I turned away from the teletype and closed my eyes for a minute, the words from one of his hit songs raced through my mind. I could almost hear him singing those words and picture him sitting there with tears streaming down his face.

The song was "I'm So Lonesome I Could Cry," and he'd called it the "biggest tearjerker" he ever wrote. Somehow its lyrics seemed to sum up the whole existence of this strange, sad, lonely young man—especially the part about "the silence of a falling star."

The greatest star in the history of country music had fallen as far as he could fall, but his songs could never be silenced.

{ 5 }

The Legacy
and the
Lawsuits

The aftermath of Hank's death was every bit as confusing and chaotic as his life had been.

It's hard to describe the grief and depression felt by millions of his fans across the country, particularly in the South and Southwest. Only a small fraction of those fans knew about Hank's addiction to alcohol and drugs or how bad his health had gotten. The suddenness of his death hit them like a sledgehammer between the eyes. Sure, they'd heard stories about him missing some performances, and they knew he liked his whiskey. But what the hell? Many of these fans knew what it felt like to drink too much and wake up with a hangover. Sometimes they didn't feel like going to work, either. So what? Stuff like that wasn't supposed to kill you.

Like me, the fans kept asking the same empty questions over and over: How could this have happened? How could somebody so young and at the peak of his career suddenly be gone forever? "Jambalaya" was at the top of the folk music charts, with "Settin' The Woods on Fire" not far behind. "Half as Much" had just been named the number-one folk record of 1952, and—talk about your irony!—"I'll Never Get Out of this World Alive" was also climbing rapidly up the charts. To his fans, there was something almost mystical about Hank dying so soon after writing and recording this last tune. It was like the fulfillment of his own terrible prophecy. Some people were obsessed with it.

Hank was still indisputably the top country singer and songwriter in America. Nobody else even came close. If the guy who wrote and sang all these hit tunes was really dead, how come you couldn't turn on a radio or listen to a jukebox without hearing his voice?

Right behind the shock and disbelief came suspicion, even anger. Some fans had a hard time accepting a heart attack as the cause of death. If Hank had been killed in a car or plane crash—so they could've seen the wreckage, or even his mangled body—maybe it would've been easier to take. But a *heart attack*, for God's sake? At the age of twenty-nine? The more people thought about it, the fishier the whole thing sounded. It was like somebody was trying to cover something up.

Was there a legitimate reason for folks to feel this way? I didn't know then, and I don't know now, but there were some real puzzles surrounding Hank's death.

One of the most troubling questions in my mind revolved around "Dr." Toby Marshall and the mixture of powerful drugs he'd been giving Hank. The show-business grapevine was humming with stories and speculation about those drugs. Marshall had traveled with Hank a big part of the time during the last month or two of his life. He also was supposed to have given Hank medical script that he could use to buy any kind of drug, up to and including morphine, anytime and anywhere. Hank had mentioned to several people that "the doctor" had given him a drug that could kill him if he drank alcohol while he was taking it. Could Hank have gotten his pills mixed up and swallowed a fatal dose of something by mistake?

Billy Walker, who was one of our rising stars on the *Hayride* in late 1952, went with Hank on a swing through Texas during this period, and he saw firsthand what was happening. He saw Marshall giving Hank some little pink pills, and he asked Marshall what they were for.

"I'm giving him pure adrenaline" Billy quoted Marshall as saying. Billy also noted that Hank got "worse and worse" during the Texas trip.

Stories have circulated that, toward the end, the constant pain in Hank's back turned him into a full-fledged morphine addict. If that's true, it must've happened very close to the time he died. I know he took pep pills to rev himself up before some of his shows and chloral hydrate tablets ("Mickey finns") to put him to sleep. I'm sure he washed a lot of these pills down with vodka, which was his drink of choice in those last months because he thought people couldn't smell it on his breath so easily. But I never saw anybody inject him with anything, except when he was given IVs in the sanitarium.

Contradictory accounts of when and how Hank actually died only added to the mystery. There's even disagreement on how he ended up with his young chauffeur, Charles Carr, in the first place. One story says Hank personally hired Carr, a freshman at Auburn University, and offered him 400 dollars to drive him from Montgomery to Charleston, West Virginia, where he was to appear on New Year's Eve. This story says they left together on the afternoon of December 30. Another story says Hank left Montgomery by chartered plane but was forced by bad weather to land in Knoxville, Tennessee. From there, Hank supposedly phoned Lilly and told her to have someone meet him in Knoxville with his Cadillac so he could go the rest of the way by car.

Whichever way it happened, the weather made it impossible to make the show in Charleston, so Hank and Carr checked into a hotel in Knoxville about 7 P.M. on December 31. Witnesses said Hank was very drunk and had to be carried to his room by porters. He was reportedly unconscious when a doctor arrived sometime later and gave him some shots. Within the next two hours, someone—nobody seems to know exactly who—phoned Carr and told him to leave immediately for Canton, Ohio, where the January 1 show was scheduled.

There's some reason to believe Hank may have already been dead when he was carried out of the hotel by porters a little before 11 P.M. that night and placed in the back seat of the Cadillac. He definitely looked dead about an hour later when Highway Patrolman Swann Kitts pulled Carr over for reckless driving and turned his flashlight on Hank, who was "lifeless and blue-looking."

"Is he dead?" Kitts reported asking Carr. Carr replied that Hank had drunk several beers and been given injections to help him sleep. He said Hank was "very sick" and asked Kitts not to disturb him, so the patrolman didn't try to wake him up. Kitts took Carr to the sheriff's office in Rutledge, Tennessee, to pay his fine. He noted in his report of the incident that Carr seemed nervous.

At least two police officers reported seeing someone else in the Cadillac with Carr and Hank that night. Kitts described this third individual as "a soldier" but didn't identify him any further. After Carr finally stopped for help about 7 A.M. the next morning, Patrolman Howard Jamey of Oak Hill, West Virginia, also saw another man in the car. The man identified himself to Jamey as Donald Surface and claimed to be a relief driver Carr had picked up earlier. He disappeared a short time later and was never seen again.

The oddest part of all was the autopsy. It was conducted by a Dr. Ivan Malinin, a Russian refugee who'd only been in the States for a short time and spoke almost no English. Incredibly, the doctor found no evidence of narcotics in Hank's body, despite the documented injections of a few hours earlier and the fact that Hank had been a "walking drugstore" for weeks. Dr. Malinin did detect some alcohol in the blood, but he described Hank's liver as normal. For anyone who'd been around Hank recently, that was extremely hard to believe. His bloating and waxy color were classic signs of liver disease.

One of Dr. Malinin's most puzzling findings was that Hank had numerous small hemorrhages and injuries on his body that indicated he'd been beaten up and possibly kicked very shortly before his death. These injuries almost had to have happened on this last trip because Hank had stayed in bed at his mother's house for several days before leaving.

The primary cause of death was listed as "acute right ventricular dilation," or failure of the right pumping chamber of the heart.

I don't know much about medical matters, and I didn't find out until much later that this is almost unheard of as a cause of death. People often die from failure of the *left* ventricle, which supplies the lungs and handles most of the heart's pumping action, but practically never from right ventricular failure.

A coroner's inquest subsequently upheld Dr. Malinin's findings, and there was no further investigation. But like the notorious autopsy performed on President John F. Kennedy almost eleven years later, this post-mortem definitely raised more questions than it answered.

Funeral services for Hank Williams began at 2:30 P.M. on Sunday, January 4, 1953, in the largest available building in Montgomery—the Municipal Auditorium where he had appeared many times before. I'd never seen a spectacle like it before, and I earnestly hope I never do again. While many of those who came undoubtedly did so out of genuine respect and honest concern, many others were drawn there by morbid curiosity. Some came to gawk and point and whisper. Some seemed to think they were at a party. Some were only interested in being part of a historical event. And some came purely to gratify their own egos.

This funeral had something for everybody, that's for sure. Audrey and Billie Jean, the two "widows" (neither of whom was legally married to Hank when he died) sat close together on the same front row. To the delight of the gossips, a young woman named Bobbie Jett sat between them. She was nine months pregnant with what was rumored to be Hank's illegitimate child, and just two days after the funeral, she gave birth to a daughter. About a month later, Bobbie Jett left for California, but the baby stayed behind with Hank's mother for adoption, allegedly as part of an agreement Hank had made with the woman.

Ernest Tubb opened the service by singing "Beyond The Sunset." Red Foley sang "Peace in The Valley" and broke into tears before he could finish it. Roy Acuff mumbled a thick-tongued introduction, then led a chorus of *Grand Ole Opry* regulars—including Red Foley, Carl Smith, Webb Pierce, Little Jimmy Dickens, Johnny Wright, and Jack Anglin—in Hank's own composition "I Saw The Light." The Statesmen Quartet sang "Precious Memories." The Reverend Dr. Henry L. Lyon, pastor of the First Baptist Church of Montgomery, eulogized Hank as "a great American" who possessed something that humanity desperately needed—"a song with a heartfelt message," then proceeded to preach a thirty-minute hellfire-and-damnation sermon on the evils of drink. In short, it was kind of like a three-ring circus where lots of people did their damnedest to upstage a corpse.

I took a group to the service from the *Hayride,* including Felton Pruett, Ray Bartlett, and several others. Henry Clay considered it an important enough occasion to let us take the KWKH company plane, a twin-engine Beechcraft, to Montgomery. That in itself was a very rare experience.

Along with other staff members from KWKH, WSM, and WSFA, I was an honorary pallbearer. So were Fred Rose and his son, Wesley, and Jerry Rivers, Hank's favorite fiddle player. The funeral turned into such a production that professional booking agent A. V. Bamford, who had set up Hank's last few shows, was hired to handle the arrangements.

Ray Bartlett got so disgusted by the "crocodile tears" and self-serving "tributes" by the contingent of stars from the *Opry* that he actually walked out of the service. Later, we bumped into Roy Acuff at the airport while we were all standing around on the tarmac waiting to take off. I'd suspected Acuff of being tipsy when he'd introduced "I Saw the Light," and he was clearly about two-and-half sheets to the wind now. He stumbled around, popping off about the fancy chartered plane the *Opry* group had flown down in and what a great sacrifice they'd all made to be there.

Ray was holding an almost-full bottle of Coke when Acuff came up and grabbed it out of his hand without saying a word and took a swig. When he handed the Coke back, Ray refused to drink it and poured it out on the tarmac instead.

Some guy who was with the Opry group rushed over to Ray, and I guess he was trying to put Ray in his place when he said: "Don't you know who that is? That's Roy Acuff."

"Oh, really?" Ray said innocently, then added with a perfectly straight face: "Does he record for anybody?"

Less than three thousand spectators could squeeze into the Municipal Auditorium in Montgomery, but between twenty thousand and twenty-five thousand others stood outside in the cold along Perry Street and listened to the proceedings over loudspeakers. Thousands more were lined up along the route to Oakwood Cemetery and at the cemetery itself. Every available policeman and fireman had been called out to handle crowd control and try to keep onlookers from stealing all the flowers.

At the grave site, I stood next to Jim Denny as Hank's ornate silver coffin was lowered into the ground.

"Look around you, Logan," Denny whispered to me. "If Hank could see these idiots now, he'd sit right up in that coffin and say, 'See, I told you sonofabitches I could draw more people dead than you could alive!' "

I smiled and nodded. Over the years, there were lots of things Denny and I didn't see eye to eye on, but I agreed with his observation 100 percent. It was true that Hank would've loved all this attention. In fact, I thought if I listened hard enough, I might be able to hear him saying those exact words.

As the burial service ended and the crowds slowly began to drift away, I found myself walking beside a cabdriver who'd been well acquainted with Hank back in his early hell-raising days.

"You know, it's just a durn good thing ol' Hank wasn't any bigger'n he was," the cabdriver remarked.

I didn't understand what he meant. "I don't see how he could've gotten much bigger where country music's concerned," I said.

"Yeah," said the cabdriver, "but I'm talkin' about, you know, physical size. When he was playin' them bloody bucket clubs around here back in the forties, he could be mean as a snake when he was drunk. I seen him hit at people in the audience with his guitar just as hard as he could. If he'd been bigger and stronger, I reckon he would've killed somebody for sure."

"What do you figure made him do things like that?" I asked.

The cabdriver kind of laughed. "He got his feelin's hurt real easy in those days," he said. "When somebody acted like they didn't like his music, I reckon that was the only way he knew to fight back. 'Course, I guess he probably changed a lot after he got to be a big star."

"Not as much as you might think," I said.

The dirt had barely been shoveled into Hank's grave when his closest survivors starting scrambling to claim his legacy and the millions of dollars it was potentially worth. In the process, they touched off a series of legal battles that lasted for years. His two "widows" both started calling themselves "Mrs. Hank Williams" and scheduling public appearances and bitterly denouncing each other. They succeeded mainly in cheapening Hank's memory and, for a time, obscuring the true value of his music.

Hank had never been worth a damn at making business decisions or managing money. After his split-up with Audrey, his financial situation became a total disaster. Hank couldn't have cared less about things like investments and security. As long as he had a big wad of bills in his pocket, he never worried about what was going to happen next week or next year. He also never bothered to make a will.

Toward the end, Hank was especially careless and forgetful about money. On a trip to Oklahoma where he earned 3,000 dollars, Billie Jean later testified that he got home with only 300 dollars. She was pretty sure the rest of it ended up in Toby Marshall's pocket, but "Dr. Toby" wasn't the only one who benefitted from Hank's carelessness. There were also numerous stories that claimed Hank had been shorted on his royalties because he not only didn't know any better; he didn't really care. However much he got, he figured Audrey was going to end up spending anyway.

I know for a fact that during the last few months of 1952 you could book Hank and his band almost any night of the week for 500 to 750 dollars. (Of course, he might not be able to stand up if and when he got there, much less sing, but it was a bargain if he did.) I don't mean to imply that this was peanuts — it wasn't. It was equal to nine or ten times that amount today. But it was also nowhere near what other top recording artists were getting for themselves alone, without having to share with a band.

It didn't surprise me to learn Hank was practically broke when he died. Of all the hundreds of thousands of dollars that supposedly passed through his hands in the previous four years, the only cash he had left was about 5,000 dollars. Most of it was in the form of a cashier's check, and the rest was in an account at the First National Bank of Montgomery. His only other tangible assets consisted of guns, jewelry, clothes, and musical instruments. He'd signed his two Cadillacs — the convertible he died in and a black seven-passenger limousine — over to his mother a few months before his death.

The only things of true, lasting worth in Hank's estate were his name and his music. In his lifetime, he'd recorded a total of fifty single songs and two albums. Now that he was dead, they were in greater demand than ever as collector's items. Less than a month after his funeral, *Billboard* reported that MGM's pressing plant was operating twenty-four hours a day to fill orders for Hank Williams records and still running behind. Meanwhile, Fred Rose had told a writer for the *Montgomery Advertiser* that there were more Hank Williams records to come.

"Hank wrote, recorded, and sang a lot of songs we haven't released yet," Rose said. "I can't say how many. It's a trade secret."

In all likelihood, Hank's records would generate far more royalty income after his death than they had during his lifetime, and it was all up for grabs. The buzzards were gathering, and the coyotes were jockeying for position. An all-out struggle for the rights to Hank's musical legacy was about to begin, and unfortunately I was going to be drawn into the middle of it.

The legal wrangling over Hank's royalties was destined to drag on for years. Within weeks after Hank's death, his mother, Audrey, and Billie Jean had all filed court cases aimed at gaining control of as much of his estate as possible.

Mrs. Stone was the first to go to court, only two or three days after the funeral, asking that she be named administrator of Hank's estate. In her action, she tried to eliminate her main competition by claiming Billie Jean's marriage to Hank wasn't valid. Her case was strengthened when a judge in Shreveport ruled the marriage illegal because Billie Jean's divorce from her first husband wasn't final until October 29, 1952, eleven days after she married Hank. Before the end of January, the court gave Mrs. Stone control of Hank's Alabama estate, but it didn't amount to much. The real wealth was in the royalties, and they weren't in Alabama.

A persistent rumor had been making the rounds ever since Hank's death, and it was about to become a key factor in the legal wrangling. The gist of the rumor was that Hank had already broken up with Billie Jean before he left on his last trip and was planning to return to Nashville, reconcile with Audrey, and reclaim his spot on the *Opry* as soon as he got back from Ohio.

Hank supposedly had revealed these intentions to several people during the last few weeks of his life. I know Hank missed Audrey terribly at times. I never could really figure out why, but I know he did. He fantasized about her a lot, and when he was drunk—as he was constantly at that time—he very well could have made comments like that. If he did, though, I'm convinced it was "blue-sky talk" without any basis in fact whatsoever.

I also know the *Opry* brass were under a lot of pressure to back down from their tough stance and let Hank back on the show. They might very well have yielded to this pressure, too, if Hank had lived. But the point was—and still is—that it wasn't their option. Hank had a contract with me that bound him to the *Hayride* every Saturday night until September 1955, and there was no way I was going to cancel that contract.

As the rumor became more widespread, people started embellishing on it. They misinterpreted the leave of absence I'd given Hank as an out-and-out release. I started hearing comments to the effect that "Horace Logan let Hank go once before, and he was ready to let him go again."

It wasn't true, though. There was absolutely no way Hank was going back to the *Opry* until his three-year contract with the *Hayride* expired. Not this time. I'd seen what Nashville and the *Opry* had done to Hank before, and I wasn't going to let them do it again.

When Audrey went to court to try to keep Billie Jean from getting any part of Hank's royalties, the rumor was an integral part of her case. Her objective was to protect the 50 percent share of royalties she'd been receiving as part of her divorce settlement from Hank and deny Billie Jean any share of the wealth. The best way to do that was to prove (1) that Billie Jean and Hank were never really married in the first place, and (2) that they were no longer living together as husband and wife when Hank died.

Meanwhile, Billie Jean filed a suit in district court in Minden, Louisiana, asking that Audrey either be barred from using the name "Mrs. Hank Williams" or forced to pay 100,000 dollars in damages for usurping Billie Jean's rights to that name. Audrey kept right on using the name anyway, even when she appeared with some *Opry* regulars in New Orleans, where the Louisiana court had jurisdiction.

"I've been using this name for ten years," Audrey said, "and I don't see why I should stop now."

In the summer of 1953, the dispute over use of the name and control of half the royalties was settled. In return for a cash payment of 35,000 dollars Billie Jean gave up both her right to be called "Mrs. Hank Williams" and any claim to Hank's royalties under the existing copyrights. The courts ruled that the split specified in the divorce decree beween Hank and Audrey would remain in effect, with Audrey continuing to get her 50 percent of the royalties. Hank Jr. was to receive the other 50 percent.

What seemed odd, though, was that the courts also upheld Billie Jean's rights as Hank's widow. Although their marriage wasn't legally valid, she was ruled to have been Hank's common-law wife. Under Alabama law, this gave her the same rights as if they'd been legally married. In light of this, it was never really clear to me why she signed away those rights and her legitimate claims to the existing royalty agreements for just 35,000 dollars.

True, that was quite a chunk of money in those days — more than lots of middle-class folks earned in ten years. But I was sure Billie Jean could've gotten a lot more if she'd just held out. I heard later that Hank's royalties paid Audrey an average of 125,000 dollars a year for the next twenty years. At the time, I guess maybe Billie Jean just wanted to get what she could, get away from the whole thing and move on with her life.

A short time after Hank's death, Billie Jean started dating another up-and-coming young artist named Johnny Horton, and within a few months they were married. Some people thought this showed a lack of respect for Hank's memory, but I never blamed Billie Jean for it. She was young and pretty, and I could understand why she didn't want to spend years mourning over a man she'd only known for a few months.

At any rate, legal sparring went on between Audrey and Mrs. Stone until Hank's mother died in February 1955. Even after that, Hank's sister Irene got involved, and the sniping back and forth continued. But when Billie Jean agreed to that 35,000-dollar settlement in 1953, Audrey probably thought she'd heard the last of her. I'm sure she hoped she had.

That wasn't how it worked out, though. In November 1968, Billie Jean filed another lawsuit in federal court in Atlanta against MGM Pictures, claiming that the movie *Your Cheatin' Heart* had damaged her reputation by portraying Hank as still being married to Audrey at the time of his death. Audrey, of course, had been a paid technical consultant for the film, and the story line most likely reflected her influence.

The movie, which was about as true to life as *The Wizard of Oz*, must've really gotten Billie Jean upset. It made her more determined than ever to be recognized as Hank Williams's last wife and to reap as much benefit as possible from that distinction. She hired herself some smart lawyers who sniffed out a very large loophole in the agreement Billie Jean had signed giving up her rights to Hank's royalties.

In 1973, she filed another federal suit in Atlanta demanding that she be recognized as Hank's wife and legal widow. Audrey, of course, contested this claim. I was called as a witness by Billie Jean's attorneys. They paid my expenses to come to Atlanta and testify.

"Were you prepared to release Hank Williams from his contract with the *Louisiana Hayride* in order for him to return to the *Grand Ole Opry* and move back to Nashville?" one of the attorneys asked me on the stand. Audrey's lawyers were basing their case on the idea that Hank had broken up with Billie Jean and was about to go back to Audrey when he died. But to do that, he obviously would've had to leave Shreveport and return to Nashville.

"Begging the court's indulgence," I replied, "hell, no."

I explained that Hank was legally bound to the *Hayride* every Saturday night for a period of three years by a standard musicians' union contract that was recognized throughout the entertainment industry, and that I'd had no intention of releasing him from it.

"If the *Opry* had wanted him any night but Saturday, he would've been free to go," I said. "But on Saturday night he belonged to the *Hayride.*"

I was also asked if, in my opinion, Hank and Billie Jean had lived together as man and wife and if I was aware of any breakup in their relationship before Hank died.

"I let Hank off early one night so he could marry Billie Jean," I said. "They lived together in Bossier City from that time until they went to Montgomery so Hank could try to get his strength back. I never heard anything about any breakup."

I was convinced in my own mind that Billie Jean had cared deeply about Hank. Otherwise, there was no reason she would've put up with him in the condition he was in. I think she believed they were legally married and never realized they weren't until after Hank died. I also think she did what she could to help him, but the situation was out of her control.

In the end, the court upheld Billie Jean's full legal rights as Hank's widow.

In the fall of 1975, more than twenty-two years after Hank's death, Billie Jean filed still another lawsuit, and I think this one caught Audrey totally off-guard. The original copyrights on Hank's biggest hits were about to come up for renewal, and Billie Jean maintained that the agreement she'd signed back in 1953 in exchange for 35,000 dollars applied only to the originals, not the renewals.

As Hank's wife and legal widow, she was now laying claim to her rightful share of the proceeds from those renewals. In other words, Billie Jean was demanding that when the copyrights were renewed, the 50 percent of the royalties Audrey had been receiving all this time be transferred to her.

Except for the change in location from Atlanta to Nashville, my testimony in the second court case was a reprise of what I'd said in the first one, at least as far as I was concerned. The key issue was again the validity of Billie Jean's marriage to Hank and whether he'd left her and returned to Audrey before his death. I was again called as a witness by Billie Jean's attorneys, and I repeated the testimony I'd given in 1973 pretty much verbatim — except for one thing.

When one of the lawyers asked my opinion about the MGM movie's portrayal of Hank and Audrey's relationship, I said: "Hank was born and he died. That much of the movie was right. All the rest of it was totally wrong."

The opposing attorneys objected loudly, but it didn't do much good. This time, it was Audrey who was going to come out the big loser.

On October 22, 1975, the judge handed down his verdict. Not only did the court recognize the validity of Billie Jean's marriage to Hank, but it also ruled that the agreement she'd signed in 1953 didn't apply to the copyright renewal royalties. As Hank's legitimate widow, 50 percent of those royalties belonged to her.

It was a crushing blow for Audrey—one of many she'd suffered recently. She'd used those royalties for more than two decades to maintain a high lifestyle and as the basis for several ill-fated attempts to make herself a singing star. With the royalties soon to be taken away, she'd have no source of income at all.

Her attempts to control Hank Jr. and his earnings had left her estranged from her own son, and just a couple of months earlier, Hank Jr. had been severely injured in a mountain climbing accident. Audrey was facing huge debts, in deep trouble with the IRS, and on the verge of losing the house on Franklin Road. She'd also developed an alcohol and drug addiction that was almost as bad as Hank's had been.

Less than two weeks after the judge's decision—and about twenty-four hours before IRS agents were scheduled to seize her house—Audrey died in her sleep.

It stirred up a lot of old memories for me when I read about her death. Regardless of all the grief she'd caused herself and other people, I was truly sorry.

In 1983, Hank Jr. and Lycrecia arranged to have their mother's remains moved from a site about thirty feet from Hank's grave and reburied beside him. Their ornate matching monuments stand on a hill overlooking Montgomery.

In that respect, at least, they're still together.

"Cradle of the Stars"

To borrow a phrase from literature, the first few days of Jan-
uary 1953 were the best of times and the worst of times for us at the
Hayride. It was a gloomy period for everybody in country music, especially those who were close to Hank Williams. In years to come,
many other prominent entertainers would meet tragic, untimely
deaths in the prime of their careers. But Hank was the first to go
out so suddenly and unexpectedly, and it was hard to shake off our
shock and sense of loss. Still, we knew the show had to go on, and
just at that dark moment, we were helped along by one of the most
exciting pieces of news in the Hayride's history.

In December 1952, after four and a half years of waiting and
negotiations that seemed to drag on forever, we learned we were finally going on the CBS radio network. The following month, CBS
launched *Saturday Night—Country Style,* an hour-long weekly series
featuring six country music shows scattered across the country
from West Virginia to Texas. The *Hayride* was one of the six and
would be heard in a thirty-minute segment every third Saturday
over the network, coast-to-coast.

At about this same time, KWKH's sister station, KTHS in Little
Rock, Arkansas, went on the air with a new 50,000-watt transmit-
ter and also began broadcasting the entire four hours of the
Hayride every Saturday night.

This breakthrough meant that millions more listeners in every
corner of the nation would be able to hear our artists. It gave our

performers far more national exposure than ever before and tremendously enhanced their chances for nationwide recognition. It also put the *Hayride* on a more competitive footing where its chief rival, *the Grand Ole Opry,* was concerned.

When Hank had left the *Hayride* and gone to the *Opry,* it started a trend that continued for years—one that saw the *Hayride* introducing and developing outstanding talent, and the *Opry* doing everything in its power to entice this talent away. Even before Hank's death, two more performers who had risen to stardom on the stage of Shreveport's Municipal Auditorium—Webb Pierce and Faron Young—had followed in Hank's footsteps and moved on to Nashville. Making it to the *Opry* was still the benchmark by which the top artists in the country music field were recognized, and we didn't kid ourselves into believing this was going to change overnight. But now we at least had more ammunition to fight back.

As a rule, the *Opry* usually succeeded in this tug of war, and few artists who went to Nashville ever returned to the *Hayride* as regulars. (I'll talk about some of the reasons for this later.) But there were also some notable exceptions to the rule—instances where some of the biggest names in country music turned down the lure of the *Opry* and chose to stay on indefinitely as stars of the *Hayride.*

Without the CBS hookup that began in January 1953, I doubt this ever would've happened. It was the national exposure on approximately two hundred network stations across the continent that helped the *Hayride* earn the nickname "Cradle of the Stars." It also allowed us to keep some of those stars in Shreveport long after they were big enough to leave the cradle and go wherever they wanted.

There were those who expected the *Hayride* to fold after we lost Hank Williams the first time. Some undoubtedly thought we might not survive losing him the second time around. Years later, many predicted that Elvis Presley's departure would bury the *Hayride* for good. But in each case we proved the naysayers wrong. We just kept on cranking out stars.

It became a contagious thing. As our reputation spread from the Atlantic to the Pacific, our show became synonymous with young, star-caliber talent. As each new star rose toward the top, another one seemed to follow in his wake. They became links in a growing chain — until there were some twenty-five of them altogether.

One star in particular led us to numerous other artists and did so very deliberately. He became the *Hayride's* unofficial chief talent scout. He was always on the lookout for promising young singers and musicians. And in a notoriously cutthroat business, he never hesitated to recommend some youngster who might be competing with him for the spotlight a few months down the road.

He was one of a kind — my friend Webb Pierce.

Whenever I think of country singers who made tremendous sacrifices to reach stardom, I always think of Webb. There's no better example of someone who used grit, persistence, and hard work to reach the top, or who was more generous once he got there in helping other struggling artists.

The climb toward fame was long and steep for Webb, but geographically it didn't cover that great a distance. He grew up in West Monroe, about a hundred miles east of Shreveport, and married a girl from Mansfield, Louisiana. His wife enjoyed singing gospel songs with Webb, but her main interest was in settling down and living a normal life. He was a personable, nice looking, neatly groomed young man who got a job at the Sears store in Shreveport after high school and worked his way up to manager of the men's clothing department.

Webb was a solid, dependable kind of guy who never had any serious problems with booze, women, or drugs as far as I know, and

I'm sure he could've moved far up the management ladder at Sears if he'd wanted to spend his whole career there. But he wanted more out of life than that. He was determined to be a singer, and the only place he knew to start was at the bottom. So, while holding down a day job at Sears, he started playing nickel-and-dime engagements at country schoolhouses, crossroads churches, and public meetings. It was a tough row to hoe, especially when it caused so much friction at home, and I know Webb came close to giving up his musical aspirations many times, but he never did.

His wife got even unhappier after he landed a job on a gospel music program at radio station KTBS in Shreveport, which at that point was a rival to KWKH but had had the same ownership until recently. As far as Webb's missus was concerned, this was just an empty distraction that was jeopardizing their financial security. And to tell you the truth, Webb wasn't really that good a gospel singer. Gospel music wasn't his strong suit, and it was only after he started trying other kinds of songs that his singing began to show promise.

It was in late 1949, a few months after Hank Williams had gone to the *Opry,* that Webb first approached me about getting on the *Hayride.* I liked him personally, but at the time I honestly didn't think he had what it took to make it as a regular on our show, and I told him so. Webb wouldn't take no for an answer, though. He kept bugging me about it for several months.

"Webb just wouldn't give up," recalled singer-songwriter Merle Kilgore. "He just kept saying, 'One of these days I'm gonna be on the *Hayride,* you wait and see.'"

As Webb himself remembered in an interview some thirty-five years later: "I met Horace Logan and kept telling him how much he needed me on the *Louisiana Hayride,* and he kept telling me I was an amateur who couldn't cut it with the pros. Finally, he said, 'Okay, I'm gonna put you on with all those professional entertainers just so you can see how bad you are.'"

I was only joking when I told him that, but there were two legitimate reasons for not giving in to Webb's badgering. In the first place, we had a rule that no one who worked for a competing station could be on KWKH. In the second place, my boss, station manager Henry Clay, had an active dislike for Webb because of an incident that took place one morning in our studios.

As I mentioned, KTBS had formerly been our sister station (before the FCC ruled that the Ewing family's ownership of two radio stations in the same market was monopolistic and required the Ewings to dispose of it), and the two stations were still in the same building and still shared one large studio. One morning, somebody moved a music stand that Webb needed for his gospel program out of the studio, and as he was looking for it, he came barging into the newsroom where I was doing an hourly newscast. The noise Webb made didn't really distract me that much, but it did interrupt the newscast, and it made Henry furious.

Because of this, when I finally let Webb make a couple of trial appearances on the *Hayride* I kept his name off the payroll so Henry wouldn't see it.

To my surprise, Webb wasn't that bad the first time, so I invited him back the following week. He was pleased, but he let me know he wouldn't be satisfied with anything less than a regular spot in our cast every Saturday.

"I'll quit my job at KTBS just for the chance to be a regular on your show," he told me. "Right now the exposure means a whole lot more to me than the money."

"Okay," I said, "if you're willing to do that, I'll give you a shot." I'd never encountered anyone so stubborn in my life, and by now I was even beginning to see some talent there.

At the same time, I was also talking to another promising young singer from Florida named Slim Whitman about joining the regular *Hayride* cast. I was impressed with both Slim and Webb, and they ended up making their debuts on the show within a week of each other — Slim on April 7, 1950, and Webb on April 14.

Landing a regular spot on the *Hayride* turned out to be both a blessing and a curse for Webb. Careerwise, it gave him the boost he needed at a crucial point in his life, but it also dealt a fatal blow to his marriage. His wife told him he was going to have to choose between his marriage and show business, and she went back home to Mansfield and filed for divorce.

Webb wasn't a fly-by-night kind of guy, and he was really devastated when his marriage broke up. For a few days, I think he seriously considered leaving the show, scrapping his career and going back to Sears if all that would make his wife reconsider. It was a hard choice—one I've seen many performers and their spouses forced to make over the years—but in the end Webb decided to stay with the *Hayride.*

Only Webb himself could've said for sure if it was the right decision or not, but in spite of the rocky beginning, everything turned out pretty well. He managed to rebuild his personal life even as his career was beginning to blossom. He started dating a girl named Audrey who worked for the telephone company in Shreveport, and she soon became his second wife. I've always been glad Webb was able to stick it out through those difficult days. If he hadn't, the world of country music would have suffered an irreparable loss.

Anyway, when Webb's name showed up on the payroll list, Henry Clay came storming into my office and jumped all over me about it.

"That guy's a pain in the butt," Henry yelled. "You can't put somebody like that on the *Hayride."*

My reaction was to get mad as hell myself. During our three-year association, I'd gotten steamed at Henry more times than I could count, but this time I was so hot I told him he could take his radio station and shove it.

"I'm the producer of the *Hayride,* and I either run the damn show or I don't work here anymore," I said. "You can call me when you decide which way it's going to be."

I walked out and stayed gone for a couple of days. That Friday morning, I guess Henry got worried that unless I came back, he'd be stuck with trying to put the show together for the following night himself. He called me on the phone, and we smoothed things over.

"Look, just come on back and do whatever you want," he said. "But I still don't see why you've got to have that sonofabitch Pierce on the show."

"Because unless I miss my guess," I said, "he's going to be one of the biggest stars ever to hit country music. He'll either succeed or kill himself trying."

To my knowledge, Henry never attended more than two or three *Hayride* performances in the entire ten years I produced the show. He didn't know the first thing about country music, and he knew even less about the people who played and sang it. Fortunately, after that, he quit meddling with my choices of performers and let me do the job I was being paid to do.

Within a few weeks, Webb's first big hit song, "Drifting Texas Sand," took off on Decca and he started making me look like a pure genius. But before that happened, he and I had one more king-sized hurdle to clear.

Like every other would-be singer, Webb had cut a couple of records for an obscure company, neither of which had sold more than a few dozen copies. He'd also signed over the rights to several tunes he'd written to the owner of the record company. Now that Webb was on the *Hayride,* Decca was ready to give him a contract that would get his voice heard on radio stations and jukeboxes all over America — but only if he could get the other record company to release him.

It was a sticky situation, one that could've delayed Webb's national success indefinitely or maybe even wrecked his career.

"This guy's got me over a barrel if he wants to get tough about it," he said. "What do you think I ought to do?"

I've always thought you can catch more flies with honey than you can with vinegar, so I suggested we butter up the president of the small company Webb had been recording for. When the guy came to Shreveport, we took him out to dinner, then made the rounds of some of the clubs in Bossier City and bought him a few drinks. We also introduced him to an attractive young lady who quickly diverted his attention to other things besides record contracts.

As the night wore on, the record company president got to feeling pretty mellow. Before the evening was over, he'd not only agreed to cancel Webb's contract but also given him back the rights to several original tunes.

The next morning, we shipped the tape of "Drifting Texas Sand" to Decca, and within a few weeks, the record was in the stores. It did very well, and Webb followed it up with "Wondering," which did even better. Webb was on his way to one of the most phenomenally successful careers any country artist ever enjoyed.

Webb described himself as "just a country boy singin' his heart out," and that was basically what he was. But he was also an intelligent, perceptive young man who learned a lot during those early months on the *Hayride*. He picked up a little something here and a little something there, and when he was done, he'd developed a certain uniqueness of style that was all his own. That's what made him a winner.

"There was a lady who used to come in and talk to me about singin' when I was workin' at Sears," Webb recalled. "She said, 'You ought to go to school and get your voice trained so it'll be smooth and you'll sound like all those famous singers.' And I said, 'But I don't want to sound like them; I want to sound like me.' "

That's exactly what Webb ended up doing. He developed a sound and style that was all his own. It was so distinctive that nobody could mistake Webb's voice for anybody else's. Part of it was a way he had of raising the pitch of his voice on his last notes, instead of coming down, the way most other singers do.

Webb also had an astute sense of timing. He held an original song of his off the market for several years, waiting for just the right moment. The name of the song was "Slowly," and when he finally released it, it became the number-one country song of 1954. Other top-of-the-charts sensations followed, including "Backstreet Affair," "It's Been So Long," "There Stands the Glass," "That Heart Belongs to Me," and "In the Jailhouse Now."

In fact, after moving on to the *Opry* in 1952, Webb put together an almost unbelievable string of hits. Beginning with "Wondering," he had thirty-two records straight that made it into the top ten on the charts. He eventually missed with one song, but then he had another string of ten top-ten hits in a row. By the end of 1953, he was recognized by the nation's jukebox operators as the number-one country singer in America. He became the heir-apparent to Hank Williams's title as "king of the hillbillies."

Webb's own great songs weren't his only major contribution to country music. He also opened the door for any number of promising youngsters who went on to become stars in their own right. Webb was responsible for bringing Faron Young to the *Hayride,* and Floyd Cramer first appeared on our stage as the piano player in Webb's band. The day after Floyd graduated from high school in Smackover, Arkansas, Webb gave him a job. Jimmy Day, who went on to become one of the top steel guitarists in the business, also started out as a sideman for Webb.

When Webb went to Nashville, where he built a big house just down the street from Minnie Pearl's, bought a custom-made convertible embedded with silver dollars, and reigned for years as one of the *Opry*'s biggest stars, Floyd and Jimmy stayed behind and became mainstays of the *Hayride* staff bands.

It was along about this time that another aspiring young musician named Jerry Lee Lewis showed up at my office one day looking for work.

"I play the piano real good," he told me, "and I really need a job."

"Sorry," I said, "but I've already got a good piano player."

"What's his name?" he asked.

"Floyd Cramer," I said.

"Never heard of him," he said.

"You will," I assured him.

A year or two later, Jerry Lee started blossoming as a singer, and before long, he was one of the top-selling recording artists in the country. He and I crossed paths many times after that, and whenever we bumped into each other, the subject of that turndown always came up.

"You sonofabitch, you wouldn't hire me," he'd say half-jokingly.

"Well, you sonofabitch," I'd respond, "you never told me you could *sing!*"

Even after he left the *Hayride,* Webb still kept his eyes and ears open for young artists he thought would add something special to our package. I remember him phoning me one night in 1952 and telling me excitedly about a singer he'd just heard perform.

"You gotta get this kid on the *Hayride,* Horace," he said. "His name's Billy Walker, and he's shy as hell, but he's gonna be really good."

On the strength of Webb's recommendation, I invited Billy to the *Hayride* right then, and he stayed with our cast for well over a year. He was a favorite with our audience, and he had the distinction of being our only regular performer to appear on shows with both Hank Williams and Elvis Presley.

I still feel honored by what Webb said about me at one of our last get-togethers with a bunch of old *Hayride* cronies back in the mid-1980s.

"There were only two people who believed in me when I was starting out," he said. "One of 'em was Horace Logan and the other one was me—and I wasn't always too sure about me myself."

Well, I'm sure of one thing today. Webb will always rank as one of the true giants of twentieth-century country music. I was deeply saddened by his death in 1991 after a long bout with pancreatic cancer, and I think it's a shame and an injustice that he's never been admitted to the Country Music Hall of Fame.

If anybody deserves to be there, it's Webb Pierce.

Faron Young was only a couple of months out of Fair Park High School in Shreveport when he landed a job on a daily show at KWKH. Right after that, Webb Pierce heard Faron sing, liked what he heard, and offered him a job with his band as a "front man" or featured singer. In October 1950, Faron made his first appearance on the *Hayride,* and from that point on, his career took off with amazing speed.

When Webb moved to Nashville, Faron set up his own band and I hired him as a soloist. He attracted almost immediate interest from Capitol Records, and I can remember him taking some of his tapes to Ken Nelson, the artists and repertoire man for Capitol, in a brown paper bag.

Capitol signed him to a quick contract, and Faron was on his way to such huge hits as "Hello, Walls" and "I Miss Her Already." Pretty soon, he followed Webb to Nashville where WSM offered him the *Martha White Flour Program,* one of its top morning shows, and a spot on the *Opry.*

Faron hadn't been gone but a few weeks when — like hundreds of thousands of other single young men at the height of the Korean War — he got drafted into the army. There was no frontline duty in store for Faron, though. In fact, his army stint hardly even handicapped him in his singing career. He was assigned to Special Services for most of his two-year army stint, making frequent radio and television appearances and doing a number of shows for the army recruiting service.

In addition to having an absolutely wonderful voice, Faron — "the Sheriff," as he liked to call himself — was an extremely handsome young man. But he was also short in stature, and like many pint-sized guys, he had a tendency to try to make up for his lack of size with loud talk and abrasive manners.

As far as sheer good looks are concerned, though, Faron didn't have to take a back seat to anybody. Women were always swarming around him and letting him know they were available if he was interested. Under the circumstances, it's not hard to understand how a guy could get a little carried away with himself, but Faron went to some real extremes. He seemed to think every female he came in contact with was ready to jump in bed with him, and he never hesitated to let them know he was ready, too.

He was without a doubt the dirtiest-talking guy I ever knew—and that's saying a lot.

He'd just walk right up to some girl he'd never seen before, give her a big grin and say, "Hi, baby, wanta screw?"

It never fazed him if the girl reacted with anger or disgust.

"Aw, come on, honey, who you tryin' to kid?" he'd say. "Hell, you got enough lather between those legs of yours to shampoo a herd of buffalo."

I thought his approach was insulting and downright crude, although I have to admit it worked sometimes. Not surprisingly, Faron had trouble maintaining long-term romantic relationships. He went through a series of relatively brief marriages and divorces.

Faron had a long, brilliant career in Nashville, and he became a very astute businessman who made money in several enterprises unrelated to music. He had a fancy house right next door to the governor's mansion, plus all the other trappings of fame. But like Webb Pierce, he was considered something of a rebel, and he was never elected to the Country Music Hall of Fame. I'm not sure how much real fulfillment he ever found, either.

The last time I saw him was at Webb's funeral in 1991, and he was still as brash and full of bravado as ever.

One of Faron's biggest hits on Capitol was "Live Fast, Love Hard, Die Young," and in some ways that seems to sum up both his philosophy and his life. Because of his good looks and his large ego, Faron was one of those people who had a tough time growing old gracefully.

It didn't get any easier when he contracted emphysema several years ago. He was still trying to perform, but his rich singing voice was failing, and it became more and more of a struggle just to get around. In December 1996, at the relatively young age of sixty-five, Faron shot himself. His death was officially ruled a suicide.

More than any other performer I know, Slim Whitman stands as living proof that any kind of music can successfully be given a "country" sound and style. Slim converted some of the most unlikely songs imaginable into some of the biggest hits in country music history. His version of "Indian Love Call"—a tune that originated in light opera—sold a million copies in 1952 and two million copies altogether. But Slim debated for a long time about recording it at all.

He and his band had been experimenting for several months with a new kind of sound, and Slim was worried that it was too much of a departure from what he'd been doing. I encouraged him because I knew he had to develop a distinctive, readily identifiable style to be really successful.

He was practicing "Indian Love Call" one day in the studio when I happened to be listening. He stopped about halfway through and asked me a point-blank question: "Do you think I ought to record this song or just forget it?"

"Well, sure, I think you ought to record it," I said. "It sounds terrific. Why not?"

"But it's just not country," he said.

"Hey, don't worry about it," I told him. "When you get through with it, it will be."

Slim had to overcome a lot of obstacles to get to the top, and the early part of his career was strictly slim pickin's. He was the son of a preacher who started out singing in the choir at his father's small church a few miles out of Jacksonville, Florida. Unknown to most of his later fans, he had a severe stuttering problem when he was young. He also was missing a finger on his left hand, so he had to play his guitar "backward"—fretting with his right hand and strumming with his left.

He worked in a shipyard before serving a hitch in the navy in World War II. After he was discharged, he played professional minor league baseball for a little while, then started singing on a small radio station. When I hired him for the *Hayride,* he'd been working on a morning radio show in Nashville for a few months as a featured vocalist. He also worked as a postman, a job he continued in Shreveport.

His yodeling ability caught the attention of RCA and he'd done a couple of single records for them. But RCA's big-name country singer was Eddy Arnold, and someone may have seen Slim as something of a threat to Eddy. Besides, Slim didn't use that high falsetto voice that later became his trademark, and he simply didn't sound much like himself. For whatever reason, the company didn't promote Slim's songs, and they never really got off the ground. By his own calculation, he'd sold a total of "only about four thousand" records when he came to Shreveport. Consequently, he was basically dead at RCA.

Even after joining our show, Slim had some rough sailing. I remember him taking his band to the small town of Vivian, Louisiana, for a performance one night in 1950 and netting exactly seventy-five cents after expenses.

Slim worked hard to change and improve his singing style during those early months on the *Hayride.* He and Webb Pierce were in fierce competition to become the principal star of our show. At first, they got along well enough with each other, but it grew increasingly obvious that an intense rivalry was building between them, and Webb was the first to score big with a hit record.

In addition to altering his style, I knew Slim needed to change record companies. I helped put him in touch with Lew Chudd, the owner of Imperial Records, which was primarily a rhythm-and-blues label based in California. Imperial had never done any country music before, but when Slim hand-carried Chudd a tape of "Indian Love Call" that we'd made in the KWKH studios, Lew got interested in a hurry. Imperial signed Slim to a contract in early

1952, and was promptly rewarded with the first million-selling record the company had ever had.

Thanks to Slim, it was far from the last. He followed up with "Rose-Marie" and "Love Song of the Waterfall," each of which also sold a million copies. The original tapes for all three of these best-sellers were made in the KWKH studios, by the way.

Slim was and still is one of the straightest, most decent individuals I ever encountered in show business. He had a strong enough character to steer clear of the bad habits that dogged or doomed so many other stars, plus the willingness to put in long hours perfecting his presentation.

I can remember only one incident in which Slim could've been accused of "putting on airs." He got the idea that his first name wasn't quite classy enough for a top recording artist, so he decided he'd change the spelling to "Slym."

He very quickly changed it back, however, after announcer Ray Bartlett and I referred to him on the air a few times as "Slime."

Steel player Hoot Raines and electric guitarist Curley Herndon, who later teamed up to form their own *Hayride* act called Hoot & Curley, were a big help to Slim in getting just the sound he was looking for.

As Slim himself explained it: "The steel players and I would go up into the high register together to create something that hadn't been done before, at least as far as I know. It was a style we perfected on the *Hayride,* and it was the turning point in my career. I've had a warm spot for the *Hayride* ever since."

Hoot put it a slightly different way. "Some folks used to say if you liked hearing a coyote howl at the moon, you'd like Slim Whitman records," he joked. "You didn't necessarily have to be good to play like that. You just had to have plenty of guts."

Along with his talent and class, Slim had plenty of guts. He demonstrated just how much when the inevitable overtures came for him to appear on the *Opry* — and he turned them down.

By then, Webb Pierce had become the *Opry*'s newest rising star.

On the strength of his smash hit with "Wondering," Webb had been invited to Nashville in 1952 as a fill-in for Hank Williams after Hank started missing shows or showing up drunk. But Slim was still caught up in the rivalry between the two of them. He was finally un-contested as top dog in Shreveport, and he soon made it clear he intended to keep things that way.

Here was a man who absolutely never used profanity, whose worst cuss-word was "blasted" ("I can't get this blasted guitar string tight," "This blasted car won't start," and so on). But he broke all his own rules of proper speech the day he rejected the *Opry* invitation.

"I'm stayin' right here at the *Hayride*," he said. "There's no way I'm goin' to Nashville."

"Well, I appreciate your loyalty, Slim," I told him, "but this is an opportunity lots of singers would give anything for. You sure you're making the right decision?"

"I'm not gonna be on any show that sonofabitch Webb Pierce is on, and that's all there is to it," he said and stalked away.

Slim was a man of his word, too. He built a beautiful home in Bossier City for his wife and daughter, bought a ranch near Tampa, Florida, as a future retirement home, and stayed right there on the *Hayride*. Even today, Slim still performs occasionally, but he never went to the *Grand Ole Opry*.

There was no such thing as a real female star in country music when the *Hayride* started, and sometimes I wonder how many there would be even today if it hadn't been for Kitty Wells. When Kitty zoomed to the top of the national charts in the summer of 1952 with her Decca record of "It Wasn't God Who Made Honky-Tonk Angels," it was something no woman had ever done before in the country field.

To be sure, any number of country bands had a "girl singer" — as female vocalists were called in those days — and we had quite a few of them on the *Hayride*. But in a totally male-dominated area of show business, women were always part of a group, rather than establishing themselves as individual performers. Most bands had to stay on the road a lot to make a living, and traveling in close quarters with a bunch of men was something most women—regardless of how much talent they might have had—weren't prepared to do.

Up till that time, any woman who gained a following in country music was likely to be a member of some family troupe like the Carter Family or the Maddox Brothers and Rose (four brothers and a sister).

Kitty Wells changed all that. She became the first female superstar of country music. In addition to claiming a large slice of fame for herself, she set the stage for the many outstanding women singers who came later—the Patsy Clines, Tammy Wynettes, Loretta Lynns, and Dolly Partons.

Kitty began her musical career the same way most other girl singers did—but she wasn't even Kitty Wells when she started out. The name she was given at birth was Muriel Ellen Deason, and her first performances were with her sisters, Mabel and Willie Mae, in a group appropriately called the Deason Sisters. In 1937, when she was eighteen, she married a cabinetmaker and would-be guitarist named Johnny Wright, and pretty soon they had a couple of kids. Johnny found an occasional job playing on the radio, but it looked like Muriel would spend the rest of her life as a housewife and mother.

Right after World War II, though, Johnny and Jack Anglin, who was married to Johnny's sister, Louise, formed a group called Johnny and Jack, working out of Knoxville, Tennessee, and performing on radio station WNOX. The act needed a female vocalist, so Muriel was pressed back into service. But Johnny decided the name Muriel Deason Wright was too hard for fans to remember, so he gave his wife the stage name taken from an old folk song called "Sweet Kitty Wells."

By 1947, Johnny and Jack and the Tennessee Mountain Boys, featuring Miss Kitty Wells, got a chance to be on the *Opry*. They appeared regularly for several months, but they were recording for the small Apollo label and their records weren't doing much of anything. After a few months, the *Opry* dropped them, and they came to KWKH to do a daily morning show even before I rejoined the station. They were on the *Hayride*'s inaugural performance and became fixtures on the show for several years before returning to Nashville. Then, in the spring of 1952, something happened that changed everything—not only for Johnny and Jack and the Tennessee Mountain Boys, but for all of country music.

Johnny and Jack had switched over to the RCA label and hit it fairly big with a record called "Poison Love." At about that same time, they hired Hubert Long of Nashville as their agent and he started trying to get them back on the *Opry*. They were in greater demand than ever before for personal appearances, and they decided to add a bass player to the band to replace Johnny, who didn't really have time to play bass and serve as the group's emcee, too. The problem was, the old DeSoto station wagon they traveled in wasn't big enough to accommodate another person, so somebody had to go.

That somebody was Miss Kitty.

There are different stories about what took place next. Johnny Wright's been quoted as saying Kitty was tired of the grind and wanted to retire and stay at home. But that's not the impression I got from Kitty herself after she was dropped from the band. Kitty was usually a very demure, sweet-tempered lady, but she left no doubt in my mind that her feelings were hurt and she was downright mad.

"Johnny can do what he wants to do," she told me, "but I want to keep singing on the *Hayride*. Can you use a female soloist?"

As I said, girl singers were in short supply. Since I was always looking for as much variety as possible on the show, I immediately hired Kitty as a separate act and used one of our staff bands with Floyd Cramer and Jimmy Day to back her. This gave her a much different and more modern sound than she'd had before.

Within a few weeks, Johnny was approached in Nashville by an executive of Decca Records, who was looking for someone to record a feminine "answer" to Hank Thompson's gigantic hit, "The Wild Side of Life." The Decca man had heard Kitty sing and he thought she'd be the perfect voice for the song. It was a public-domain tune with lyrics by songwriter J. D. Miller that rebutted Thompson's chorus line: "I didn't know God made honky-tonk angels . . ."

The recording session was held in Nashville in early May 1952 with Johnny on bass and Jack on guitar. By July, "It Wasn't God Who Made Honky-Tonk Angels" had displaced "The Wild Side of Life" as number one on the charts. It went on to sell well over a million copies, and many of the fans who bought the record heard the song on the *Louisiana Hayride* well before the record was released.

"I didn't think much about Hank Thompson's record, or that it needed an answer," Kitty said later. "I guess it just turned out to be the right song at the right time."

It did, indeed. With two follow-up number-one hits that same year — "I Heard the Jukebox Playing" and "A Wedding Ring Ago" — Kitty was on her way, and she never looked back. From that point on, Johnny and Jack were, in essence, working for her.

Never before had a woman country singer boldly talked back to menfolk about their philandering and misbehavior. It was simply unheard of — so much so, in fact, that the patriarchs of the *Opry* refused for a long time to let Kitty sing there. The part of her first big hit about a trusting wife turning into a fallen angel made them nervous, I guess. But the only thing that meant to me was that we were able to keep her on the *Hayride* that much longer.

The *Opry* couldn't ignore her forever, though, and her staying power as the Queen of Country Music was nothing short of phenomenal. For thirteen out of the next fifteen years, Kitty had at least one record that reached the top of the charts, and she was voted *Billboard*'s number-one female country artist for eleven straight years.

Not bad for a "retired" lady, right?

In my estimation, Jim Reeves ranks right up there with Frank Sinatra, Bing Crosby, Perry Como, and Nat "King" Cole as one of the greatest male vocalists of this century. His career was cut short by tragedy, but nobody had a smoother, finer voice than Jim.

That's why it still amazes me, even today, to remember how Jim came to KWKH in 1952 — as an announcer, not as a singer or musician. At the time he contacted me about a job, he was a deejay on a little 250-watt station in Henderson, Texas, and I don't think he even had any serious aspirations about a singing career.

It also amazes me how one man's downfall can indirectly trigger another man's rise to fame. If Hank Williams had stayed sober and healthy enough to perform, Jim might never have gotten a chance to sing on the *Hayride*. It was as an emergency stand-in for Hank that he made his first appearances on the show.

Actually, as a farmboy growing up in the "Piney Woods" of East Texas, Jim had shown considerable promise as a singer, but I didn't know anything about that when I hired him. He'd been a big fan of Jimmie Rodgers, the "Singing Brakeman," and tried to imitate him, singing and picking on an old guitar with several of the strings missing. Jim's family encouraged his interest in music, and at ten he'd even done some singing on the radio. But then his voice changed and his attention shifted to other things—most notably baseball.

Like Slim Whitman, Jim had been a hotshot baseball player when he was in his teens. He compiled a dazzling win-loss record as a right-handed pitcher at Carthage High School and earned an athletic scholarship to the University of Texas. After college, he was signed to a professional contract by the St. Louis Cardinals and sent to their minor-league farm club at Lynchburg, Virginia. But in his second year of pro ball, Jim tore up his knee sliding into second base. The injury brought his baseball career to an abrupt end.

When Jim first applied at KWKH, I didn't have an opening, but

I liked his voice and his delivery, and I told him to stay in touch. Finally, something opened up and I hired him as a regular member of our announcing staff. I also assigned him to the announcing team that worked the *Hayride*. During my time as its producer, there were eight announcers in all who handled segments of the show. Besides Jim and myself, they included Ray Bartlett, Norm Baile, Bill Cudabac, Frank Page, Hi Roberts, and Jeff Dale. Like every other aspect of the show, we liked to have variety in our announcers, so we always alternated four members of the announcing staff on each hour of the broadcast.

Jim had made a record on something called the Wagon Wheel label and paid for it himself. But at that point, he had what I'd classify as a pleasant-but-ordinary singing voice. There was none of that intimate, silky-smooth quality that he developed later, and until Hank's problems got to the critical stage, I never gave any thought to letting Jim sing.

One night when Hank couldn't stagger out to the microphone for the second show, I hurriedly asked Jim if he wanted to sing something. He said "Sure," and that was how it began. He filled in several times over the next month or two, and I frankly don't even remember anything he sang. Whatever it was, it was okay—nothing exceptional but okay.

But in addition to having a marvelous voice hiding inside him somewhere, Jim also had a good head on his shoulders. He was smart, and he watched what other artists did to emerge from obscurity and become famous right there on that same stage. I'm sure he told himself, "Hey, I can do that, too!" As it turned out, he could.

One day early in 1953, he came into my office and talked to me at length about it. That was when I realized for the first time how much Jim had his heart set on being more than just an announcer or a stand-in.

"I think I've figured out what these other guys are doing that makes them successful," he said. "They've all got something special about their style, something that makes them easy to recognize when you hear 'em. It's something they do that's a little bit different, like their own personal trademark."

"You've hit the nail on the head, Jim," I said. "When you hear a record by Hank or Lefty Frizzell, you know instantly who it is. There's no question in your mind."

"For somebody like me, I think it's also important to pick the right songs," he said. "If the song doesn't fit my voice and style, it's not going to work."

"You're right," I told him. "It'd be ridiculous for Slim Whitman to try to sing bluegrass or boogie. His fans wouldn't know who the hell he was."

"I've got an idea," he said. "I'm going to work on it."

We both understood one of the basic precepts of professional announcing: the deeper the masculine voice, the more soothing the effect on the listener. So what Jim started doing was gradually lowering his voice and getting closer to the mike to let the amplifiers do the work and allow him to sing more softly with no vocal stress.

It was intriguing to watch as he worked to perfect this technique, and I could often detect improvement from week to week. He also found a song he liked—a tune written by a young man from Nacogdoches, Texas, named Mitchell Torok. It was called "Mexican Joe." The two of them worked out a deal to let Jim record the song, but he still faced a major stumbling block. To market the song, he'd have to hook on with a recognized record company. The Wagon Wheel label just wasn't going to get the job done this time.

I put Jim in touch with Fabor Robison, who owned a small California company that sold records under the Fabor and Abbott labels. It wasn't a well-known outfit, but it had helped a number of other fledgling singers get started, and Jim just wasn't good enough or well-known enough yet for a major label to consider signing him.

We recorded "Mexican Joe" in the KWKH studios after work one night with musicians from our staff bands. The next morning we shipped it off to Fabor Robison, who released it on the Abbott label. Within a few weeks, it was obvious that Jim had a major hit. He quickly followed up with "Penny Candy" and "Bimbo," and all three songs reached the national charts. "Bimbo" alone sold more than 600,000 copies.

Jim's days as an announcer were suddenly a thing of the past, but Jim was a cautious sort of guy. He asked me for a leave of absence to do a prolonged cross-country tour and see how well he could draw in person. But before he left, he made it clear that he didn't want to burn any bridges behind him.

"This may not work out, Hoss," he said, "and I'd sure like to think I could come back here if it doesn't."

I responded with a line I was getting used to using with fast-rising stars of the *Hayride*. "As long as I'm here, you'll be welcome at KWKH anytime," I said.

Jim's tour was a resounding success, of course. It led to a recording contract with RCA, a summer job replacing Red Foley on the *Ozark Jubilee* television show, and an invitation to join the *Grand Ole Opry* in September 1955.

By that time, Jim's voice had matured and ripened, and he had become extremely adept at picking songs that fit his velvety smooth tones. He also became one of the first artists to carry his own sound system with him wherever he went. This allowed him to produce exactly the sound he was looking for through amplification. It's a common practice today, but it was highly unusual then.

The first record to show the full effect of Jim's vocal trademark was the hauntingly beautiful "Four Walls." Then came the aptly named "Touch of Velvet," followed by "Guilty," "Heartbreak in Silhouette," "I Could Cry," "I'll Follow You," and many others. In 1960, his RCA release of "He'll Have to Go" sold more than three million copies.

Some people called him a "new Eddy Arnold," but Jim was more than that. He was not only the number-one male artist in country music, but also claimed a huge crossover audience in the pop field. He did more to erase the barriers in popular music than anyone until Elvis.

He achieved greater popularity overseas than any country singer up to that time. The fans in South Africa especially idolized him, and he drew crowds in the tens of thousands whenever he toured there. He even recorded some songs in the Afrikaans language and starred in a South African–produced adventure movie.

Jim's most important attribute, though, was that he was an all-around nice guy. I heard rumors later that Jim went through some problems with alcohol and drugs. One of his former band members once told me, "We got Jim off whiskey and onto pills, but he got to be such a pillhead, we thought maybe we ought to try to get him back on whiskey again."

Personally, I think any problem Jim may have had along those lines was short-lived and fairly minor. I know how things get exaggerated sometimes. At any rate, I never saw any evidence of drug or alcohol abuse as long as he worked with me. In my experience, Jim was a straight-arrow kind of guy who was devoted to his wife, Mary, loyal to his friends and fans, and dedicated to his career.

The only unpleasantness I ever remember him getting involved in was when a girl in Shreveport — a notorious groupie who'd bedded down with a half-dozen members of the *Hayride* cast — turned up pregnant and loudly accused Jim of being responsible.

I think she just picked on him because she thought he was a soft touch and she could worm some money out of him. But she definitely picked on the wrong guy. In the first place, those of us who knew him well knew that Jim was sterile. He and Mary had tried unsuccessfully for years to have children. And in the second place, when this girl's baby was born, it was obvious to everybody who the real father was. The kid was the spitting image of the fiddle player in one of the *Hayride* bands.

The whole thing might have been laughable except for the fact that it cost Jim the membership he'd been seeking in the Masonic Lodge. Because of all the controversy, the Masons blackballed him, and Jim was deeply hurt by the snub.

On July 31, 1964, at the height of his career, Jim and Dean Manuel, his manager, flew from Nashville to Batesville, Arkansas, in a rented four-seater Beechcraft Debonair to look over some property Jim was thinking about buying. On the return flight that evening, the small plane crashed into a hillside near Brentwood, Tennessee, during a summer storm.

It took searchers two days to find the scattered wreckage and recover the bodies of Jim and Dean from a densely wooded area on a hill called Old Baldy.

I was in Dallas when I heard the news, and it came as a terrific blow to me. I had lost another friend to an abrupt, untimely fate, and America had lost one of the greatest singing voices it had ever heard.

Often show business seems to be one giant melee where thousands of people grapple for fame and only a few manage to grasp it. But if you stay in the business long enough, you discover, as I did, that it's really a tapestry, where careers overlap and interlock in peculiar ways. It's a fabric where even the most colorful threads are dependent on all the others for support and substance.

The list of performers whose careers were nurtured by the *Hayride* between the late forties and the mid fifties goes on and on. Some became megastars, and some found only a few fleeting moments of glory. Others had to spend their lives literally playing second fiddle. Still others had to settle for a spot in the background contributing to someone else's success. But, in all, hundreds of different performers had a role in making the *Hayride* a one-of-a-kind show.

Sonny James got his start on our stage as a guitarist and featured vocalist with Slim Whitman's band. He stayed with the *Hayride* only a few months, but it became his springboard to a Capitol recording contract (his "Young Love" sold over a million copies) and stardom, first at the *Big D Jamboree* in Dallas, then at the *Opry*.

The Browns—Jim Ed and Maxine—were a brother-sister act from Pine Bluff, Arkansas. They came to the *Hayride* in May 1954, and were later joined by their younger sister, Bonnie. They had a humorous little song that Jim Ed and Maxine had written themselves called "I Was Looking Back to See," but they'd offered it to almost every major record company and been turned down by all of them. Fabor Robison arranged a contract for them on the Fabor label, and we recorded their song in our studio with Jim Reeves on rhythm guitar and Floyd Cramer on piano. It became the first in a long series of national hits, including their unforgettable version of "The Three Bells" on RCA.

The Wilburn Brothers — originally made up of four brothers, Leslie, Doyle, Lester and Theodore — were among the first regulars to join the *Hayride* when it started in 1948. The Korean War split up the group, and the brothers worked separately in various bands for a while. But Doyle and Teddy eventually got back together, revived the Wilburn Brothers name and signed a contract with Decca Records, where they turned out one hit after another. Loretta Lynn got her start as the "girl singer" for the Wilburn Brothers, and they became one of the fixtures on the *Opry*.

Jimmy C. Newman was an authentic Cajun singer out of Big Mamou, Louisiana, who was appreciated in his native state long before Cajun music attained any national popularity. I gave him a job on the *Hayride* at a time when none of the big record companies would even talk to him about Cajun music, and he became a favorite of our audience. He signed with Dot Records in 1954 and scored a major hit with a composition of his own, "Cry, Cry, Darling." Just over a year later, he was off to the *Opry* and later had a crossover hit called "A Fallen Star."

These acts and many others were vital parts of the *Hayride* family in the ten years I served as its producer. Each one contributed in its own way to our overall success. Each one brought something special to America's musical culture.

And each one helped to earn the *Hayride* its title as "The Cradle of the Stars."

The Feud
with the Opry

Before I go any further, I want to make one thing clear: I've always had great respect for the Grand Ole Opry as an institution, and I still do. Nothing I'm going to say in this chapter is meant to demean the Opry's contribution to America's musical heritage or deny the value of the entertainment it's provided for tens of millions of listeners over the past seventy years.

The *Opry* traces its roots back to late 1925 when promoter George D. Hay launched a show on WSM, a new station in Nashville owned by the National Life and Accident Insurance Company (the station's call letters stood for the company's slogan, "We Shelter Millions"). Hay called his show the *WSM Barn Dance*, a name he borrowed from the *WLS Barn Dance* in Chicago, which predated the WSM version by a few months. The name of the program was changed to the *Grand Ole Opry* in 1928, after WSM became an NBC affiliate. A chance remark by a WSM announcer at the close of a network show called the *Music Appreciation Hour* is said to have triggered the change. The announcer introduced the *WSM Barn Dance*, which came on next, with these words: "For the past hour, we have been listening to music taken largely from Grand Opera. From now on, we will present the Grand Ole Opry."

Actually, the *Opry* was the second nationally broadcast radio show to feature an all–country music format, not the first. Chicago's *WLS Barn Dance* was first heard on NBC in 1933, with cowboy singer Gene Autry as its star. That was six full years before the *Opry* hit the network. The network portion of the Chicago show was soon renamed the *National Barn Dance*. Although WSM's powerful 50,000-watt clear-channel signal carried the *Opry* to a large part of the South, it wasn't until 1939 that it made its debut on NBC.

That's just a minor footnote to history now, though. By the end of World War II, the *National Barn Dance* had faded away, but the *Opry* survived the war and grew steadily stronger. One main reason for this was that Nashville was in the heart of the South while Chicago was somewhere "up north," and country music and the South were as inseparable as black-eyed peas and cornbread.

Today, as an institution, the *Opry* is to country music what the Super Bowl is to professional football, what the Louvre is to art, what the Kentucky Derby is to horse racing, and what Mt. Everest is to mountain climbing. As a cultural force, its impact on worldwide musical tastes and styles is practically incalculable. For those who play and sing country music, and those who love to listen to it, the *Opry* is the ultimate, the top. Nothing ranks above it.

The same, unfortunately, can't be said, in my opinion, for some of the greedy, arrogant, mean-spirited SOBs who called the shots at the *Opry* between the late 1940s and the middle 1950s.

For about six or seven years during that period, the *Opry* had a real battle on its hands. It was the only time in the past half century that the *Opry* and Nashville's power structure faced a genuine threat to their absolute control of the country music industry. The threat came from the *Louisiana Hayride,* and the *Opry* hierarchy didn't like it one damn bit. I don't blame them for fighting back. The only thing I blame them for is not always fighting fair.

Without the example of the *Opry*'s great success, of course, there probably never would've been a *Louisiana Hayride* in the first place. It's silly and pointless to argue otherwise. Like all the other Saturday night country music shows that sprang up on radio stations across the nation after the war, we imitated the *Opry* to some extent when we started out. But unlike those other shows, the *Hayride* moved beyond the status of mere imitator. We became a challenger and a rival to be reckoned with.

I made up my mind to be deliberately different, innovative, and free-spirited where the *Opry* was predictable, cut-and-dried, and sometimes downright stodgy. This formula made us the second most popular show of our kind in the United States. For a while, we were breathing down the *Opry*'s neck, and that made the Nashville power brokers very uncomfortable.

At KWKH, we always tried to be good-natured about the Shreveport-Nashville rivalry. We joked openly about it on the air, and I referred countless times to the *Opry* as "the Tennessee branch of the *Louisiana Hayride.*"

Sometimes, though, it was hard to ignore the *Opry*'s closed mindedness and petty politics. It was hard to overlook the jealousy and arrogance that often characterized the *Opry*'s attitude toward the *Hayride* and its dealings with its own performers. It was hard to forgive its pompous inflexibility as the self-appointed guardian of the "purity" of country music.

George Hay and his successors were determined to keep the *Opry*'s music as simple and earthy as it had been in the 1920s. This meant nothing but traditional instruments were acceptable — guitars, banjos, mandolins, fiddles, basses, pianos, occasionally an accordion or harmonica, but no horns, drums, or "newfangled gadgets." When a musician named Sam McGee had the audacity to play an electric guitar on the *Opry* for the first time in 1939, Hay met him when he came offstage.

"That's real pretty, Sam, but it's too modern," Hay said sternly. "We want to keep the show down to earth."

McGee left his electric guitar at home after that, and it was a long time before this type of instrument was allowed on the show.

To me, this made about as much sense as it would've made to stick with the crude sound systems of the 1920s or ignore electronic improvements in recording technology or make every performer on the show wear knickers and sailor straw hats. Not only did it rigidly limit the kind of music you could hear on the *Opry,* but it also slammed WSM's doors in the face of some of the outstanding artists of the time. I was determined from the start that there would be no such narrow-minded restrictions on the *Hayride*.

Our goal was to entertain our audience, and we didn't have any qualms about experimenting. If we saw a trend emerging, we tried to make the most of it—and we didn't mind starting some new trends, either. We knew we were like David taking on Goliath, and we were always looking for fresh weapons. Sometimes we had to laugh just to keep from crying, but we preferred to concentrate on the continuous high quality of our show and the occasional victories we won, rather than the numerous stars we lost to the *Opry* in the forties and fifties.

As author Chet Hagan noted in writing about this period in his 1989 book *Grand Ole Opry,* "More and more the *Louisiana Hayride* in Shreveport was providing new acts for the *Opry.* Some eyes viewed it as a training ground, a minor-league farm club, so to speak, for the *Grand Ole Opry.*"

We definitely didn't think of ourselves that way, however. And the thing that rankled most with us, I think, was the *Opry*'s refusal to admit publicly that the *Hayride* even existed. The people who ran the *Opry* shamelessly raided our talent over and over again, then ordered the stars it took away from us never to mention the *Hayride* while performing on the *Opry.* I guess they thought if they ignored us long enough, we'd finally go away.

Literature circulated by the *Opry* about Hank Williams after his death graphically illustrates what I'm talking about. It said only that "Hank came to the *Opry* from Montgomery, Alabama," and made it sound as if the *Opry* owned him and created him all by itself. It never mentioned that the *Hayride* launched Hank's national career, much less that he came back to the *Hayride* after the *Opry* dumped him.

I think the powers-that-be at the *Opry* were more embarrassed by Hank's return to Shreveport than anything that had ever happened to them before. When we signed Hank to a contract that would've kept him off the *Opry* for three full years and gave him access to our show's vast radio audience right after the *Opry* had punished him for breaking the rules, it was a real slap in the face to the bigshots at WSM. If Hank had lived and regained his health, I can only guess how hard they might have tried to get him back.

Nobody had ever bucked the *Opry* that way before, and they decided, by God, they'd teach us a lesson. It was the beginning of a long and sometimes bitter feud.

Two of our other notable victories in the feud were in keeping Slim Whitman and Johnny Horton in Shreveport. Both turned down invitations to the *Opry,* and even after each of them had gotten as big as a country music star could get, they chose to remain as long-term mainstays of the *Hayride.*

Our greatest triumph of all, of course, was in signing Elvis Presley and keeping him for eighteen months after the *Opry* gave him the cold shoulder. The *Opry* and its power brokers could only watch helplessly as the focus of the whole entertainment world turned to the *Hayride,* where Elvis was changing popular music forever. Their narrow concepts of musical "purity" cost them dearly in that instance, and Elvis never forgave them for what they did.

"I wouldn't ever go back there," Elvis told me more than once. "Not even if they offered me ten thousand dollars to sing one song."

After CBS started broadcasting the *Hayride* at the beginning of 1953 and the Armed Forces Radio Network began airing a special thirty-minute segment of our show the following year, the feud between the shows intensified. The *Opry* brass retaliated with what I consider some really shoddy tactics. They established an unwritten law that no artist who was under contract to the *Hayride* could appear on the same program with any *Opry* artist. Since the vast majority of the biggest names in country music were on the *Opry,* this was a heavy blow to our young performers.

Every week, *Opry* stars fanned out across the continent to play engagements booked by the *Opry*. These tours put money in the artists' pockets, it's true, but their underlying function was to promote the *Opry* itself. Appearing with these major stars was one of the most important ways for an up-and-coming regional performer to gain stature and exposure, and losing that opportunity was a big disadvantage for our artists. I think it was a blatant attempt to dry up our sources of talent and force aspiring singers and musicians to stay away from the *Hayride.*

If it was, it was also shortsighted and stupid. To use Chet Hagan's terminology, it was like a major league team trying to shut down its own farm club. For every top star that didn't go on to the *Opry* after a stint on the *Hayride,* at least a half-dozen did make the move to Nashville. *Hayride* "graduates" became the lifeblood of the *Opry.* Shutting down the *Hayride* or reducing it to the status of just another local country music show would've been like blocking a main artery to the *Opry*'s heart.

The *Opry* was and is a showcase of established talent. In the forties and fifties it certainly had no tolerance for nobodies who were trying to become somebodies. People who hadn't already made a name for themselves with a hit record or two never got invited to the *Opry* in the first place. Never once in its long, glorious history has the *Opry* ever created a single star or launched a single career that I know of. The *Hayride,* on the other hand, created dozens of stars and launched hundreds of careers.

I'm proud of that difference.

We might have been able to put up a lot stronger fight — and things might even have turned out much differently — if we'd had even a few of the facilities that were essential to advance the careers of the stars we developed. But Shreveport had no booking agencies that operated on a national scale. It had no artists' service bureaus or music publishers or record companies.

Because of the *Opry*'s long dominance in the country music field, Nashville had accumulated these related enterprises. It was the presence of these facilities, as much as the opportunity to perform on the Ryman Auditorium stage on Saturday nights, that drew aspiring artists to "Music City" like moths to a flame.

As early as 1951, when we were in the process of losing Webb Pierce to the *Opry,* I tried to persuade the management of KWKH to set up the same type of artists' service bureau as WSM operated, but I ran into a brick wall. Henry Clay wasn't interested. Neither was John Ewing, the station's owner.

I urged the station to support efforts then being made to bring a recording studio, a talent agency, and a music publishing firm to Shreveport. They didn't want to do that, either. They were afraid if local operators succeeded with these kinds of businesses, it would undermine KWKH's control of the talent in our region and somehow end up costing the station money. The last thing the Ewings wanted was competition on their home turf.

The fact is, Webb and I went ahead and set up a small music publishing venture, anyway. We became partners in a company called Ark-La-Tex Publishing, and in the short time it was in business, we both made a significant amount of money out of it. It's now common practice for artists to own their own music publishing firms and recording studios, but back then these functions were mostly controlled by a few powerful companies.

When Webb left, we sold the company, and Henry Clay advised me not to try to start another one. But once he was established at the *Opry,* Webb went into partnership with Jim Denny, who had basically the same job at the *Opry* as I did at the *Hayride,* and formed another publishing company.

The management at WSM eventually gave Denny an ultimatum. They told him either to get out of the music publishing business or lose his job at the *Opry.* By this time, Denny had seen how lucrative his moonlighting business was, and he elected to stay with the publishing company. He ended up also starting his own artists' service bureau and making a lot more money than he'd ever made at the *Opry.*

They couldn't afford to give the same kind of ultimatum to

Webb, because by then he was the hottest country singer in America. But I suspect their underlying resentment toward Webb was one factor in Webb's failure to win a spot in the Country Music Hall of Fame.

Eventually, my frustrations over the lack of support services for *Hayride* artists played a part in my own painful decision to leave the show. While I was mentally debating what to do, I was approached informally about going to the *Opry* as Denny's replacement. I guess I should've been flattered, but I never really gave it any serious consideration.

I didn't want to live in Nashville. And even if I had, it would've been like selling out to the enemy in time of war. I would've spent the rest of my life feeling like a traitor.

From the very beginning, I wanted the *Hayride* to have an identity all its own. I didn't ever want it to settle into a repetitious routine the way the *Opry* had. I believed then, and I still believe today, that the main ingredients of our success were variety, unpredictability, audience involvement, and a fast pace.

As I've mentioned before, we never advertised our cast in advance for any particular show. There was always an element of surprise, and the audience liked that. Where the *Opry* demanded conformity, we encouraged every act to make itself as distinctive and individual as possible. Where many *Opry* performers were backed by the same staff band, we liked for every featured act to have its own band because we didn't want everything to sound alike. We also made every effort to keep the show moving along at a rapid clip. The *Opry* might let Roy Acuff or Red Foley hold forth on center stage for a half-hour, but anytime our artists went beyond two numbers, they had to earn that privilege through audience approval.

The performers and announcers on the *Hayride* did a lot of clowning around strictly for the entertainment of our live audience. One night, we had a group harmonizing on the old Sons of the Pioneers classic, "Cool Water," and Ray Bartlett and I started bringing cups of water out to the singers. Finally, we hauled out a whole water cooler and plopped it down on the stage, and the audience roared.

We never gave our radio listeners any indication of what was happening when we pulled stunts like this or when Ray Bartlett was doing his jumping-jack act during a number. The idea was to let the radio audience hear these unexplained bursts of laughter and cheering and get curious enough about what was causing them to come down to the auditorium the next Saturday night and find out for themselves. This is one of the reasons we averaged drawing over thirty-three hundred paying customers a week during the whole ten years I produced the *Hayride.*

To this day, many country music fans have the idea that those big-name stars they heard on the *Opry* forty-odd years ago were drawing big-time salaries for being there. The truth is, the *Opry* paid many of its performers even less than the *Hayride.* Both shows used straight union scale, but *Hayride* soloists were always allowed to do at least two songs, which guaranteed them 18 dollars per performance. The *Opry,* on the other hand, frequently limited artists who weren't part of the regular family to a single number, then handed them a check after the show for just 9 dollars.

If you made it to the stage of "the Greatest Country Music Show on Earth," you were supposed to be too grateful to even think about the money. That was the idea, but it just didn't fly with some people.

In 1949, Hank Thompson, one of the all-time greats of country music, stormed out of WSM and never returned to the *Opry* after receiving his 9-dollar paycheck for singing his hit tune "Green Light."

"I wish they'd had Xerox machines back then so I could've made a copy of it," Thompson said many years later. "I said then I ought to frame the sonofabitch, but I had to cash it to get out of the hotel we were in. Hell, I could've made more on the street corner passing the hat with a tin cup nailed to my guitar."

Although he wasn't voted in until 1989 — much later than he should've been — Thompson made it to the Country Music Hall of Fame without any help from the *Opry* and largely in spite of it. Not only was the pay unrepresentative of "the Greatest Country Music Show on Earth," its hidebound standards that prohibited drums, wind instruments, and just about anything unorthodox also irritated Thompson.

"I just didn't like the politics," he said. "That wasn't the way I did things. If I'd stayed at the *Opry*, I'd never have established the musical sound I wanted. I think I did the right thing by walking away."

I couldn't agree more. The fact that he did walk away from the *Opry* made it possible for the *Hayride* to book Hank Thompson for a number of guest appearances.

Bob Wills, another immortal Texas-born star of country music, was never really welcome at the *Opry* because of the unusual instrumentation he used. When the runaway popularity of his hit record "San Antonio Rose" virtually forced the *Opry* to put him on a time or two, Roy Acuff predicted dire consequences. The electrified fiddles used by Wills's Texas Playboys would "ruin" the *Opry* forever, Acuff predicted. Despite his huge following and the indelible mark he left on popular music, Wills's western swing wasn't "pure" enough to satisfy the judges in Nashville.

Webb Pierce was at the peak of his popularity when he decided he simply couldn't afford to spend every Saturday appearing on the *Opry* and making next to nothing for being there.

"It was just too much," he said. "If we were going to make any money on personal appearances, most of it had to be on Saturday night, and any time we were on tour, we had to turn around at the end of the week and be back at the *Opry*. I don't care if we were in Canada on Friday, the *Opry* expected us to be in Nashville the next night."

Webb walked away, too—yet another reason for his image as a rebel.

After the *Hayride* ceased to operate as an every-Saturday-night show in late 1958, leaving the *Opry* with no serious competition at the national level, the greed and possessiveness of WSM's management really became apparent. They tried to squeeze more and more out of the *Opry*'s regular performers while giving less and less in comparison to what they were getting elsewhere.

I'd been gone from the *Hayride* about six years and was working at the *Big D Jamboree* in Dallas when WSM president Jack DeWitt staged his notorious "purge" at the *Opry* in 1964. He kicked a dozen major artists off the show at one time and prohibited them from using the *Opry* name in their outside billings.

The purge grew out of DeWitt's demand that these performers—including Faron Young, Kitty Wells, Johnny Wright, Ferlin Husky, Ray Price, and George Morgan—sign contracts agreeing to appear in person on the *Opry* twenty-six Saturday nights a year. They refused to sign the agreement, and they had every reason to refuse.

"I put a pen to it and figured it out," Faron said at the time. "I was gonna lose one hundred eighty thousand dollars a year to work at the *Opry* those twenty-six weeks."

The reason, of course, was that the *Opry* still expected these stars to perform basically for free when they could be earning thousands of dollars for a night's work anywhere else.

WSM first included Chet Atkins's name in the group of ousted stars, only to be forced to admit several days later that Atkins hadn't been officially connected with the *Opry* for years. It was a high-handed fiasco all the way around.

My good friend Willie Nelson, who wrote the songs that made a half-dozen other country singers famous before he found fame as a singer himself, also had major problems with Nashville's narrow mold and the *Opry*'s grasping ways. After holding him at arm's length for years, the *Opry* finally made Willie a regular in 1964, but he was never very comfortable there. In the early seventies, he also walked away. His disillusionment with Nashville gave rise to Willie's famed "outlaw" movement, which has influenced the whole course of country music in the twenty-five years since.

But without the slightest doubt, the most historically noteworthy parting with the *Opry* took place one Saturday night in October 1954.

That was when a dejected teenager from Memphis walked off the Ryman Auditorium stage for the first and last time with Jim Denny's advice to go back to driving a truck still ringing in his ears.

Just a week later, the "Elvis era" began on the *Louisiana Hayride*. After that, nothing would ever be the same again.

{ 8 }

The Act Nobody
Could Follow

Elvis didn't exactly set the world on fire that first night on the *Hayride* in October 1954. When he finished his first singing stint and came offstage, you could tell by the look in his eyes he wasn't sure he'd even ignited a spark. He knew something wasn't right, that he hadn't really connected with the audience the way he wanted to. His nervousness had dissolved into doubt and uncertainty. I could almost hear him wondering, "Oh, Lord, have I screwed up again?"

But I knew our audience well enough to guess what was behind their response—or more correctly their lack of one. Most of our regular patrons were traditional country music fans, a big percentage of them in their thirties, forties, fifties, and even older. This kid's music was so different from anything these people had ever heard before they didn't know how to react. "Blue Moon of Kentucky," one of Elvis's two songs that night, was an old Bill Monroe tune, but there was absolutely no comparison between the way Elvis did it and the way the "Father of Bluegrass" had done it. With a little encouragement from Frank Page and me, Elvis drew a subdued round of applause from the older fans and some enthusiastic cheers from several hundred teenagers in the auditorium. But it didn't come anywhere near encore level.

There were other factors that worked against Elvis in that initial performance, too. With his oily, slicked-back hair, his odd little bowtie and well-worn sportcoat, he looked out of place on a stage where almost everybody else was dressed in Western garb. Even Scotty Moore and Bill Black, his sidemen, were wearing cowboy-style shirts.

But the main thing was, the whole time he was at the microphone, Elvis was so nervous his knees were almost knocking together, and his jerky leg motions added to the strange, wild look about him. There was electricity there, but he communicated as much uneasiness to the audience as he did talent. I think they wanted to like him, the same way I did, but a lot of them weren't quite sure what to make of him.

Among young people in the Deep South, though, word was already spreading fast about this kid singer with a style so unconventional it defied definition. Some college students from Texarkana had found out Elvis was going to be there and several dozen of them had come down for the show that night. I'm pretty sure there were even a few faithful fans from Memphis who made the long trip to Shreveport for the biggest moment yet in the kid's career.

All these youngsters hung around for the second portion of the show, while a few of the older fans left after the first part. By the time Elvis was introduced by Frank Page for his second appearance of the evening, he was a little less uptight. He'd had a chance to meet Merle Kilgore, Tibby Edwards, and several of our other artists backstage, and maybe that helped. The change may also have had something to do with knowing he wouldn't be on CBS this time. He even managed to stammer his way through a bit of small talk with Frank before his numbers.

"You all geared up with your band—" Frank started to ask.

"I'm all geared up!" Elvis blurted, interrupting.

"To let us hear your songs?" Frank finished.

"Well, I'd like to say how happy we are to be out here," Elvis said. "It's a real honor for us to have—get a chance to appear on the *Louisiana Hayride*. And we're gonna do a song for you—Uh, you got anything else to say, sir?"

"No, I'm ready," Frank assured him and got out of the way.

As Elvis hunched up to the microphone, he got a more enthusiastic reception from the crowd than he had the first time. I was watching from backstage, and I could see his confidence starting to build.

"I think they were a little scared of him at first," Merle Kilgore said later. "They thought he was gonna jump off the stage or something, but when he came back out, they were more prepared for him."

Elvis still didn't encore the second time around, but the change I saw in him from the first show, plus the way the kids in the audience responded—especially the girls—convinced me we'd found something really special.

We put Elvis in the slot in the middle of our lineup usually occupied by the duet of Jimmy Lee and Johnny Mathis (not the famous singer of "Chances Are" by the same name). Tillman Franks, who handled bookings for Jimmy and Johnny, had a lucrative show date for them that night in Carlsbad, New Mexico. But I told Tillman the only way they could miss the *Hayride* was for him to find a replacement for them. That was his main reason for wanting me to give Elvis a try in the first place.

At the time, the thought of putting Elvis on the show as a closing act never crossed my mind. You always saved one of your hottest performers for the grand finale—the best for last, in other words. You didn't want people drifting away after their favorite performers had left the stage. On the *Hayride,* the closing role was normally filled by Slim Whitman or Johnny Horton, never by a teenage newcomer with greasy hair, an undersized guitar, and a secondhand jacket.

But within a couple of weeks, Elvis and his parents would sign a contract making him a regular on the *Hayride* (he was still a minor, so his signature alone wasn't legally binding). As word got around that he'd be on our show all the time, young people from a half-dozen states started flocking to the Municipal Auditorium on Saturday nights. They grew in numbers and volume every week, and they soon made it obvious that nobody but Elvis would be closing our show as long as he was there.

Once those teenagers became a dominant force in our audience, they refused to listen to anybody else after Elvis started to sing. In Hank Williams's prime, his audiences were wild and exuberant, but with Elvis they were much more intense. Nothing like this had ever happened in American public entertainment. Young females in the audience exploded with excitement. They screamed themselves into hysteria until the noise level became deafening. They made so much noise Elvis could've lip-synched the words and nobody would've known the difference. It was sheer bedlam.

"I'd never seen anything like it before," said Jimmy C. Newman. "We'd just stand in the wings and shake our heads and say, 'It can't be. It can't last. It's got to be a fad.' "

But it did last, and it just kept mushrooming.

Once Elvismania took hold in Shreveport, our other top artists were smart enough to see what was happening, and they had no desire to contest Elvis for the closer's spot. No other *Hayride* regular — no matter how popular he might've been with our audiences in the past — dared walk out on that stage and try to succeed Elvis. Not as long as this frenzy went on.

But in some other places the message took longer to sink in, and when Elvis went out with touring package shows in months to come, it sometimes led to huge embarrassments for other big-name country music stars.

Before that winter of 1954–55 was over, Elvis had become the act that nobody could follow.

I let Elvis get two more *Hayride* performances under his belt — on October 16 and 23 — before I made the final decision to sign him to a one-year contract as a regular member of the cast. During that two-week period, there was a noticeable change in the makeup of our live audiences as more and more teenagers heard about the

"Cat from Memphis" and came to see and hear him in the flesh. We played and plugged his Sun record daily on KWKH, and sales of the record skyrocketed in our listening area.

At the same time, I could see clear evidence that some of our longtime fans—and even a few of our cast members—resented Elvis and disliked his music. A small percentage of our more mature fans expressed their displeasure by staying away from the Municipal Auditorium. But we still had a varied, balanced package of talent with something for everybody, including plenty of traditional country music, so we gained a lot more ticket buyers than we lost.

Elvis did a lot of leg and torso motions during his songs in those early days, but he hadn't yet started those pelvic gyrations that caused so much controversy and condemnation a little later. Most of the songs he was singing at this time, in addition to "That's All Right, Mama" and "Blue Moon of Kentucky," were styling variations of old country or rhythm-and-blues tunes. He also did some brand new things in the emerging rock-and-roll field. "Good Rockin' Tonight" was a number he'd recorded for Sun a few weeks before his *Hayride* debut, and it was getting some radio play, but it wasn't widely available yet. Once in a while, though, Elvis tried something that was pure mainstream pop. He had a rare gift for being able to sing just about any kind of song. He could alter his style and sound drastically different from one number to the next, yet still be unmistakably Elvis.

"I love Hank Williams and Hank Snow," he confided to me one day, "but Dean Martin's one of my favorite singers, too. That low, sexy voice of his is really cool, and I'd sure like to be able to sound that way."

At the time, his comment surprised me, but a couple of years later, when I heard him sing "Love Me Tender" for the first time, I understood what he meant. I think the Dean Martin influence was pretty obvious in many of the romantic ballads he did later on.

I know Elvis appreciated our willingness to let him do what he wanted on the *Hayride*. He asked me often during those early weeks, just as he had before his debut performance, what I thought he ought to sing, and my answer was always the same: "Sing whatever you feel good about singing, whatever you think you do best. Just get out there and be yourself."

You could feel him gaining confidence each time he stepped up to a microphone. When he sang, his shy innocence melted away, and there was something fierce, almost cocky, about him. Offstage, though, he was still as polite and reserved as ever, and he was unfailingly respectful toward everybody. It was always "sir" or "ma'am," even with people in his own age group.

"Ever'body at the *Hayride*'s treated us real good, Mr. Logan," he told me after his second show, "and me and the boys really 'preciate it. You got a nice crew here. Ain't a single one of 'em accused me of bein' crazy. At least not yet."

And on the way back to Memphis that weekend, Scotty Moore remembered him expressing similar sentiments. "They're a whole lot friendlier in Shreveport than they are in Nashville," Elvis remarked. "I don't even wanta think about them sumbitches at the *Opry* anymore."

After the October 23 show, I approached Elvis, Scotty, and Bill backstage and told them I was ready to offer them a contract.

"We give our performers five Saturday nights a year off," I said, "and if something really major comes up, we might be able to arrange a little extra free time. Otherwise, you'll have to be here every Saturday for the next twelve months. You think you can do that with no problem?"

"Yes, *sir*, Mr. Logan!" Elvis said, grabbing my hand and shaking it. "This is just what we been hopin' for."

I let them miss the show the following Saturday night (October 30) to fill a commitment they'd made several weeks earlier at the Eagle's Nest, a club in Memphis where they'd been playing on weekends for several months. But I told them to show up early for their next scheduled *Hayride* performance on November 6 to sign the contract.

"And since you're a minor, Elvis, we're going to need your mama and daddy's signatures, too. You think they can come down with you that weekend?"

"Sure, we'll bring 'em along," Elvis said. "I want my mama to see my first show as a regular on the *Hayride,* anyway."

Despite his spreading fame across the region, Elvis was still hanging onto a five-day-a-week job in Memphis as an electrician's apprentice. Scotty and Bill had regular daytime jobs, too, and both sidemen also had wives to support. But on the strength of my contract offer, they all decided the time had come to quit and devote their full energy and attention to their musical careers.

All three were a little nervous about cutting themselves loose from the security of "real" employment, and Elvis told me his daddy didn't take kindly to the idea at all.

"My daddy's kind of old-fashioned, Mr. Logan," the kid said. "He's seen a lot of guys who called themselves musicians and were basically just bums. He's been tellin' me for a long time I was gonna have to choose between pickin' a guitar and makin' an honest livin'. He says he never saw a guitar player that was worth a damn."

"Well, he's right about one thing," I said. "You can't stay out all night playing shows and still work all day — not if you want to do a decent job of either one. You think your daddy's going to be willing to sign this contract, or is that going to be a problem?"

"Aw, he'll sign it," Elvis said. "He probably won't like it much, but he'll do it."

This here's my mama and daddy, Mr. Logan," Elvis said. "They been lookin' forward to meetin' you."

"Welcome to the *Louisiana Hayride,*" I said as we shook hands. "I hope you folks had a good trip down from Memphis."

It was late afternoon on November 6 when the six of us — Elvis, Scotty, Bill, Mr. and Mrs. Presley, and me — met backstage at the auditorium in a dressing room that doubled as my office to sign what turned out to be the most important document in the history of the *Hayride*. It was a standard union contract that called for Elvis to receive 18 dollars per Saturday and Scotty and Bill to receive 12 dollars apiece.

It was my first meeting with Elvis's mother and father. They were staying at the best hotel in town, the Captain Shreve, and they mentioned something about how nice their room was. I wondered at the time how they managed to afford such fancy accommodations, but for obvious reasons, I never asked. Later I decided Sam Phillips, the owner of Sun Records, had probably come up with a little expense money for the occasion. Elvis's brief association with the *Hayride* had certainly done more to boost Sam's company than anything that ever happened to it before.

Vernon Presley struck me as a typical redneck who had almost nothing to say and very little faith in his son's ability to succeed as a professional entertainer. Gladys Presley was a doting mother who was already upset by the fact that some people thought Elvis's singing style and gestures were "vulgar." She told me several times what a "good, God-fearing boy" Elvis was.

They both seemed relieved when I explained that the contract was, in effect, an agreement in which Elvis would be apprenticed to me for a period of one year to further his musical education and prepare him for a professional career. Both signed the document with no objections, and I gave them a copy to keep for themselves.

"I'll put it in the scrapbook I'm making for Elvis," Mrs. Presley said, beaming at her son.

That night, with his parents watching from the audience, I had no doubt that Elvis would encore, and he did. It was the first of more than fifty performances he did while under contract to the *Hayride,* and he never again failed to encore. In fact, within weeks, we were having even more trouble getting him off the stage than we'd ever had with Hank Williams. The audiences got bigger, louder, and more unruly with every performance.

During those first few weeks, Elvis went home to Memphis fairly often. He still had a steady girlfriend there named Dixie Locke. They'd been dating ever since high school and were more or less engaged to be married at the time Elvis started to get famous. I think Elvis really cared about the girl and missed her at first. But before long, girls were swarming around him by the hundreds, making him forget his homesickness for Dixie.

Elvis, Scotty, and Bill usually stayed at the Al-Ida Motel, one of the cheaper places along the gaudy Bossier City "strip." And beginning that fall, long lines of teenage girls would form outside their room every Saturday night after the show. Lots of them just wanted a chance to see Elvis close up or say something to him. Others had more intimate encounters in mind. But regardless of their motives, Elvis always gave each of them at least a minute or two of his time. Regardless of the hour or the circumstances, he was courteous and considerate to everyone in those days.

It was a brand new experience for him, and he was flattered by the attention. He also was absolutely crazy about girls. He loved them—both figuratively and literally. They kept his adrenaline pumping, and he never seemed to get tired of having them around. During that period in his life, I never saw Elvis take an alcoholic drink of any kind, and I frankly doubt if he ever did. I think he had very strong moral convictions against drinking. By the same token, I never saw him take so much as a puff from a regular cigarette, much less a marijuana cigarette. But he had an insatiable addiction to girls.

As odd as it may seem today, I think one of the main reasons Elvis was eager to come to the *Hayride* was a cute little folksinger named Carolyn Bradshaw, who recorded on the Abbott label. Carolyn had joined our show in 1953 when she was just sixteen years old, and she was easily the smallest member of our cast. She stood less than five feet tall and probably weighed around ninety-five pounds. But she was a very attractive girl with an exceptional enough figure to win the 1954 title of "Petite Miss Physical Culture" for the whole state of Texas.

One of the first questions Elvis asked me when I met him at the auditorium that first afternoon in October was, "Is Carolyn Bradshaw gonna be on the show tonight?"

When I assured him she was, he grinned. "Is she as good lookin' in person as she is in her pictures?"

"Even better, I'd say," I told him. "But I'll let you decide for yourself."

When he saw her in person, I think he was even more taken by her. I don't know how much they saw of each other outside the show itself, but I'm pretty sure they went out together at least a time or two. But as soon as he started being mobbed by teenage girls everywhere he went, I guess he lost interest. I don't know what ever happened to Carolyn. She made quite a few personal appearances in the South and Southwest, but then her career seemed to stall. She was never able to move on to a higher level, and she left the show a few months after Elvis got there.

The girls were only part of what Elvis liked about Shreveport. He soon came to feel more at home in these new surroundings than he felt back home. In Memphis, he was still "that kid from the projects" to a lot of people, and he hated that. (One of the first things he did once he started making some decent money was move his parents out of their rent-subsidized apartment and into a rented house of their own.) Among his ex-classmates and old acquaintances, even his Memphis fans, he was never quite sure where he really stood or what they really thought of him. Despite the way he acted on stage, he had a lot of insecurities bottled up inside him— insecurities that no amount of wealth and fame could ever erase.

In Shreveport, it was a whole new ball game. He could assume a whole new personality if he wanted to, and nobody knew the difference. Most of his fellow *Hayride* performers readily accepted him as their peer. Some were well-established artists in their own right, and this fed his ego. After nineteen years of never being far from his mama's apron strings, he was finally on his own, and he relished the freedom.

He especially liked hanging out with Merle Kilgore and Tibby Edwards. They spent countless hours talking about music and their musical idols.

"He reminded me of Hank Williams," Merle said. "There was something about his eyes."

Not everybody appreciated Elvis, though. Some other performers despised him and were jealous of his success. Country music traditionalists, both on the stages and in the audiences, were already scratching their heads over him. Many of these same people would soon be loudly denouncing him as "lewd" and "obscene."

That fall, Elvis met D. J. Fontana, a drummer in one of our staff bands who also sometimes played show dates with Hoot Raines and Curley Herndon. The first time D. J. ever heard Elvis sing was when I played his recording of "That's All Right, Mama" in my office one day. From then on, Fontana thought Elvis's music was great. They got along well from the beginning, and D. J. would soon become the third member of Elvis's Blue Moon Boys. But their friendship indirectly led to an incident that showed just how much Elvis's music turned some people off.

For several years, Hoot and Curley had been playing regularly at the Lake Cliff Club outside Shreveport, and they'd developed a strong following among the clientele. One night when they had a show scheduled at the club they got a chance for a big payday somewhere else, and D. J. offered to play with Elvis, Scotty, and Bill if they'd fill in for Hoot and Curley. Unfortunately, nobody bothered to tell the paying customers about the change.

"It was a real fiasco," D. J. recalled later. "At first they just kind of sat there looking at each other like they couldn't believe what was happening. Then the place started emptying out, and the longer we played, the more people headed for the exits. By the time we got done, I don't think there was a soul left in the place."

It was the last gig the Blue Moon Boys ever did at the Lake Cliff Club. For a long time after that, I don't think any of them even felt comfortable driving past it.

As the end of 1954 approached, Elvis was a potential multimillion-dollar property without a manager. A Memphis disc jockey named

Bob Neal had been impressed enough with Elvis's first record to help him line up a few show dates in the immediate area. I don't know what kind of agreement they had at that point, but Neal was still acting as a manager of sorts when Elvis joined the *Hayride,* and he came to Shreveport with Elvis a time or two.

Problems soon developed between them. As I understand it, Neal didn't like the rock-and-roll element in Elvis's music or his on-stage antics. Neal thought tunes like "Good Rockin' Tonight" and "Baby, Let's Play House" were too raunchy to be on the radio. He wanted Elvis to identify himself with "pure" country and conform to established Nashville standards. Their relationship was an informal one, and it seemed doubtful that it would ever progress beyond that.

Because he was older, Scotty Moore took on most of the organizational duties for the group. He handled expenses, kept tabs on the schedule, generally played "mother hen" to Elvis, and lined up an occasional show date. But Scotty didn't have the contacts or experience to be a real manager. Somebody had to start making the critical decisions that could move the kid's career into high gear. Without sustained public exposure, the whole Elvis phenomenon could easily fizzle.

Tillman Franks was a big help to Elvis in the early going. Tillman booked him on package shows with other *Hayride* regulars all over Texas, Arkansas, and Louisiana. Through Tillman and Pappy Covington, the booking agent for the *Hayride,* Elvis made appearances during November 1954 in such towns as Longview, Lufkin, and New Boston in East Texas and as far west as Odessa. In December, Elvis and the Blue Moon Boys got an enthusiastic reception in Houston.

During late 1954 and early 1955, Elvis talked several times to Tillman about becoming his manager, and Tillman could undoubtedly see the vast potential this kid represented. But Tillman was already managing several other artists, including Johnny Horton, who was also one of the nation's most promising young country music stars. Tillman had solid contacts throughout the South and Southwest, but he lacked the national influence that a budding talent like Elvis—especially one with such limitless crossover possibilities—needed to land the really big bookings. As tempting as the prospect must have been for Tillman, he ended up letting the opportunity pass.

At least three or four times, Elvis even asked me if I was interested in managing him. He and I had gotten along really well from the very beginning. I wore a pair of six-guns as a standard part of my costume as emcee of the *Hayride,* and Elvis was intrigued with guns. We were always clowning around and trying to outdraw each other (the guns were never loaded, of course). Pretty soon, we formed a close friendship, and he often turned to me for advice and reassurance. But when he first mentioned this manager idea, it came as a complete surprise to me. I did know a lot of people in the business, but I'd never had any experience doing that kind of thing, and I'd never even given any thought to it.

"I couldn't do that, Elvis," I said. "I've got a full-time job at KWKH."

"But I need somebody I can trust, Mr. Logan," he said, "and I know I can trust you. I just wish you'd think about it before you say no."

"Well, I'll do whatever I can to help you find somebody good," I told him. "But I'm afraid I'm not the man for the job."

Every time Elvis brought up the idea after that, it got harder and harder to dismiss. Within a year or two, I firmly believed he'd be one of the biggest attractions in show business. But, of course, I had no way of realizing just how big. Meanwhile, I knew the window of opportunity wouldn't stay open long. That had been one of my main reasons for moving quickly to sign him to a *Hayride* contract in the first place—to keep somebody else from grabbing him. With the kid getting bigger every day, there were too many people who could smell the money he was going to make. One of them was going to latch onto him, and soon.

I finally made up my mind, though, that it wasn't going to be me. I'd been on the road with *Hayride* performers enough to know what a grind it was, and this was only a drop in the bucket compared to what I'd be facing if I took on the job of managing Elvis. It would mean traveling all over the country and being gone from my home and family for weeks at a time. I'd seen too many families broken apart by long absences and professional pressures. I had three young children at home. I didn't want them to forget what I looked like.

In all the years since, I've never regretted my decision. I know I missed out on millions of dollars, and some people would think what I did was sheer stupidity. But I was there to see my children grow up, and that was worth any financial sacrifice on my part.

Cashbox and several other music industry publications ran reports early in 1955 that Elvis and his parents had signed a management deal with Bob Neal, but I never had the feeling it was going to last. Neal was, first and foremost, a disc jockey—just as I was a radio station program director and the producer/emcee of the *Hayride*. Maybe Neal was willing to do some things I wasn't willing to do, but overall he was no more qualified to manage Elvis than I was.

Meanwhile, the kid just kept getting bigger by the day. In and around Memphis, his records were selling like hotcakes, with "Blue Moon of Kentucky" at number five on the area charts and "Good Rockin' Tonight" at number eight. But this was only the beginning. "Baby, Let's Play House," released by Sun on April 1, 1955, would become his first record to crack the national top ten on *Billboard*'s charts three months later, and Elvis would start drawing serious attention from RCA.

Neal did help him get some fairly good bookings around Memphis, and he continued to be packaged with other *Hayride* artists for show dates in places like Hope, Arkansas, and Bastrop, Louisiana. He played before some of his biggest and loudest crowds in Lubbock and other West Texas towns, where he teamed with *Hayride* regular Billy Walker. By now, he was averaging three or four personal appearances a week, and although none of them were yet outside the South or Southwest, it was only a matter of time.

Often on these shows, Elvis was packaged with Jim Ed, Maxine, and Bonnie Brown, established stars of the *Hayride.* They had a big following in Texas, Arkansas, and Mississippi, and once in a while they were actually able to top Elvis as the crowd's favorites. But the day was fast approaching when Elvis would steal every show he was on.

Into this fermenting situation came one of the crudest, most overbearing, most universally detested men in show business. He called himself "Colonel" Tom Parker—although he was no more a real colonel than I am. And he came with just one purpose in mind: to take total control of Elvis Presley and claim half of every dollar the kid would ever make.

That's exactly what he did, too. And God forgive me, I was an unsuspecting accomplice in this piece of grand larceny.

Tom Parker was a blustering, overweight huckster—an ex-carnival barker whose background remains a mystery to this day, and who may not even have been an American citizen. But I've got to give the devil his due. He had an impressive track record for successfully promoting top show business figures, including Roy Acuff, Eddy Arnold, Gene Austin, and Tom Mix. He also had an uncanny knack for squeezing large amounts of money out of almost everybody he came in contact with.

As Eddy Arnold's manager, he'd already transformed "The Tennessee Plowboy" from an unknown soloist with Pee Wee King's band into one of the three or four biggest country music stars of the past decade. Parker had kept his eagle eyes on Elvis ever since the kid started on the *Hayride.* Now he was circling like a buzzard and waiting for the right moment to close in for the "kill."

Inadvertently, I helped give him that moment.

With the combined help of the *Hayride,* Sam Phillips, Bob Neal, and others, Elvis started getting some pretty impressive bookings. In late February, he took his first trip north to play at Cleveland's Circle Theatre. In April, he returned to Cleveland and made his first trip by plane to New York, where he suffered a major disappointment when he tried out for the popular TV show, *Arthur Godfrey's Talent Scouts*. Not only was he turned down, but he also never got a chance to see Godfrey in person. As usually happened when he faced any kind of rejection, Elvis went into a funk for a day or two, but he quickly recovered.

"Come on, Elvis," I told him when he got back. "Forget about New York for right now. They'll be begging to book you there one of these days, but right now we're taking the *Hayride* to Dallas to put on a special show for the *Big D Jamboree*. They'll love you at the Sportatorium."

Indeed, they did. But when he returned to Dallas the following year, he'd totally outgrown the Sportatorium, a four-thousand-seat wrestling arena. By then, it would take the Cotton Bowl to hold the crowd.

Elvis's first association with Tom Parker came when he was invited to join a tour featuring Hank Snow as its headliner and including Mother Maybelle and the Carter Sisters and comedian Whitey Ford (known far and wide to *Grand Ole Opry* fans as the Duke of Paducah). By this time, Eddy Arnold had fired Parker, and the "Colonel" had started booking shows for Hank Snow. Elvis joined up with the Hank Snow All-Star Jamboree in Roswell, New Mexico, then went on to play dates in Lubbock and Odessa, Texas, where he was already one of the hottest acts going.

The promoters were impressed enough to ask Elvis along in May when they put together an even more ambitious tour. This was to be a three-week swing through twenty cities covering the whole mid-South with more than thirty artists participating altogether. Elvis and other younger talent were to be featured during the first half of each show, followed by the headliners (Slim Whitman and Faron Young had been added to the earlier lineup) during the second half. The tour's organizers had enough sense to put Elvis at the end of the "young talent" half of the show as the last act before intermission—but as it turned out, that wasn't enough.

Elvis's new Sun record of "Baby, Let's Play House" and "I'm Left, You're Right, She's Gone" had just been released when the tour started in New Orleans on May 1. From there it went to Baton Rouge, Mobile, Birmingham, Macon, Daytona Beach, and Orlando. Elvis tore 'em up everywhere they went. There were near-riots in several towns. Hordes of screaming girls awaited him at each stop. After the show they chased him down the street as he cruised around in the new pink and white Cadillac he'd just bought.

The climax came in Jacksonville, Florida, on May 13 at a Gator Bowl stadium jammed with fourteen thousand screaming fans. This time, the show never got past Elvis. The frenzied mob of teenage girls refused to listen to anyone else. They booed when anyone else set foot on stage, including Hank Snow. The whole place quivered with shrill cries of "Elvis! Elvis!"

Finally, just to try to get off the stage — and knowing Elvis, I have to believe it was just his idea of an innocent joke — he waved and yelled into the mike: "Girls, I'll see you-all backstage."

Unfortunately, the girls took him at his word. As he ducked behind the curtain, thousands of them came swarming after him. By this time, according to first-hand accounts I got from Faron Young and other eyewitnesses, they were more like a giant pack of wolves than adoring fans. Within a matter of a minute, a full-blown riot had broken out.

The cops whisked Elvis down into a locker room in one of the stadium dugouts. They thought he'd be safe there, but they underestimated those girls. They found some open windows and hundreds of them started pouring into the backstage area, trampling policemen and performers who got in their path.

Several hundred of them cornered Elvis and started ripping at his clothes. They tore his ruffled pink shirt to tatters, shredded his jacket, and even ripped off his boots and socks. They were making every effort to get his pants, too, when police reinforcements finally arrived.

"Elvis was scared," Faron said later. "He'd climbed up on top of a shower stall trying to get away from 'em, but they were all jumpin' up and grabbin' at him. That was one time he had all the girls he wanted—and then some."

Tom Parker was among the witnesses to this bizarre scene, and I think he saw something much different from what everybody else saw that night. He saw a lot more than a bunch of crazy teenagers and a very unnerved young singer. He caught a glimpse of the power generated by this twenty-year-old kid. It was like a preview of the Elvis Presley tidal wave that was about to break across America.

What Tom Parker saw was the biggest gold mine in entertainment history, and he was determined to grab as much of it for himself as he could.

I'd already known for years that we had to find an effective way to market the talent we developed on the *Hayride* if we were to have any hope of holding onto a significant part of it. Time after time, I'd seen us lose artists as they began to peak in their careers, but by that spring of 1955, I was convinced we were going to suffer our greatest loss ever if we didn't find a way to effectively display and promote Elvis on a national scale.

This kid wasn't just another star. With all due respect, he was more than a Webb Pierce or a Faron Young or a Kitty Wells. He was more even than a Hank Williams, I strongly suspected, because he cut across all the existing boundaries of popular music. He was country, he was rock-and-roll, he was pop—he was everything. He was sizzling hot everywhere he went, and this was barely the beginning. Elvis was going to be one of the biggest show business names of the century, and for the moment he "belonged" to the *Hayride*. But unless we acted with speed and decisiveness, he'd slip away from us, and in a few months, he'd be gone.

Ironically, there was no danger this time of losing him to the *Grand Ole Opry*. Elvis had made that much clear again and again.

He'd never have anything to do with the *Opry* again, and that, at least, was to our advantage. But the stakes were even bigger this time. The power structure of the whole entertainment industry would be looking to turn a profit on the Elvis phenomenon, and the biggest giants in the business would be competing for his talents.

The solution was to set up an effective artists' service bureau to market *Hayride* talent across the nation. More than anything else, having that type of operation was what enabled the *Opry* to keep most of its stars for as long as it wanted them. And not having it was what caused us to lose most of ours.

But to set up an artists' service bureau, we needed help from someone who was accustomed to booking top names into top venues in major cities. In other words, we needed someone like Tom Parker. On a personal level, I didn't like the guy at all, but he was the one person I thought might be able to do the job for us. Needless to say, I also didn't know at the time how intent he was on capturing Elvis as his own prize.

So I called Parker and asked him to come to Shreveport to talk with Henry Clay and me. I felt like kicking myself about it later, but by then it was too late. In all likelihood Parker would've somehow managed to get Elvis signed to an exclusive contract with him, anyway. He was just that kind of wizard at wheeling and dealing. But by inviting him to town and laying our cards on the table we made it a lot easier than it might have been otherwise.

Parker demanded 1,200 dollars in expenses, and I finally talked Henry into paying it. We offered to provide him office space at the radio station, pay for his phone and other essentials, and give him access to all our artists if he'd set up the bureau and run it. But Parker wanted 12,000 dollars out front to get the operation started. He wouldn't budge from that figure, and, predictably, Henry balked.

"The guy's trying to rob us," he said, "and there's no way he's going to get away with it."

Admittedly, it was a considerable amount of money for the time — about two years' worth of salary for an experienced announcer, for example. In fairness to Henry, he wasn't the only one guilty of being penny-wise and pound-foolish where Elvis was concerned. I heard from reliable sources that Columbia Records, one of the biggest labels in America, turned down an offer from Sam Phillips to sell Sun's rights to Elvis for 18,000 dollars, which would've been the steal of the century.

But the point is, the 12,000 dollars Parker wanted wasn't even a drop in the bucket compared to what we could've made booking Elvis over the next two or three years.

Every time I think about it, even today, it makes me sick.

From that point on, although Bob Neal retained the title of Elvis's manager, Parker began calling more and more of the shots. Beginning in the summer of 1955, practically all of Elvis's major show dates were arranged by Parker's Jamboree Attractions, based in Madison, Tennessee. It was only a matter of months until Parker would shove Neal aside and take full control of Elvis.

Actually, Parker might have succeeded much sooner if Elvis's mother and daddy hadn't been a little suspicious of him. Until January 1956, when Elvis turned twenty-one, he still had to have his parents' signatures on all contracts and other legal documents.

Elvis even complained to me about it.

"The Colonel's a real smart man, Mr. Logan," he said. "He's got connections ever'where — in Hollywood, even. He says he can get me in the movies, but my mama don't wanta change things right now, and my daddy just keeps sayin', 'We don't know very much about this man, and we could be makin' a big mistake.' "

"Well, it's none of my business," I said, "but I think you'd be smart to listen to your mama and daddy. If you sign the wrong paper now, it could hurt you for the rest of your life."

During the next few weeks, the Colonel turned up the pressure on Vernon and Gladys Presley. He called them almost every day and soon wore down their resistance. On August 15, 1955, they and Elvis signed a document that made Parker a "special advisor" to

Elvis for a period of one year with two one-year options. Parker was to receive 2,500 dollars a year plus expenses "to negotiate and assist in any way possible the build-up of Elvis Presley as an artist." More importantly, Parker got exclusive rights to book a hundred appearances for Elvis over the next year at 200 dollars each, including Elvis's three sidemen.

After that, there was never any real question about who was in charge of Elvis's career and his future.

By late summer, I sensed the possibility of serious problems with the Colonel when Elvis's contract came up for renewal in November, and I made up my mind to move quickly before Parker had a chance to muddy the water. During the first week in September, I showed Elvis a copy of the new contract and suggested that he might want to think about signing it early. I was also hoping he'd be impressed with the fact that I was offering him almost twelve times what he'd made during the first year.

"We want to raise you to two hundred dollars a show," I said. "I think you've earned it."

His eyes got kind of wide. "That's real generous of you, Mr. Logan," he said.

"The station won't let me put the new fee into effect until November," I said. "But if you want to go ahead and sign it, we can lock in that figure and get the formalities out of the way."

That's exactly what we did. Parker did his best to persuade Vernon Presley not to sign the new contract "until we see what kind of record deal we can get," but Elvis and both his parents signed anyway. When his second one-year contract went into effect on November 5, it raised Elvis's fee for each Saturday night performance from 18 to 200 dollars — over Henry Clay's loud objections, I might add. I had to explain to Henry that Elvis's deal with Parker guaranteed him 200 dollars per performance elsewhere, so we really had no choice. The truth was, as I told Henry, we were damned lucky to be able to retain the every-Saturday-night services of the nation's hottest new star for that amount.

Just over two weeks after the new contract took effect, I think even tight-fisted Henry could see the wisdom in what we'd done. On November 21, RCA purchased Elvis's contract with Sun Records for 35,000 dollars in a deal engineered by Parker. RCA was the label of both Eddy Arnold and Hank Snow, and Parker had been working with Steve Sholes, head of the company's artist-and-repertoire department in Nashville, for more than ten years. Included in the deal was a 5,000-dollar bonus for Elvis representing unpaid previous royalties.

But the new contract with RCA accomplished even more for Parker than it did for Elvis. Its cagey wording gave Parker full authority to act as Elvis's agent and employer. It basically left Bob Neal standing outside in the cold, although he didn't realize right away that he'd been displaced. An arrangement continued between Neal and Parker for a few more months, but he was never again a factor in Elvis's career. After that, it was the Colonel's show exclusively. Parker even managed somehow to ditch Hank Snow, his partner in the All-Star Jamboree, and leave him high and dry. The two never spoke to each other again.

The amount of money Tom Parker made off Elvis, both during his lifetime and after his death, is simply incalculable. On the strength of my own close association with the people involved, plus what I've been told by dozens of other knowledgeable sources, I believe Parker took considerably more than half of everything Elvis earned from late 1955 until Parker's death in early 1997.

In some cases, those early shows that paid Elvis and his band a flat fee of 200 dollars, for instance, may have brought the Colonel ten times that much—money he was free to keep under the terms of the agreement. It's true that, once Elvis landed in the movies, Parker was able to drive his fees up to fantastic levels. But the money Parker made for himself out of these deals was out of all proportion to his service to Elvis. Elvis was too trusting and naive, too unsophisticated about financial matters—and by now too obsessed with the idea of being a movie idol—to question anything Parker did.

Scotty Moore, Bill Black, and D. J. Fontana—the sidemen whose sacrifice, hard work, and musical skills helped establish Elvis as a star and give him the distinctive sound he had to have to stay on top—were treated like dirt by Parker. At a time when Elvis was commanding 1,500 dollars or more for a performance, Scotty, Bill and D. J. were being paid a pathetic straight salary of 200 dollars a week. Since they often played seven nights a week, this came down to less than thirty bucks per show.

I think that's disgraceful. These guys weren't just three musicians Elvis picked up off the street. They were loyal friends, and for whatever part he played in the shabby treatment they got, Elvis should've been ashamed.

When Elvis returned to the *Hayride* in late May after the melee in Jacksonville, Florida, I could see an immediate difference in the way our audiences reacted to him. They were wilder and more out of control than ever before. When Elvis came onstage, the teenagers in the crowd ran totally amok.

Keeping fans from disrupting our schedule during the CBS segment of our show was one of our biggest problems. The network segment had to be kept tight and fast-moving, but the moment Elvis put in an appearance, pandemonium broke loose. It had reached the point where if the fans' screaming didn't totally drown out Elvis's singing, he felt like he wasn't doing his job.

At first, most of us had thought the screaming was kind of funny. I guess we also thought as soon as the "new" wore off, the kids would quiet down a little. Instead, they just got louder, and the uproar was no joking matter anymore.

After the shows, the lines of girls outside the Al-Ida Motel now stretched for blocks. Out of curiosity, I sometimes drove by the motel myself before I went home, and personally saw as many as three hundred girls there. Members of the skeleton crew who staffed KWKH on Sunday mornings often saw a few of them still hanging around outside the motel as they came to work at dawn.

It still amazes me to think about it. This was the mid-1950s — a time when parents were supposed to be keeping much closer tabs on their kids than they do today — and most of these girls were sixteen, seventeen, and eighteen years old. Now and then angry mothers and fathers would show up looking for their daughters and cause a major scene. But for the most part, nobody seemed to care where these girls were in the small hours of the morning.

Elvis was no longer as indulgent of these worshipping throngs as he'd been at first. Some nights he'd pick out three or four girls who caught his eye, then load them into his car and drive off, leaving the rest of them standing there. Occasionally, he and his "chosen few" would show up at some other motel across town and have a private party for a couple of hours.

When he performed out of town, it was much the same situation, except that not as many of the girls knew where he'd be staying the way they did around Shreveport. But they were always there, always ready. And Elvis was always willing to accommodate as many of them as he could.

During the sixteen months he was on the *Hayride,* Elvis went to bed with dozens of girls in cities and towns across the South, but as far as I know, these were all brief encounters. If he ever had any serious romances, I never heard about them. Like most other young studs of nineteen or twenty, he was just on the prowl and looking for fun. But unlike the rest, Elvis scored whenever he wanted to. He screwed around with so many girls he'd never seen before and never saw again that I'm surprised he didn't catch something and die.

I know of at least one woman in Houston who had a daughter by Elvis as a result of these late-night frolics. She called me one day in May 1975 when I was working for a radio station in Monroe, Louisiana, and I've often wondered how she managed to locate me after so many years. Elvis was scheduled to appear that night at the

Monroe Civic Center. The performance was sold out, but the woman was desperate to get two tickets.

"You're bound to remember me, Mr. Logan," she said. "Elvis and I were always together when he was playing in Houston back in fifty-five. My daughter and I drove up to Monroe especially for this show, and I've just got to get tickets."

I *didn't* remember her, but I tried to be polite. Houston had been one of the first big cities to catch the Elvis craze. He'd appeared there a number of times on package shows with other *Hayride* artists during 1955 and always drawn good crowds.

"I'm afraid I can't be much help," I said. "I could probably walk in the back door myself without getting thrown out, but I just don't have any way of getting tickets. It's a complete sell-out, like all his shows are."

"Oh, but it's so important," she said. "My little girl's eighteen now, and she's never seen him. It'd mean so much to me if she could see her daddy just one time."

"Does she, uh, know he's her daddy?" I asked.

"No," she said, "I never could bring myself to tell her, but I thought maybe if she could see him I might be able to get up my nerve—"

"I'm sorry, ma'am," I told her. "I understand how you feel, but there's really nothing I can do. Maybe it's better to let sleeping dogs lie, anyway, if you know what I mean."

I could hear her crying softly as I hung up the phone.

The Grand Ole Opry didn't take kindly to those Elvis fans booing Hank Snow off that stage in Jacksonville. Only a few days after the incident, the *Opry* let it be known throughout country music circles that its regular performers would no longer be allowed to appear on any show that included any Hayride artists.

The ban was a cheap shot, as I've already said, because it hurt everybody associated with the *Hayride* and it was a high-handed attempt to choke off our talent supply. But if the ban had applied only to Elvis, I have to admit it would've been a whole lot more justifiable.

The ironic thing was that Hank Snow was one of Elvis's idols, and Hank's son, Jimmie Rodgers Snow, was one of Elvis's best friends. There's no way Elvis would ever have embarrassed Hank Snow on purpose.

Part of the ban was just sour grapes, I think, because the *Opry* had let Elvis get away from them, and now there was no way to get him back. But part of it was genuine concern for their established stars, too. There's nothing more demoralizing for a headliner than to have a houseful of people flat out refuse to listen to his music.

For the rest of the time Elvis was on the *Hayride*, I only remember one small exception to the *Opry*'s new rule. It happened at the annual Jimmie Rodgers Memorial Celebration held each May 25 in his hometown of Meridian, Mississippi.

There was already some bad feelings toward the *Opry* among some *Hayride* artists because of what had happened at the memorial celebration the year before. It was customary for top country artists to volunteer their services for a special show each year to highlight the celebration. In 1954, a group from the *Hayride* had made the long drive to Meridian — it was about three hundred miles — strictly to help pay tribute to Rodgers, the man generally recognized as the "Father of Country Music."

But when they got there, artists from the *Opry* had taken over the whole program, and they were told rather rudely that there was no room for them. Not a single one of our *Hayride* people got to perform, and everybody on our show had been hacked off about it for the whole year since.

This time, we didn't take any chances. We made definite arrangements with the organizers of the celebration. The middle hour of the three-hour program was to be devoted entirely to artists from the *Hayride* and a few acts from other CBS shows, with the first and third hours allotted to performers from the *Opry*. Our hour of the show was being carried by CBS, so it didn't bother us that the also-rans from the *Hayride* only got half as much time as the "big-time acts" from the *Opry*. At least they had to recognize our existence, and I had a feeling things might balance out a little before the night was over.

Naturally, we brought along Elvis, our newest star, this time. And naturally, since nobody on the *Hayride* dared follow him, we put him right at the end of our portion of the show — and right before the *Opry*'s second hour was supposed to start.

It was less than two weeks after the mess in Jacksonville, and I never could figure out how those *Opry* stars let themselves be suckered into an arrangement like that. It looks like they would've known better.

But it still tickles me that they didn't.

I was sitting in a car talking to Little Jimmy Dickens, one of the stalwarts of the *Opry*, after Elvis came out on stage and the crowd had erupted in whistles, cheers, and high-pitched squeals.

Dickens looked at me and kind of grinned. "So this is the boy they booed Hank Snow off the stage over down in Jacksonville," he said. "I been wantin' to get a look at him. What's so special about him, anyway?"

"He's got the hottest sound going," I said. "It's like nothing anybody ever did before. The kids go crazy when he gets started, and they don't want to hear anybody else. All they want is more Elvis."

When Elvis broke into "That's All Right, Mama" and started those gyrations of his, the screams got loud enough to shatter glass. I thought to myself it was a good thing this was an outdoor concert. If it had been indoors, the roof would've blown off for sure.

Elvis stayed on stage for ten minutes, then fifteen. You'd have thought the kids' vocal chords would've been starting to wear thin by now, but if anything the noise just got louder. I knew that Dickens was scheduled to open the *Opry*'s second hour of the show, and I could tell he was getting a little worried.

After nearly twenty minutes of Elvis, Jimmy looked at his watch.

"Hey, ain't his time about up?" he said. We were parked in a back-stage area a good hundred feet from where Elvis was singing, and Jimmy had to practically shout to make himself heard above the up-roar.

"Hell," I yelled back, "he's been trying to get off the stage for about ten minutes, but they won't let him budge. I don't envy you having to go out there and try to follow him. I'll tell you right now nobody on the *Hayride* can do it."

"Well, *I* can," Jimmy snorted. "I can follow *anybody.*"

If he hadn't been acting like such a smart-aleck, I might have felt sorry for Jimmy. He'd been coasting along in a comfortable rut for so long, he just didn't realize what he was up against. As it was, though, his attitude irritated me a little.

"Jimmy," I said, "if you'll get out of this car and climb up on my shoulders, I'll carry you up onto that stage and give you the finest introduction you ever had in your life. Then I'll stand back and watch you fall flat on your butt."

"Get off my back, Logan," he huffed. But he didn't make a move to get out of the car.

After another minute or two, Elvis finally fled from the stage, but the screaming continued without letup for at least ten more minutes before the kids in the crowd finally gave up.

There were a few catcalls, and dozens of the kids started leaving as soon as Jimmy came out, cracked a corny joke, and started singing "Sleepin' at the Foot of the Bed." About all I can say about the *Opry's* second portion of the show that night was that it was a very short hour and a very quiet one.

The *Hayride* had had a rare moment of revenge, but there was much more significance to what happened that night than just getting back at the *Opry*. The arena where we all lived and worked was changing. It was changing fast and it was changing drasti-cally—and this twenty-year-old, 18-dollar-a-show kid was the one responsible for the change.

Webb Pierce was there that night as one of the *Opry's* headlin-ers. Webb was always pretty perceptive, and he said something as everybody was packing up to leave that hit the nail right on the head. I think it pretty well summed up what must have been running through the minds of a lot of those pampered Nashville stars at that moment.

"Unless we learn to keep up with him," Webb said, "that kid may put us all out of a job before it's over."

{ 9 }

Freeing the King

to Claim

His Throne

By the end of that summer of fifty-five, Elvis was starting to get used to the idea of being a star and a headliner. His stage presence had become nothing short of awesome, as each performance gave his ego another boost. The energy he projected as he gyrated his hips and punched the air with his fists was breathtaking. His suggestive, no-holds-barred antics on the stage had many a preacher up in arms, and more than a few of the big names in show business were condemning his act (In an interview, Frank Sinatra called his music "deplorable"). But this only served to heighten the teenagers' interest and make them more eager than ever to see Elvis in person.

He developed an uncanny ability to read an audience. If it wasn't as responsive as he thought it should be, he'd work that much harder to win it over.

"He'd study a crowd," said Tillman Franks, "and when he saw he'd gotten through to them, he'd give them a little bit more. He had the same kind of electricity Hank Williams had. The difference was, Hank just got out there and gave everything he had and didn't worry about it. But Elvis was a genius at making the most of any given situation."

In sharp contrast to his onstage demeanor, Elvis remained the picture of respectful, reserved innocence in nonperformance settings. Media representatives were inevitably amazed at how polite and unassuming he was during interviews. Sometimes he still had trouble believing all this was really happening, but he was already the undisputed star of the *Hayride* and was getting top billing on personal-appearance tours in certain areas, particularly West Texas and Oklahoma. Audiences in cities like Lubbock, Amarillo, Midland, Odessa, and Abilene positively adored him. So did fans in Lawton, Altus, and Guymon, Oklahoma. He met Roy Orbison on an Odessa radio show and gave Buddy Holly's infant career a boost when he appeared with him in Lubbock.

In early August, Sun released Elvis's third single with "Mystery Train" on one side and "I Forgot to Remember to Forget" on the other. Within weeks, the new record gave Elvis his first number-one hit on the country charts and brought him a flurry of new bookings in the North.

In October, he performed in Omaha, then at Cleveland's Circle Theatre with Roy Acuff and Kitty Wells (he and Acuff didn't get along because of the chilly reception Elvis had gotten at the *Opry*). Then, the very next night, he appeared on another show in Cleveland with Pat Boone, Bill Haley and the Comets, and the Four Lads.

Those two engagements in Cleveland dramatically illustrate how Elvis was blurring the lines between rock and roll, rhythm and blues, country music, and straight pop. Acuff and Kitty Wells were as "pure country" as you could get. Pat Boone had gained a big following doing R&B tunes with a "white pop" flavor like "Ain't It a Shame." Bill Haley was billed as the "creator of rock and roll" for his 1951 version of "Rock Around the Clock." And the Four Lads' big hit, "Moments to Remember," was strictly mainstream pop.

Boone, a singer with a country background who was married to Red Foley's daughter, Shirley, had also blended the black blues sound with pop stylings to score with several crossover hits. As he watched Elvis perform, he was admittedly fascinated.

"Elvis looked like he'd just gotten off a motorcycle," Boone said. "He sang his first song and the kids loved it. I was really surprised. Then he opened his mouth and said something, and he sounded so hillbilly that he lost the crowd. Then he sang another song and won them over again."

Better than any of his previous records, "Mystery Train" illustrated how impossible it was to define Elvis's music. It blended elements of blues and country so smoothly that nobody could tell where one stopped and the other started. It was probably the greatest commercial success Sun Records had ever had, and there's no question it drove up the price RCA had to pay to buy out Elvis's contract.

As much as Elvis and Sun Records had done for each other, though, it was clearly time for him to move on. The next phase in the Presley phenomenon was beyond the scope of Sam Phillips's small company. The only thing standing in the way of international superstardom for Elvis was the lack of a major record company contract, and that last remaining obstacle was about to be removed.

The headline on *Billboard*'s December 3 story on Elvis signing two contracts with RCA pretty well says it all:

> Double Deals Hurl
> Presley Into Stardom

In November, about a week before Elvis went to New York for the RCA signings, the Country and Western Disc Jockey Association had named him the Most Promising Country Artist of 1955. It was a big honor, one that accentuated the *Hayride*'s good fortune in having him under contract for another full year. But within a matter of months, such a limited distinction would seem downright insignificant. Elvis was about to become the most promising artist in all of popular music, period.

Early that December, Elvis started rehearsing a new number that would eclipse everything else he'd put together. It was a somber song that was cowritten by Mae Axton, singer-songwriter Hoyt Axton's mother, and based loosely on the words in a note left by a suicide victim. When RCA released the tune on January 17, 1956, it became one of the landmark records of the century.

It was unlike anything Elvis had sung before, and because of its gloomy lyrics and mournful melody, some people thought it wasn't a good "fit" for him. Sam Phillips went so far as to call it "a morbid mess," but I think that was mostly sour grapes. By spring, helped along by six appearances on Jimmy and Tommy Dorsey's popular TV program, *Stage Show,* it zoomed to number one on both the country and pop charts.

Before long, everybody in America under the age of twenty-five seemed to be humming Elvis's phenomenal new hit and dancing to its infectious beat.

Its name, of course, was "Heartbreak Hotel."

There's no way to exaggerate Elvis's contribution to the *Hayride's* national popularity. Nothing that ever happened to our show was more important than he was. But that doesn't mean we were putting all our eggs in one basket during the Elvis era in Shreveport. If I'd discovered anything over my eight years with the *Hayride,* as of early 1956, it was that all good things eventually have to end. And when they do, you have to replace them with other good things. Otherwise, if you're in the entertainment business, you're in a helluva lot of trouble.

I'd known for months that Elvis would soon be too big to be bound to any one stage or locale on Saturday nights. So I kept on working as hard as ever to keep the stream of new talent flowing, to find and develop other star-caliber artists.

About seven months after Elvis first joined the *Hayride,* our association with Sam Phillips and Sun Records brought another promising but unproven new artist our way. His voice and personality were totally different from Elvis's, but he too was experimenting with new variations in style and sound. Where Elvis was flamboyant on stage, this young artist was quiet and reserved. Where Elvis poured seething, sensual energy into his music and demanded maximum volume from his band, this artist's music was so sparse and simple and lean that it was almost like something out of the distant past.

His uniqueness was obvious the very first time I heard his demo tape of "Folsom Prison Blues," a song he hadn't even released on record yet. He was destined to attain worldwide fame as one of the most exciting, innovative, and durable performers of the next forty years. But to me, he was even more than that. He was and still is one of the most honest, decent, upright individuals I ever encountered. He and I formed a friendship that continues to this day, at least on my part.

I'm talking, naturally, about Johnny Cash.

Johnny was another one of those guys who started as close to the bottom of the ladder as you could get and worked his way to the top the hard way. He grew up in a sharecropper's cabin on a dirt farm near Kingsland, Arkansas. By the time he was twelve, he was spending many of his days picking cotton and a lot of his nights trying to write songs. In high school, he did a little singing on a radio station in Blytheville, Arkansas. But then the Korean War broke out, and Johnny enlisted in the air force.

Instead of going to the Far East, he ended up in Germany, where he bought his first guitar and spent his spare time learning to play it. After his discharge, he found a job as an appliance salesman, married a girl named Vivian and started having a family. He was going nowhere fast, but he signed up for a radio announcing course, met a couple of other struggling musicians, and talked Sam Phillips into giving them an audition.

Johnny's first Sun record was released in June 1955 about the same time he came to the *Hayride*. It had "Hey Porter" on one side and "Cry, Cry, Cry" on the other. Both were Cash originals and both were solid tunes. When the record became a hit, Johnny gave a lot of the credit to the exposure he'd gotten on the *Hayride*.

He followed up on this early success with a string of major hits that became the salvation of Sun Records after Elvis left. Four of his numbers reached the top ten in 1956, including "So Doggone Lonesome," "There You Go," "I Walk the Line," and "Orange Blossom Special."

I'll be talking more about Johnny's career on the *Hayride* in a later chapter. But even as Elvis was taking the nation by storm, we were still as busy as ever grooming other young artists for the future.

We had no intention of abandoning our role as America's most prolific producer of stars.

In late September 1955, we took the *Hayride* on the road for one of our periodic swings through part of our prime listening area — in this case, Texas. Elvis had just wound up a two-week tour of Virginia, North Carolina, and Tennessee that caused him to miss one Saturday night on our Shreveport stage. On September 26, he made a quick trip to Wichita, Kansas, where he and the Blue Moon Boys drew a huge crowd, then drove all night to meet the rest of our troupe in Bryan, Texas, the following day.

From Bryan, we made the short drive to Conroe, Texas, for a September 28 show that turned out to be an event of major historical significance.

We had advertised the Conroe show that afternoon on a radio station in Houston, which was only about forty miles away. It was a Wednesday night, not the best night of the week to draw a crowd, and we hoped our ads would help build up our attendance, but we got an unexpected response from one young man.

A couple of hours before curtain time, this guy showed up at the high school football stadium where the show was to be held and asked to talk to me. He was young and kind of skinny with a crew-cut, and he looked to me like he was still in his teens, although I found out later he was actually twenty-four years old and a Marine Corps veteran.

"Howdy," he said. "I'm George Jones and I'd sure like to audition for a spot on your show tonight."

I wasn't too enthusiastic about it. With the red-hot Elvis, Johnny Horton, the Browns, David Houston, and several other solid acts, our lineup was pretty well set.

"What do you do for a living?" I asked.

"I paint houses most of the time," he said, "and sing whenever I get a chance."

"Well, we don't usually put anybody on unless they've got a record out," I said. "Have you ever recorded anything?"

He kind of laughed. "Yeah, I done a song on the Starday label called 'There Ain't No Money in This Deal,' and that sucker ain't done nothin' but live up to its name. But I know how to sing, Mr. Logan. If you'll listen to me, I think you'll like what you hear."

I was vaguely familiar with the Starday label. I knew it was owned by H. W. "Pappy" Daily, and I knew Daily had been kicking around the music business for a long time. I didn't think he'd release a record by someone with no talent at all.

"Okay," I said. "Let's hear what you've got."

"This is one that me and a friend of mine wrote ourselves," he said. "The record ain't out yet but it should be soon. It's called 'Why Baby Why.' "

It was a damn good song—one that would crack the top ten and put the then-obscure Starday label on the map within a few months—and George really put his heart into it.

"You're on," I told him. "Since you're a local talent, I'll let you open the show."

We had quite a scare that night, as it turned out. Our "stage" was the back of a flatbed truck out in the middle of the football field, and Elvis slipped as he was coming up the steps to it. He fell and knocked himself out cold, and we had to delay the start of the show for about ten minutes until we could get him conscious again and make sure he wasn't seriously hurt. When he sat up and shook his head and said he was okay, I breathed a huge sigh of relief.

Anyway, George got out there and put on quite a show. He stomped and hollered and really got into it. His songs were original and showed a touch of the rockabilly influence that was becoming so strong. But George sang them with a sharp-edged old-time twang that reminded me a little of Hank Williams.

After the show that night, I offered him a regular job right there on the bed of that truck, and the very next week he made his debut on the Municipal Auditorium stage in Shreveport.

As every country music fan knows, George developed into one of the all-time greats in the field. But like Hank Williams, he had severe problems with alcohol, problems that began to surface soon after he joined the *Hayride.* George ended up losing everything he had and almost dying before he managed to turn his life around — but the important thing is that he *did* turn it around. Today, his list of top-ten hits is almost endless, and he ranks as an entertainment legend in his own lifetime.

He also stands as another living monument to the *Louisiana Hayride*'s unique star-making ability.

Elvis entered one of the busiest, most hectic periods of his whole career as 1956 began. He was already traveling far and wide, but his personal-appearance schedule was reaching a frantic pace. By spring the demands on his time would often leave him exhausted, sleepless, and irritable.

On January 7, Elvis sang for a standing-room-only crowd at Shreveport's Municipal Auditorium. The next day was Elvis's twenty-first birthday, but there was no time for cake and candles. He and some other *Hayride* regulars hit the road that morning for another brief tour.

Two days later, Elvis was in Nashville, accompanied by Scotty Moore, Bill Black, D. J. Fontana, and Floyd Cramer, to cut "Heartbreak Hotel" for RCA. They were joined for the recording session by guitarist Chet Atkins and backup singers Gordon Stoker, Ben Speer, and Brock Speer. At the same session, Elvis recorded "I Got a Woman," "I'm Counting on You," and "I Was the One."

Then it was right back to the *Hayride* again for another Saturday night show.

The nonstop grind was starting to take a noticeable toll on Elvis.

He'd always been jumpy and high-strung, ever since that first Saturday when I came down early to let him into the auditorium. Lately, though, as the pressures of fame intensified, he'd gotten even edgier.

He had a temper, too. For the most part, he kept it well-concealed, but I learned to spot some of the danger signs. Sometimes he clenched his fists so tight his knuckles turned white when some guy started heckling him. Once in a while, that temper would flash suddenly and without warning.

One night, one of the helpers backstage bumped into Elvis just as he was getting ready to go on. Almost like a reflex, Elvis whirled around, smacked the guy in the jaw and knocked him flat on the floor.

The stagehand was sprawled there on the seat of his pants when Elvis realized what he'd done. I've never seen anybody turn so contrite in such a hurry. The next thing I knew, Elvis was down on the floor beside the guy apologizing and trying to help him up.

"God, I'm sorry," he said. "I—I don't know what got into me, man. Are you hurt?"

The guy finally got up, but he wasn't too steady on his feet. He leaned against the wall and mumbled something I couldn't hear.

"I'm really sorry," Elvis said again. "Hey, hang on. I'll get somebody to call a doctor."

"Nah, I'm all right," the guy said.

"You sure?"

"Yeah, I'll be okay."

Elvis was still white as a sheet when he walked out on the stage a minute later for his first song.

Every Saturday night brought a new sellout at the auditorium, and a lot of latecomers had to be turned away. But from the very beginning, our crowds had averaged being close to capacity almost every week, so there actually weren't many more people in the auditorium now than there were before Elvis came along.

What was different, though, were the demographics of a typical audience. The average age was much younger, and the largest single group was made up of girls between the ages of thirteen and nineteen. They made a hellacious amount of noise, but there was never any major disturbance in the auditorium during a *Hayride* performance. Some people later implied we had a riot or near-riot on our hands there every Saturday, but that just isn't true. There was always efficient crowd control and ample security, and anybody who did anything that seriously disrupted the show or endangered someone else was quickly removed.

Because of his heavy schedule, I gave Elvis permission to miss three straight *Hayride* appearances during late January and early February. Since these absences were excessive under the terms of his contract, Henry Clay demanded that Elvis pay 400 dollars to KWKH for each performance he missed over and above the five he was allowed each year (at the rate of one every sixty days).

I didn't think it was fair, because Elvis really had no choice in the matter. Besides, in order to get Elvis to sign that last contract, I'd hinted that we might bend the rules a little because of his special circumstances. Now I felt like Henry was forcing me to go back on my word to the kid.

"We never charged anybody else a penalty for missing shows," I said. "Why can't we just dock him two hundred dollars for every time he's not here and let it go at that?"

But Henry was adamant. "I hear he's getting up to twelve hundred fifty dollars for those television appearances," Henry said. "At prices like that, he can afford to pay us."

"Maybe so, but that doesn't make it right," I said and walked away.

During much of this period, Elvis was in New York cranking out new RCA releases as fast as he could. Of the dozen or so songs he recorded on this trip, the one that became his biggest hit was "Blue Suede Shoes," written and recorded originally by Carl Perkins.

Elvis also made his first appearances on network TV. In addition to the Dorseys' *Stage Show* on CBS-TV, where he was featured for six straight weeks, he was signed to appear on the *Milton Berle Show* in April. The Colonel also approached Jackie Gleason about a guest spot for Elvis on Gleason's highly rated show, but Jackie wasn't impressed.

"He can't last," Gleason declared. "I tell you flatly, he can't last."

I tell you flatly, he did.

On April 1, Elvis and the Colonel were in Hollywood, where Hal Wallis gave the kid his first screen test. Five days later, he signed a seven-picture contract with Paramount. There were lots of rumors about the amount of money involved. Some said Elvis would earn up to 200,000 dollars per picture, but those of us who knew Tom Parker thought he'd end up getting a helluva lot more than that. In his career, Elvis would make thirty-three feature films all told, and estimates of his total income from these movies runs as high as 200 million dollars—at least half of which went to Parker.

This was all still somewhere off in the future, of course. But for a guy who'd been making 18 dollars per Saturday night a few months ago, Elvis wasn't doing bad right now. According to reliable sources, he earned the biggest paycheck of his career to date—5,000 dollars—for appearing on the April 3 *Milton Berle Show*. He sang "Heartbreak Hotel," "Blue Suede Shoes," and "Shake, Rattle, and Roll" to an audience of servicemen and women from the deck of a U.S. Navy ship in San Diego harbor, then took part in a silly comedy skit in which he and Berle played twin brothers.

This was just the beginning for Elvis, but he'd reached the end of the road as far as the *Hayride* was concerned. He signed the Paramount movie deal on April 6, then flew back to Shreveport in time for the Saturday *Hayride* performance the following night. It was to be his last as a regular member of our cast.

I'd known for several weeks what was coming, and obviously I'd hoped to stall it as long as possible. But when I saw him before the show that night, I knew the time had come, and I wasn't really surprised. It had come earlier than I wanted it to, but it was there, and there was no sense denying it.

"I'm gonna have to buy out the rest of my contract, Mr. Logan," he said. "I really hate it 'cause ya'll been really good to me, but the Colonel says I got no choice."

I want to emphasize that the contract we had with Elvis was legal in every respect. There's absolutely no question we could've held him to it if we'd wanted to get tough about it. But my position all along had been that just because something was legally binding didn't necessarily make it right. Forcing Elvis to keep working for 200 dollars when he could make twenty or thirty or forty times that much for a Saturday performance somewhere else would've been wrong, and I didn't want any part of it.

"I understand," I said. "I don't like it, but I understand. Where do you go from here, Elvis?"

"Colonel Parker's talkin' to some people in Las Vegas. It looks like we'll be headin' there pretty soon." The excitement was clear in his voice.

"I wish you luck," I said.

"I've got seven months to go on my contract," he said. "That's about thirty weeks in all. At four hundred dollars a week, that means I owe you twelve thousand dollars, right?"

"Yeah, but if you'll do me one last favor, I think we could round it off at an even ten thousand dollars." As I said it, I could almost hear Henry yelling, but I didn't care.

"Sure," he said, "what's that?"

"I want you to come back and make one final appearance on the *Hayride*. You can do it anytime between now and the end of the year. Just give us a couple of weeks' notice so we can do it up right and let all your Louisiana and Texas fans know. We'll donate all the proceeds after expenses to some charity. What do you say?"

"You got it, Mr. Logan," he said, and we shook hands.

Two days later, I received a 10,000-dollar check signed by Elvis and made payable to "Horace Logan." I thought at the time this was a little strange, but it was only later that I figured out why he'd done it. Since I was the one who negotiated and signed the contract, I guess Elvis assumed all the money went to me.

It was more than a year before I got a chance to set him straight and explain that KWKH got every last cent of that 10,000 dollars. In the meantime, the whole thing with Elvis really bothered me.

It bothered me that we'd lost Elvis in the first place. And the way we'd treated him bothered me, too. It also bothered me — as it had for a long time — that nobody seemed to care if we kept the stars we developed or not.

By this time, a lot of things about the policies, management, and ownership of the radio station where I'd spent most of my adult life were really starting to eat at me.

For the first time in the nearly ten years since I'd returned to KWKH, I was beginning to seriously wonder if it wasn't about time for me to move on, too.

The day after Elvis's last show as a *Hayride* regular, Parker closed a deal with the New Frontier Hotel in Las Vegas. It called for a four-week engagement at 12,500 dollars a week, starting April 23. But it turned out to be too big a jump too soon. Vegas wasn't ready for this rough-edged kid, at least not yet. After two weeks, the New Frontier had had enough, and they canceled the rest of the dates. *Variety* branded Elvis's show a "failure," and I'm sure he brooded over it for a few days.

But the flop in Vegas turned out to be his only major setback of the year. Everything else was coming up roses.

The King was free, and the sky was the limit.

By fall, he was being seen by tens of millions of TV viewers on the *Ed Sullivan Show* and by tens of millions of moviegoers in his first feature film, *Love Me Tender.* The theme song from the movie hit number one on the charts in early November. It followed "Hound Dog" and "Don't Be Cruel," both of which had held the top spot earlier in the year. "Love Me Tender" had presold more than 850,000 copies before it was even released.

While rumors flew about serious romances between Elvis and actresses Debra Paget, Ann-Margaret, and Natalie Wood, he was featured in articles in *Look, Newsweek, Collier's, Cosmopolitan, Photoplay, TV* and *Radio Mirror* and other major magazines. Press reports said he was now being paid 25,000 dollars and up for personal appearances, eclipsing the 10,000-dollars-a-night fees earned by Dean Martin, Jerry Lewis, and other top names in show business.

In the midst of all this, it was mind-boggling to remember that Saturday afternoon almost exactly two years ago when I'd met a shy, nervous kid from Memphis face-to-face for the first time. I couldn't help but chuckle when I recalled how excited he'd been back then at the idea of earning 18 dollars per show from the *Hayride.*

I wondered if he'd figured out yet how many hamburgers he could buy with 25,000 dollars.

With Elvis gone, there was never any question of going back to the way things had been before he came. As I said before, he changed everything, and if the rest of us in the music business were going to survive, much less prosper, we had to adapt to those changes.

Many people outside the business tried to convince themselves that Elvis was an isolated phenomenon—a fad that would go away. But for those of us who depended on reading and responding to musical trends for our survival, taking an attitude like that would've been suicide. If we tried to con ourselves into thinking we could go back to "Red River Valley" and "You Are My Sunshine" and forget about the musical revolution Elvis had started, we'd find ourselves abandoned and dead in the water.

I had no intention of trying to turn every act on the *Hayride* into a rockabilly Elvis imitator. But at the same time, I knew the only way to keep the teenagers who'd become such a key part of our audience during Elvis's tenure in Shreveport was to offer them some kind of replacement for what they'd lost.

In keeping with the policy I'd followed ever since the *Hayride* began, my first priority when Elvis left was finding someone to fill the gap he left behind. We already had Johnny Cash, who was a tremendous favorite with the youngsters as well as with more mature fans. Johnny, too, was part of the cutting edge of musical change, but his style was totally different from Elvis's. He'd never be a "new Elvis," and he had no desire to be.

I had enough sense to know that nobody could really replace Elvis. But what we needed was a fresh young talent with a cute enough face and a strong enough voice to take the girls' minds off Elvis for a while.

In the early summer of 1956, just a few weeks after Elvis's departure, I thought I spotted those qualities in the person of an eighteen-year-old kid who'd just graduated from high school in Kilgore, Texas.

He first came to the *Hayride* as a member of a male quartet who called themselves the Four Diamonds. But he was a good enough singer that he'd won a talent contest in Tyler the previous spring, and when the other three members of the group decided to go back to school that fall, I offered to try him out as a soloist.

He was also handsome, muscular, athletic (an outstanding baseball player at Kilgore High School), and very personable — what I think girls nowadays might call a "real hunk."

His name was Bob Luman, and at the time I hired him, I broke one of my own long-standing rules. Bob had almost no track record as a professional performer. He'd never made a record and had no prospects of any kind of recording contract. But I gave him a job in spite of those things. One reason was that I had a gut feeling about him, and my gut feelings had proved right before. I also took an instant liking to this young man, and he never gave me any reason to feel different. Besides, like I said, the times were changing, and sometimes you just have to go with the flow.

I had no illusions about his potential as "Elvis II." It would've been totally unrealistic to think I'd ever find another King hidden among the pine groves and oil fields of East Texas. But if the teenyboppers of the Ark-La-Tex would just accept Bob Luman as the next prince of the *Hayride*, I'd be more than satisfied.

Horace Logan, drum major,
as pictured in his high school yearbook.

Hayride announcers Frank Page (left) and Norm Bale
(center) with Horace Logan.

Louisiana Hayride performers assemble for a curtain call.

[Photo by Langston McEachern]

Gene Autry and his horse Champion pose with Horace's oldest son, Lee, before Autry's guest appearance on the *Hayride* in 1950.

Hank Williams poses with his stepdaughter, Lycrecia, and his "new" Packard in front of their home in Bossier City.

Hank Williams in one of his last *Hayride* publicity photos.

In one of the few photos of Hank Williams without his hat, he and Billie Jean exchange vows for the third time in twenty-four hours.

Faron Young was known as the "Deputy" during his years as a *Hayride* star.

Slim Whitman was a postman by day and a yodeler on Saturday nights.

After rising to stardom on the *Hayride*, Webb Pierce helped launch the careers of Floyd Cramer, Faron Young, Billy Walker, and others, but he and Slim Whitman became bitter rivals.

Whitman recorded three million-selling singles after-hours in the KWKH studios.

Horace greets Jim Reeves as he lands at Barksdale Air Force Base after a tour of South Africa.

(Photo by Langston McEachern)

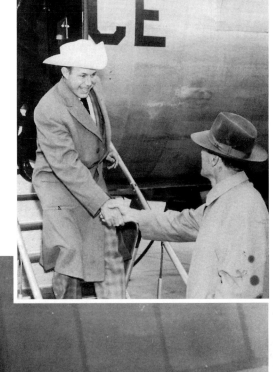

Elvis belts out a song as Bill Black plays the bass and D. J. Fontana and Horace lurk in the background.

(Photo by Langston McEachern)

AGREEMENT, HE SHALL BE LIABLE TO A SUIT FOR INJUNCTION AND DAMAGES.

11.

ARTIST ACKNOWLEDGES THAT HIS SERVICES ARE UNIQUE, AND HE HEREBY AGREES AND COVENANTS NOT TO ACCEPT ANY EMPLOYMENT, AS MUSICIAN OR SINGER, WHICH WILL INTERFERE WITH OR PROHIBIT HIS APPEARANCE ON THE PROGRAM HEREIN SPECIFIED, AND THAT IN THE EVENT OF HIS FAILURE TO COMPLY WITH THIS CONTRACT, AND IN ADDITION TO THE LIABILITY FOR ALL DAMAGES CAUSED TO STATION, ARTIST CAN BE RESTRAINED BY INJUNCTION FROM PROCEEDING WITH SAID OTHER EMPLOYMENT DURING THE PERIOD OF THIS CONTRACT UP TO AND INCLUDING _____

6 November 1955

IN WITNESS WHEREOF THIS AGREEMENT IS EXECUTED IN DUPLICATE ORIGINALS THIS 6th DAY OF _____ November _____, 1954.

WITNESSES:

Vernon E Presley
Gladys Presley

STATION
INTERNATIONAL BROADCASTING CORP.

BY *H. L. Fryar*

ARTIST

✝ *Elvis Presley*

✝ *Winfield Scott Moore*

✝ *William Black*

Copy of Elvis's original

Hayride contract

Elvis Presley's original contract with the *Hayride* was signed by his parents, Vernon and Gladys Presley.

Carolyn Bradshaw, a 17-year-old folksinger who was billed as the smallest regular member of the *Hayride* cast (95 pounds and under five feet tall), attracted immediate interest from Elvis when he joined the show.

(Center)
Elvis sings under the approving eye of "Two-Gun" Logan.

(Photo by Langston McEachern)

(Right)
Elvis poses against a cinder-block wall backstage at the *Hayride* for his first publicity photo connected to the show.

Elvis and Horace practice their fast draws backstage as visiting disc jockey Ed Hamilton tries to "settle things peaceably."

Elvis examines a six-shooter that Horace won in a bet with Webb Pierce.

The future "King" strikes a sexy (or menacing) pose for Shreveport fans.

Young *Hayride* fans grab at Elvis in early 1955.
[Photo by Langston McEachern]

These photos of Elvis and Johnny Cash on the *Hayride* stage were taken on the same night in late 1955. Johnny's portion of the show was sponsored by the makers of a well-known laxative.

[Photos by Langston McEachern]

Johnny Horton and
Johnny Cash have a
laugh backstage.

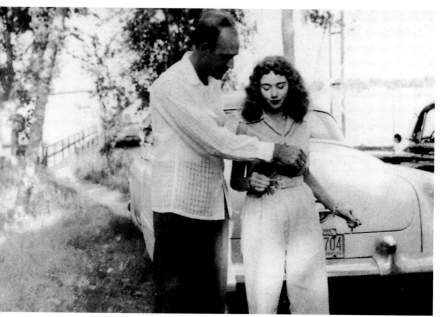

Johnny Horton, caught in an informal moment without his hat or
toupee, with his wife Billie Jean.

Johnny Cash (left) and Johnny Horton fish at Caddo Lake.

A very young George Jones (with guitar) poses with fellow *Hayride* performer James O'Gwynne.

Teenage fans swarm around Bob Luman in 1957.

"Hossin'" around on the set of *King of the Mountain*. The hand holding the gun belongs to David Houston.

The Municipal Auditorium, home of the *Louisiana Hayride*, still stands in downtown Shreveport.

Horace (right) and Billy Walker enjoy a recent visit.

Elvis made his triumphant return to Shreveport and the *Louisiana Hayride* stage on December 15, 1956. It was also his final farewell. As agreed, all proceeds from the show after expenses would go to a local charity. The Shreveport YMCA would receive a brand new swimming pool out of this deal, and thousands of hysterical girls would have a night to remember for the rest of their lives.

The main thing I got out of it, though, was a demolished automobile.

We'd decided months beforehand to hold Elvis's "last hurrah" at the Hirsh Coliseum, also known as the Youth Center, at the state fairgrounds, and it was a good thing we had. It was by far the largest audience ever to attend a *Hayride* performance — more than thirteen thousand people, the vast majority of them young and female.

I can safely say that not a one of them heard a single word Elvis sang that night. From the moment he stepped onto the stage until he waved both arms and ran back behind the curtain about thirty minutes later, everything was completely drowned out by the ceaseless roar from the crowd.

As the *Shreveport Times* reported the next day:

> The gyrating rotary troubadour was seldom if ever heard by an audience screaming like Zulus every time he moved a muscle. . . . No entertainer in history has worked under greater audience handicaps, not even Sinatra at the Palace. Elvis's mere appearance on the *Hayride* stage last night set off a veritable atomic explosion of photographic flashbulbs and squeals from teenagers which crescendoed into pandemonium.

It was more than a show. It was one of the major local news events of the year. *Times* staff writer Bob Masters called it "one of the finest displays of mass hysteria in Shreveport history."

Security was heavy prior to the show. "Probably [Russian leaders]

Khrushchev and Bulganin wouldn't have been better guarded than was the young singer during most of the day," Masters wrote. Elvis's suite at the Captain Shreve Hotel was protected by cordons of police, hotel security personnel, and private bodyguards.

But the situation deteriorated during a scheduled hour-long press conference, where newspeople were overrun and outflanked by hordes of fans, autograph hunters, and curiosity seekers.

By now, Elvis was encountering this kind of reaction everywhere he went, and Tom Parker and the promoters he worked with were getting more and more unnerved by the out-of-control mobs of teens. Tragically, the time when Elvis could perform freely and in close proximity to large general-admission audiences was rapidly coming to an end. It was just getting too dangerous.

I made a point of visiting privately with Elvis before the show. There was something I'd been wanting to tell him for months, and this might be my last opportunity for a long time. By now he was the highest paid superstar in America, and the 10,000 dollars he'd paid to buy out his *Hayride* contract probably seemed like chicken feed to him. But it was still important to me that he know the truth.

"You made the check out to me, but every dollar of that money went to KWKH," I said. "Maybe it doesn't matter now, but I just wanted to set the record straight."

He grinned kind of sheepishly. "I guess I'm pretty stupid about business stuff," he said. "I shoulda made the check out to the station."

"That's not important," I said. "If it'd been up to me, I wouldn't have charged you a dime to get out of that contract. I would've torn the contract up and let you go for nothing, but my boss didn't see it that way. That's what I want you to understand."

"You always treated me fair and square, Mr. Logan, and I appreciate it." His tone was as polite as the first day I met him. "I knew you were only doin' what you had to do."

"Well, how does it feel to be the most famous guy in America?"

"I dunno," he said and kind of shrugged. "Sometimes it feels real good, and sometimes it feels, well, scary. Sometimes I wish me and the boys was still back at the Al-Ida Motel. I never realized what a good time I was havin' back then till it was all over. Now I gotta hide from the girls. I don't like that."

I laughed. "From the sound of that crowd out there," I said, "they don't like it, either."

In setting up for the show that night, we'd tried to create a thirty-five-to-forty-foot buffer zone between Elvis and the audience by keeping that much distance between the first row of seats and the stage. Unfortunately, though, we were using portable chairs, and all the kids just picked them up and moved them forward as far as they could, until they were pressing right against the stage.

The fire marshal took one look at this arrangement and told me in no uncertain terms that the show couldn't begin until that buffer zone was reestablished.

"How the hell am I supposed to get all those kids to move back?" I said. "They're packed in there like sardines. The ones in front can't move back till the ones behind them get out of the way. It's a human logjam."

"Well, I don't know what to tell you," the fire marshal said. "But unless we have enough space to get emergency equipment to the stage in case of a problem, there won't be any show—and that's final."

I was beginning to feel a little panicky. Trying to call off the performance at this point would be something like spraying gasoline on a forest fire. It could touch off a riot that might go on all night.

I was also getting angry.

"All right," I said, "I think I've got a plan. But I'm warning you now, if it doesn't work and I have to tell all these kids the show's being canceled, I'm also going to tell them who's responsible for canceling it."

I waited a second or two to let my meaning sink in. Then I smiled and added only half-jokingly, "They'll tear your ass to pieces. There won't be enough of you left to fill up a Dixie cup."

At the heart of my plan were a half-dozen young polio patients in iron lungs who were being transported to the show in ambulances from a local hospital. I'd found out they were coming an hour or so earlier.

About ten minutes before the show was supposed to start, I went to the microphone in the center of the stage and made an announcement.

"Ladies and gentlemen," I said, "we have some young polio patients in iron lungs with us tonight, and we need to get these children down here in the area immediately in front of the stage. That's the only way they're going to be able to see the show. So I'm asking all you folks to please pick up your chairs and move them back far enough so we can get these iron lungs in here. The quicker you can do that, the faster we can get the show started."

There were some low mutterings and grumblings, but then everybody started standing up and trying to move. The problem was, most of them couldn't.

"If you'll all just pick up your chairs and move them back about ten or twelve steps to the rear, that'll give us the room we need," I coaxed. "You folks further back will have to move first so the ones in front can move back, too. Just as soon as you clear the way and we can get these children in here, we'll get our program under way."

They finally got the idea and over the next two or three minutes, a massive relocation took place. As soon as there was enough space, the ambulance attendants rolled the iron lungs into position right in front of the stage, and we were able to start our first act almost on time.

Not only did my little ruse satisfy the fire marshal and allow the show to go on, but the row of iron lungs created an effective barrier between the screaming teenagers and Elvis. The kids were too far back to even think about grabbing at Elvis or reaching up and trying to touch him. Even the most eager and frantic fans weren't going to run the risk of bumping one of those iron lungs to get closer to the stage, and the crippled kids were able to get a great view of Elvis too.

The noise the crowd made was enough to peel paint. A few girls fainted from sheer excitement, but there were no major incidents, and everybody was generally well behaved — at least as long as they were inside the coliseum.

Once Elvis had finished his part of the show, though, it was a completely different story. The audience went totally berserk and started running wildly through the building. I tried repeatedly to calm them down a little, and finally, in sheer desperation, I said something into the microphone that's been repeated so many times in the years since that it's become an inseparable part of the Elvis phenomenon.

"Ladies and gentlemen, please," I implored. "Elvis has left the building. Now if you'll just return to your seats, we'll go on with the show."

It took a while for it to sink in, but the pandemonium inside the coliseum gradually subsided. The same wasn't true outside. Hordes of shrieking girls who either hadn't heard my announcement or didn't believe it circled the place like packs of hungry wolves, looking for any way to reach the backstage area and the dressing rooms. Anywhere they found an opening that might lead them to Elvis, they swarmed around it like ants on a picnic lunch.

That was how I got a very nice 1955 Mercury hardtop totally trashed that night.

I'd parked the car at the rear of the coliseum in a place that seemed out of the way and perfectly safe. I'd noticed the row of high windows that ran along the wall just above my parking space, but the windows were a good twelve to fourteen feet above the ground. I never gave any thought to somebody trying to climb through them.

Well, somebody did — several hundred somebodies, in fact — and they used the top, hood, and rear deck of my car as a launching pad for their assault on the windows.

When I came out to get the car an hour after the show, the area outside the coliseum was deserted. There wasn't a single teenage girl in sight, but one glance at my Mercury told me instantly what had happened. It looked like an elephant had danced a jig on it.

The top was pushed in so far it was practically touching the backs of the seats. The hood and deck were mangled. God knows how many girls had been on that car at one time. They must've used it as a trampoline, jumping and bouncing and trying to reach those windows from it. I've seen cars that looked better after they were rolled three or four times.

"I guess it's a good thing you're gone, Elvis," I sighed as I surveyed the damage. "I don't think I could afford many more shows like this."

As it turned out, though, Elvis and I weren't quite done with each other. In fact, it was only a few months later that Johnny Horton, Tillman Franks, and I stopped off in Memphis on our way to Nashville. Elvis was spending a good part of his time in Hollywood then, but we decided to drop by his home and see if he was there. This wasn't long after I'd read about him buying an old rundown mansion called Graceland, but it was still being remodeled and wasn't ready to move into yet.

In the meantime, Elvis and his parents were living in a house on Audubon Drive in Memphis that should've been big and fancy enough for almost anybody. I'd heard some of their rich neighbors were raising all kinds of hell over the commotion Elvis's fans kept causing. The fuss the neighbors were making upset and embarrassed Elvis's mother. She claimed they were picking on her son, but the minute we pulled up in front of the place, it was obvious that the neighbors had a point.

It was early evening — just about dusk — and there must've been two or three dozen teenage girls ganged up outside the house yelling "Elvis! Elvis!" as loud as they could. The house was surrounded by a six-foot stone and wrought-iron fence, and every inch of the premises was brightly illuminated by floodlights. There were also uniformed guards at all four corners of the property and another one at the gate. There was no way the girls were going to get any closer than they were, but there was no way they were going to leave, either. I got the feeling this kind of thing went on about eighteen hours a day.

When we told the guard at the gate who we were, he called the house and almost immediately opened the gate and directed us inside.

Elvis welcomed us like his long-lost brothers. He seemed really excited to see us.

"Man, what a surprise," he said. "Come on in. I want you to meet some friends of mine." He gestured toward a young blond guy who looked vaguely familiar and a beautiful dark-haired girl that I recognized instantly.

"This is my ol' motorcycle buddy Nick Adams," Elvis said, slapping the guy on the shoulder. "And this is . . ." He turned to the girl and hesitated for a second. "This is Natalie Wood."

The three of us sort of ignored Adams, I'm afraid. We were too busy gawking at Natalie Wood to pay much attention to anything else. She was every bit as gorgeous in person as she'd been in the movie *Rebel Without a Cause.*

"Pleased to meet you, ma'am," we said, more or less in unison. Johnny Horton was grinning at her from ear to ear. It was a good thing Billie Jean wasn't around to see that, I thought. Johnny never would've heard the last of it.

Later Elvis took me out to the six-car garage behind the house and showed me the pink-and-white Cadillac he'd bought for his mother and the new pickup he'd bought for his daddy. He also had several of his own cars in there, including a Lincoln Continental that was missing part of the back seat as well as the hood ornament and various other pieces of trim.

"Some girls got ahold of it," he said. "Gonna have to put it in the shop for a day or two."

"I guess that's part of the price of fame," I said. "Do you ever get tired of it?"

He frowned thoughtfully for a second. "Aw, sometimes, I guess. I mean, it's funny, you know. I used to be the one that did the chasin'. Now the girls're always chasin' me. It's hard to get tired of somethin' that's so much fun, but once in a while I do."

"I keep reading all this stuff about your big romances," I said. "You think you might get married sometime soon?"

He almost broke up at that. "Are you kiddin', Mr. Logan?" he said. "It's like my daddy says: Why would anybody want to buy a cow when they already got all the free milk they can drink? Hey, did you see that story about me in *Confidential* magazine—the one that said I was in bed with three girls at one time?"

"Yeah, as a matter of fact, I did. Was it true?"

"No sir, absolutely not," he said.

"Well, how many was it really?"

"Six," he said with a broad grin. I glanced over at Vernon Presley and saw him beaming proudly at his son.

"You must be trying to set some kind of record," I said.

"Nah, not really. Stuff like that just seems to happen to me nowadays. I don't even have to work for it, it just happens. I tell you the truth, Mr. Logan, I been in bed with girls I never even dreamed I'd meet—girls I figured I'd never get any closer to than a front-row seat at some movie."

My curiosity got the best of me for a minute. "Like who, for example?"

He grinned again. "How 'bout Kim Novak? How's that for an example?"

"But what about Miss, uh—?" I jerked my head toward the house.

"Aw, Nat and me're real good friends, and I like her a lot," he said. "But this big love affair of ours is mostly just somethin' the publicity people cooked up. Bob Wagner's the guy she's really stuck on."

By the time I left I knew the Elvis I was talking to now wasn't the same shy kid who'd driven into Shreveport that October day two and a half years ago. He was more mature for one thing—he'd just turned twenty-two a couple of months earlier. He was also more financially secure than he'd ever thought of being back in 1954.

He'd gone from wondering where his next hamburger was coming from to being able to buy anything that struck his fancy. And the money had only just started to flow. In a few days, he said, he'd be going to California to start shooting his new movie, *Jailhouse Rock*. Meanwhile, his latest hit record, "All Shook Up," was number one on the charts. It was appropriate that Elvis had started wearing a gold lamé outfit at his concerts. Everything he was touching was turning to gold.

But there was more to the change I saw in him than that. He also seemed more self-assured. He still cared about what other people thought of him, but he didn't fret about it as much. Now he could accept the dreams of the past as the realities of the present. He didn't have to pinch himself anymore to make sure he was awake. He didn't have to eat all the hamburgers, bed all the girls, or buy all the cars today, because he'd still be able to do the same thing tomorrow.

He was smoother, more polished, worldlier, a little wiser, and not quite as happy as he'd once been. He was just now able to see the disillusionment that lurked on the dark underside of success.

Up until that moment, I don't think Elvis had ever taken any drug stronger than the Dexedrene pills that many performers took to stay alert and energized for endless strings of show dates. He'd never used alcohol or tobacco, either, which gave him a sizeable advantage over most other artists. And now he didn't even have to tour the hard way anymore. The grind of one-night stands and exhausting car trips in between was a thing of the past. He was averaging one or two huge personal appearances a week in major cities, and despite his fear of planes, he'd learned to fly first class. He was playing fewer dates than ever before, so there was no reason for him to get trapped in the deadly cycle of uppers and downers. That's what I told myself, anyway.

He'd changed a lot, but hidden somewhere under all the kingly trappings, I knew the shy kid was still there. He hadn't died or disappeared. He'd just gone dormant for the time being. I was pretty sure he'd always be around.

What I didn't know was if this "inner kid" would help keep Elvis honest, straight, and down-to-earth in years to come or if he'd only make it easier for the old fears, doubts, and insecurities to come back and drag Elvis down.

Would he end up being a blessing or a curse?

Elvis and I would cross paths several more times during his career, and I'd have a chance later on to answer that question for myself.

{ 10 }

Johnny Horton:

Fisherman's Lament

I've probably mentioned Johnny Horton's name a couple of dozen times in this book so far. I've mentioned his long-running stardom on the Louisiana Hayride, his marriage to Hank Williams's widow, his refusal to leave Shreveport even after he got as big as a recording artist can get, and the tragedy that took his life at the peak of his career. But these have all been just passing references—brief asides made while the main subject was something or somebody else. Up to now I haven't actually talked at all about the real Johnny Horton. I haven't made any attempt to dig into the character and personality of the man behind those gigantic hit songs. I haven't told you how he became perhaps my best friend, next to Hank, in the country music business.

Now I think I know why I haven't. Maybe I've been avoiding the subject because it's still so painful. Even now, thirty-seven years after Johnny's death, it hurts like hell to think about it, much less try to write about it.

But at the same time, no book about the *Hayride*—or about American music in the fifties and sixties in general, for that matter—could be anywhere near complete without the story of Johnny Horton. I've wished a million times for some way to rewrite that story and change the ending. But, of course, that's impossible. So I'll just have to tell it like it is.

From my perspective, Johnny was as straightforward and unpretentious as any person I ever met. He never once struck me as the "man of mystery" many people made him out to be. But there are some puzzles and unanswered questions in his background, starting with the date and place of his birth. Nobody seems to know for sure if he was born in California or Tyler, Texas. A souvenir book on Johnny's career, issued after his death, lists his birthplace as Los Angeles. But our *Hayride* promotional material referred to him as "a native of Tyler," and since he never bothered to correct us, I'll go with that option. There's also some doubt as to whether he was born in 1925 or 1929, but I'd tend to go with the earlier year. The date was April 30.

The fact that Johnny never made so much as a single appearance on the *Grand Ole Opry,* and, in fact, declined repeated invitations from the *Opry,* undoubtedly rubbed certain powerful people the wrong way. The fact that he began dating Billie Jean Jones so soon after Hank Williams's death also may have given him a black eye in some quarters. This may help explain why he's sometimes excluded from the lists of country music "greats" and why the questions about his background haven't been cleared up long before now. The authoritative *Encyclopedia of Folk, Country & Western Music,* which includes entries on more than six hundred artists from Roy Acuff to Steve Young, doesn't contain a single word on Johnny Horton.

Regardless of where he was born, John LaGale Horton spent at least part of his growing-up years around Tyler. After high school, he enrolled at Lon Morris Junior College in Jacksonville, Texas, for a while and later attended Baylor University on a basketball scholarship. He also attended the University of Seattle and worked in the commercial fishing industry in Alaska and California. His Alabama-born father, John Horton Sr., was an itinerant carpenter who moved wherever construction work was available, and Johnny apparently inherited his daddy's rambling tendencies. He roamed from one corner of the continent to the other, picking fruit in Florida, working in the mailroom at Selznick Studios in Hollywood, and doing construction work in Alaska. Somewhere along the way, he started writing songs, picking a guitar, and trying to sing.

By 1950, Johnny had migrated back to East Texas, where he got his first break as a singer. He won a talent contest at the Reo Palm Isle nightclub in Longview. (The host of the contest, by the way, was a deejay from nearby Henderson named Jim Reeves.) This small victory gave Johnny the impetus to go back to California and start trying to sing professionally. By now, he was married to a girl named Donna Cook, and she was amazed by his decision.

"I'd never heard him sing," she remarked later, "but he could pound out a little boogie-woogie on the piano."

He started entering just about any talent contest he could find and was encouraged to make a record by songwriter Les McWain, co-owner of a tiny label called Cormac. Johnny resisted at first, but McWain finally talked him into it. "He was very shy, and he didn't think he could sing," McWain said, "but I liked the little yodel he worked in at the end of a line, and I thought he had a very pleasant voice."

Johnny landed a spot on *Hometown Jamboree,* a radio show in Pasadena, California, that was hosted by Cliffie Stone and featured such future stars as Tennessee Ernie Ford and Merle Travis. It was on this show that Johnny was first billed as "The Singing Fisherman." He soon caught the attention of Fabor Robison, who helped get so many struggling artists started later, and when Cormac records went out of business, Robison picked up some of Johnny's songs and put them on the Abbott label. His early Abbott releases included Johnny's own compositions, "Done Rovin'," "In My Home in Shelby County (Down Near Memphis, Tennessee)" and "Talk Gobbler Talk." None of these records went anywhere commercially, but they allowed him to meet one of our main requirements for putting an artist on the *Louisiana Hayride.*

Johnny made his first appearance on the *Hayride* in May 1952, and he quickly became a favorite with our audience. He was tall, gregarious, good-looking, and wore immaculately tailored western shirts that his sister, Nola, had made. But within a few weeks of his debut, his determination to remain a regular on the show cost him his marriage.

Donna told Johnny she was tired of him being gone all the time and urged him to go back to California with her and get a "real job." When he refused, she went by herself. For several weeks, he tried to work out a reconciliation, but she insisted that he move back to Los Angeles as the first step, and Johnny wouldn't do that. She filed for divorce and Johnny moved into a duplex with Fabor Robison and his wife.

From that point on, Johnny's rambling days were over. He made Shreveport his home for the rest of his life.

For the next two or three years things were really rough financially. Johnny played lots of nickel-and-dime dates within fifty or sixty miles of Shreveport, and he had a lot of devoted fans on the *Hayride*. But his recording career seemed to be stuck in neutral, and his audience appeal outside our area was just about zero.

Johnny and Hank Williams worked together on the *Hayride* for several months after Hank's return in August 1952. Johnny was a big fan of Hank's, and Billie Jean recalled Hank telling her many times that Johnny had real talent.

"Hank would stop the car to listen when Johnny came on the radio," Billie Jean said. "I remember the last record Hank heard him sing. It was 'The Child's Side of Life,' which was a real dog. After it was over, Hank turned it off and said, 'No, son, this one ain't gonna make it.' But he told me that one day Johnny would be one of the biggest stars in the business."

The tune she mentioned — an "answer" to Hank Thompson's "Wild Side of Life" that never made it into the same league with Kitty Wells' "It Wasn't God Who made Honky-Tonk Angels" — was fairly typical of the stuff Johnny was recording in those days. A lot of it was bad, some was ill-advised, and some of it just didn't click.

In early 1953, Johnny tried hard to move up to the next level. He dropped Fabor Robison as his manager and got a chance to sign with the Mercury label and record several of his own compositions, including "First Train Heading South," "Mansion You Stole," "All for the Love of a Girl," and "Train With the Rumba Beat." They were good songs, but again, none of them made much of an impact on the market, and Johnny remained in a state of professional limbo somewhere between mediocrity and the charts.

To make matters worse, the backup musicians who'd been working with Johnny started quitting, and he ended up having to use pick-up bands or Billie Jean's brothers, Alton and Sonny Jones, on his show dates—which weren't many. In fact, they were so few that Johnny actually quit touring for a while and took a Monday-through-Friday job with a local tackle company.

At least this job kept him in close touch with his favorite activity in the whole world—fishing.

I know one thing for sure about Johnny. He came by his nickname, the "Singing Fisherman," honestly. He liked everything about the outdoors, but he loved to fish better than anybody I ever met. He was always happiest when he was in a boat on some lake or stream with a fishing rod in his hand. If he passed a likely looking fishing hole on his way from one show date to another, he was as likely as not to pull off the road and give it a try for an hour or two. For several years, he worked for tackle manufacturers, testing various types of fishing equipment.

And he could catch fish, too. Lord, could he ever catch fish! He was one of those guys who made ordinary fishermen like me want to eat our hearts out.

I especially remember one time in 1956 when a group of us from the *Hayride* were on a five-day tour down in Mississippi. Elvis had left the show by that time, but the troupe included Johnny, Tillman Franks, George Jones, Jimmy C. Newman, Tibby Edwards, Hoot and Curley, the Browns, David Houston, and some others. As usual, most of our artists were traveling a little light on cash and looking forward to collecting their share of the gate receipts from our first show to put a little money in their pockets. Unfortunately, though, as we were checking into an inexpensive motel in Biloxi, the desk clerk noticed some of our musical instruments.

"Oh, you're musicians," he said. "That means you're gonna have to pay in advance. It's motel policy. We've had too many musicians skip out on us in the middle of the night."

That really put us in a bind. I had about sixty dollars, which was a reasonable amount to carry on a trip like this in those days. But we needed a half-dozen rooms altogether, and some of the guys didn't have but two or three bucks to their names. We pooled our resources and let Johnny serve as the "banker" — which shows how much all the rest of the group trusted him.

The idea was for everybody to put whatever money they had in the pot, and just about everybody did — except for George Jones. George held back enough money to buy a bottle of booze, but we didn't find out about it until he turned up drunk and we discovered the empty bottle. The irresponsible streak that would earn him the unwanted nickname of "No-Show Jones" was already making its presence known.

We managed to come up with enough cash to satisfy the clerk. The problem was, our first show wasn't scheduled until the following night at Hattiesburg, and we had almost no money left to eat on in the meantime. We'd have gotten awful hungry over the next thirty hours or so if it hadn't been for the "Singing Fisherman."

"There's some mighty good bass fishin' in the backwaters in these bayous," Johnny told me, "and I know where we can get hold of a couple of boats. We ought to be able to catch enough fish for a meal or two at least."

We split up into two groups in order to cover as much territory as possible. Johnny and Tillman Franks and some others went in one boat, and I took a second group in another boat. As we were getting set to leave on our expedition, we ran into Billy Gray, the front man for Hank Thompson and his Brazos Valley Boys, who were also doing a show in the area, and Billy came along in my boat.

Johnny caught more fish than anybody that day, as usual, and I caught two or three nice ones, too. But Billy Gray snagged the biggest one of all — a bass that weighed close to four pounds. When he first pulled it into the boat, I think Billy had the idea of taking it home and maybe having it mounted as a trophy, but I let him know pretty quick that I had other plans for it.

"You're not keeping that fish," I said bluntly. "We need it for our dinner."

When I explained the situation, Billy was a good sport about "donating" his prize catch. He'd gone through some lean times just like the rest of us, and he knew how it felt to have your empty belly rubbing against your backbone.

We used the last of our money to buy some cornmeal, potatoes, onions, and lard. Then we went back to one of the kitchenettes at the motel and had ourselves one helluva fish fry. I don't think I ever enjoyed a meal more than that one, and it kept us going until we could make a payday. I doubt that Jesus himself could've found any leftovers when we got through.

In some ways, Johnny was almost as perceptive about people as he was about fish. He was among the earliest observers to see something special in Elvis. Shreveport singer-songwriter Claude King recalled being introduced to Elvis by Johnny in the office of bandleader Pappy Covington, who booked acts for the *Hayride.* King was unimpressed when Elvis sang a song called "Milkcow Blues," and he told Johnny so after they left.

Johnny laughed when King made some disparaging crack about how Elvis would be smart to hang onto his "daytime job."

"I'm gonna tell you something, Ace," he said to King. "That young guy's gonna be the biggest singing star that ever lived—bigger than Sinatra or Crosby or anybody."

"Oh yeah? What makes you think so?" King asked.

"When he goes out on stage, he does this little bop step, and all the teenagers go nuts," Johnny told him. "It's gonna be that way all over the world."

Johnny's fascination with Elvis's appeal caused him to test the rockabilly waters himself toward the end of his three-year association with Mercury Records. In his last session for Mercury, Johnny recorded several fast-paced numbers, including "Ridin' the Sunshine Special," "Hey Sweet Thing," "Big Wheels Rollin," and "You

Don't Move Me Baby Anymore." But it was still another Horton experiment that failed to generate any broad market appeal. Eventually, it led only to another dead end.

When Mercury and Johnny parted company, neither side had any great feelings of regret, because neither side had realized much of anything from the other. Walter D. Kilpatrick, Mercury's hard-driving young folk and western repertoire chief, admitted that he didn't understand Johnny.

"Every time you'd see Johnny Horton, you'd discover something about him you didn't know before — another part of his life," Kilpatrick said. "He had more compartments in his life than anyone I've ever known. I never could get in a groove with Horton. I never blamed him for it, I was just trying to get on his frequency, but I never did . . . there was something about him I could never lock into."

Johnny was very versatile and had a sharp, agile mind. If something didn't work for him, he was always willing to try something else. Some people saw him as a mass of complexities, but I always thought of him as a basically simple guy whose main priorities were his family, his home, his career, and being able to get away from the grind and relax.

Truthfully, though, Johnny might have spent his whole career floundering around from one musical style to another and never really finding a niche for himself if it hadn't been for Tillman Franks. Tillman gave Johnny the guidance and direction he'd never been able to get from anybody else — and that's what finally made Johnny a national star.

Johnny and Tillman were both down on their luck when Johnny came out to Tillman's house on Summers Street in Shreveport one day in the spring of 1955 and asked Tillman to be his manager. According to Tillman, Johnny and Billie Jean had spent the money she'd gotten from the settlement on Hank Williams's royalties, and they were broke. Never one to mince words, Billie Jean told Johnny to "get your ass out and make us some more money." He was trying his best to do it, but he wasn't having much luck.

Tillman didn't mince words during that first conversation, either. "I told him I just flat didn't like the way he sang," Tillman recalled later. "He said, 'No problem, I'll sing any way you want me to.' And he was serious."

The thing was, Johnny *could* sing just about any way anyone asked him to. His lack of success had nothing to do with a lack of talent. It was because he'd just never picked the way that was right for him yet. But with Tillman calling the shots, all that was about to change.

Tillman's first move was to get Johnny released by Mercury and picked up by Columbia, a label with a deeper commitment to country music and the changes that were taking place in it. Tillman enlisted help from Webb Pierce, who was now a partner with ex-*Opry* boss Jim Denny in Cedarwood Publishing. Pierce talked to Denny, who in turn talked to Troy Martin of Golden West Melodies. Martin and Denny then approached Don Law of Columbia, who agreed to give Johnny a standard one-year deal with a 2 percent royalty.

It was no bonanza and no guarantee of success, and although it was a step in the right direction, it did nothing to solve Johnny's immediate problems. Johnny's car note and his rent were both overdue when he headed to Nashville in a borrowed car for his first Columbia recording session. On the way, Johnny actually stopped in Memphis and asked Elvis to loan him ten dollars — which Elvis gladly did. That's how broke Johnny was.

All through this difficult period, Johnny used fishing as his number one escape from the drudgery and disappointments of life. I couldn't begin to count the afternoons when he and I slipped away from the radio station to spend a few hours at one of the nearby lakes. Many times, it was just Johnny and me, but Tillman and Johnny Cash and a few others sometimes came along, too. Mostly, we went to Cross Lake, which is just outside Shreveport. But when time allowed, we'd make the thirty-mile drive over to Caddo Lake, the only nonmanmade lake in the whole state of Texas and one of the best fishing lakes anywhere.

I'll never forget the day Johnny walked into my office and laid a brand new fishing rod and an expensive reel on my desk.

"This is for you, Chief," he said. "Just so you won't have any excuses the next time I catch more fish than you do."

The rod and reel I'd been using were pretty bad, I admit, and the sight of that new rig really made my eyes light up. But I also knew what a tough time Johnny was having financially. This equipment he was giving me must've cost close to a hundred bucks. I was touched, but I felt guilty about accepting it.

"You shouldn't be spending your money on something like this for me," I said.

"Aw, don't worry about it, Chief," Johnny said. "It didn't cost me any *real* money. I just put it on my charge account."

Those first Columbia releases marked the beginning of Johnny's rise to stardom. He recorded four songs in all in his first session with Columbia in January 1956, but the two that propelled him toward greatness were "I'm a One-Woman Man" and "Honky Tonk Man." Tillman made Johnny keep working on the songs over and over until he was satisfied enough to say, "Boy, that's a smash!" They kept recutting the songs until almost midnight.

Tillman and guitarist Tommy Tomlinson also helped Johnny perfect his new style and sound on the stage. In addition to being his manager, Tillman played bass for Johnny, and he had a way of loosening the bottom string to make it sound a little like a snare drum. Tommy, meanwhile, would cover both melody and rhythm on the lead guitar. Like Elvis with Scotty Moore and Bill Black, they could get a lot of sound out of just three pieces.

By May 1956, "Honky Tonk Man" put Johnny on the charts for the first time in his career. Almost immediately, the demand for personal appearances skyrocketed. A. V. Bamford, the same booking agent who handled Hank Williams's last shows, got Johnny some very lucrative tours. All of a sudden, Johnny was getting up to 500 dollars for a Saturday night engagement when he wasn't on the *Hayride*.

His struggles weren't over, though. There were still some rough times ahead—a repossessed Cadillac, troubles with the IRS, and days spent playing pinball machines for pocket money. But in 1958, he scored with another major hit, "All Grown Up." It spent two months on the charts, moving as high as number eight, and the flip side, "Counterfeit Love," also got wide airplay.

That was the same year that I ended my ten-year relationship with the *Hayride*. When I left, Johnny Horton was the top star and mainstay of its cast. His good friend Johnny Cash had left for Nashville and guest appearances on the *Opry*, but Horton stayed on until the *Hayride* ceased to exist as a live every-Saturday-night show toward the end of 1958.

By then, Johnny was ready for bigger things anyway. In November 1958, he recorded the first of his so-called saga songs, "When It's Springtime in Alaska." Although it held the number-one position only briefly, it stayed on the charts for about six months and was by far his biggest hit yet. It also broke over into the pop field, but its success was only a drop in the bucket compared to what was coming next.

"The Battle of New Orleans" was one of those watershed songs that only comes along once in a blue moon. It became the best-selling record of 1959 and spent ten weeks on top of both the country and pop music charts. It had the kind of beat and lyrics that stuck in people's minds. It seemed like everybody from coast to coast was singing or humming or whistling it. Columbia reported sales of about 2.5 million copies of it. Along the way, the tune—based on singer-songwriter Jimmy Driftwood's revision of an old ballad called "The Eighth of January"—inspired a host of imitators, but none of them came close to matching its appeal.

Johnny had finally found his niche, and he made the most of it. His personal appearance fee jumped to 2,000 dollars a show, plus a share of the gate. He appeared on the Ed Sullivan and Dick Clark television shows and collected 10,000 dollars for one booking in Indianapolis. He bought a beautiful new home in an exclusive area of Shreveport called Shreve Island.

He followed up "The Battle of New Orleans" with another major hit, "Johnny Reb." Then came "Sink the Bismarck," which climbed to number six on the charts despite its historical inaccuracies. It was followed by "Johnny Freedom," which reached the pop charts but not the country charts.

Many people thought "Sink the Bismarck" was the theme song for the movie of the same name. It actually wasn't, but it was tied into promotions for the film, which undoubtedly boosted record sales. Even more important, it opened some very big doors in Hollywood for Johnny. A few months later, 20th-Century Fox invited him to compose and sing the title theme for the John Wayne epic, "North to Alaska."

In less than two years' time, Johnny Horton had established himself as one of the five or six biggest names in American music. Next to "The Battle of New Orleans," "North to Alaska" was destined to be his biggest hit ever.

Tragically, it was also his last.

Over the years, Johnny took a lot of kidding about his interest in spiritualism and psychic phenomena. Personally, it always struck me as odd that someone who seemed so down to earth in so many ways could be so fascinated with seances, reincarnation, premonitions, meditation, hypnosis, and other spooky stuff. But he unquestionably was, and his interest deepened after he got to be friends with Johnny Cash and Merle Kilgore. They both shared Horton's fascination with the supernatural, and the two Johnnys did a lot of experimenting with hypnosis and ESP.

I distinctly remember the time Cash and Horton decided to hypnotize David Houston, who was an up-and-coming young *Hayride* artist at the time. They went through this long, involved ritual that was supposed to put David into a deep trance. Then they started asking him questions and trying to get him to go back and relive his childhood.

This went on for a half-hour or more before David finally got tired of playing possum. When he sat up all of a sudden and yelled, "Fooled you!" Horton and Cash both practically jumped out of their skins. David got a big laugh out of it. He said later he'd been wide awake the whole time.

Tillman Franks recalled a hypnotic experiment with more serious implications, though: "Horton hypnotized Cash and took him back to when he was six years old in a classroom at school," Tillman said. "Cash would tell what color the teacher's dress was and sing the first songs he ever wrote. But when Horton tried to take him into the future, Cash started screaming about a dark, scary room. 'Don't make me go in there,' he kept hollering."

Maybe because he was married to Hank Williams's widow, Horton seemed especially obsessed with the idea of communicating with Hank's ghost. He talked about going to seances somewhere in Mississippi to try to contact Hank. As one disbeliever joked: "Every time the window would rattle, Johnny'd think it was Hank trying to get in touch."

Even today, the strange parallels between the lives and deaths of Johnny and Hank strike me as eerie and unexplainable. They go far beyond merely being married to the same woman. They also shared many physical characteristics and personal traits. Both were prematurely balding, and both were highly sensitive about it. Neither was worth a hoot at managing money. And both were tormented by visions of their own death.

During the last three or four years of his life, Johnny became more and more convinced that he was going to die young. The conviction may have been intensified by the death of his father in August 1959. Within a year after that, Johnny was openly warning close friends and members of his family that his days were numbered. He asked his sister Marie to "pray for Billie and the girls" (his daughters, Melody and Yanina) and told her he knew he was going to die a violent death.

In late October 1960, Johnny paid a visit to Merle Kilgore's house to deliver a similar message of doom.

"He said the spirits had told him he was going to die within a week and he wanted to see all his old friends," Merle said. "He said, 'I want you to have this old guitar. Don't ever sell it.' I promised him I wouldn't, but I told him he wasn't going to die. He was adamant. He said a drunk man would kill him, and he thought it would be in a bar at one of the places he was fixing to play in Texas."

Johnny reportedly stopped by Rusk, Texas, on Wednesday, November 2, to visit with his mother, who was also having premonitions about his death. She told relatives that they looked through the family photo albums and talked about earlier days. Then he told her he was going to the "highest plane" where he would sit at Jesus' right hand.

He warned Billie Jean, too, but she didn't want to hear any of it. "We were laying in bed and he asked me what I'd do after he was gone," she said. "I said, well, I can't hardly go on the road and sing 'North to Alaska.' Then he raised up in bed and said, 'Bill, I'm fixing to die. It's close. I've got to prepare and so have you.'"

I was living in Dallas at the time, working as emcee of the *Big D Jamboree*. I hadn't seen Johnny very often for the past couple of years, but we talked by phone fairly often and once in a while we'd manage to get together and do a little fishing. I never remember him mentioning any of these premonitions to me, but that's not really surprising. For the most part, Johnny seldom talked about his spiritual beliefs except to people he knew shared those beliefs. When he and I talked, it was usually about bass lures or fishing boats or duck hunting.

According to Billie Jean, Johnny phoned Johnny Cash on his last morning at home—or at least tried to. He wasn't able to get through to his friend, and Billie Jean was later quoted as saying Cash was stoned at the time and refused to take the call.

Early that afternoon, November 4, 1960, she remembers Johnny kissing her on exactly the same spot where Hank Williams had kissed her when they parted for the last time. Johnny hugged his older daughter, Yanina, tightly as he started out the door. Then he climbed into his Cadillac and drove off to keep a show date, just as Hank had done nearly eight years earlier. Johnny's destination was the Skyline Club in Austin, Texas — the same club where Hank had given his last performance.

A little more than twelve hours later, Johnny Horton was dead.

Johnny was driving when the wreck occurred. It was about 2 A.M. on Saturday, November 5, and the Cadillac was crossing a bridge just north of the small town of Milano, Texas. Tillman was dozing in the front seat of the passenger side of the car, and Tommy Tomlinson was slumped in the rear seat about half awake.

Tommy usually drove the Cadillac, but Johnny had wanted to drive himself this time, even after doing two shows. They stopped for coffee just outside of Austin, then headed northeast on U.S. 79 for the 220-mile trip back to Shreveport. They took the most direct route, and Tommy remembers Johnny being in a hurry. He was eager to get to one of his favorite fishing and hunting spots, a huge swamp near Spanish Lake in southern Louisiana that he'd nick-named the "Alligator Hole." Johnny was planning to spend most of the next week there hunting ducks. His fishing buddy Claude King was already at the lake waiting for him.

"Johnny was driving too fast," Tommy recalled after the accident. "All he had on his mind was getting to the lake. The guy who hit us was drunk and weaving all over the road. He hit the bridge once on each side before he hit us."

Tillman remembered waking up a split-second before the crash. "Johnny was fighting the steering wheel," he said, "and then I saw that pickup truck coming in on us. When we hit I felt like I was floating on a cloud. When I came to, I was lying against Johnny, and I asked Tommy what happened. He was moaning in the back seat and he said, 'Tillman, we been in a bad wreck and Johnny's in a real bad way.' Then I went out again."

Tillman, who'd just gotten out of the hospital after a hernia operation, suffered head and chest injuries. Tommy's leg was so badly smashed that medical efforts to save it failed and it had to be amputated several months later. An ambulance attendant thought Johnny was still breathing when he was pulled from the wreckage, but there was no way he could've survived his massive head injuries. He was pronounced dead on arrival at a hospital in Cameron, Texas.

Ironically, nobody who knew Johnny well would've ever expected him to die in a head-on collision because he was so adept at defensive driving. "Johnny had trained himself to take to the ditch," Tillman said. "He always said, 'Ain't nobody gonna hit me head-on.' He'd probably spent hundreds of hours preparing himself for something like that, and he'd actually hit the ditch a time or two. But this time, he was on that overpass and there was no place to go."

The driver of the pickup truck was identified as a nineteen-year-old kid from Brady, Texas. His only injury was a cracked rib.

"The last day he lived I think he was the happiest I have ever seen him," Tillman wrote about Johnny a few weeks after his death. "He had practiced on his duck caller practically all the way to Austin. As he didn't much like to play dances, he stayed back in his dressing room most of the evening except when he was on stage. Not that he didn't like mixing with people and seeing his friends, but he just didn't like to be around a place where they sold whiskey and beer."

Some of his friends wondered aloud why Johnny had been playing the Skyline Club in the first place. As Tillman said, he'd never liked the honky-tonk atmosphere and the drunkenness that went along with it. His 800-dollar fee for that Friday night gig would've seemed like big money to Johnny a few years earlier. But it was strictly small potatoes for a national star who'd just released a smash-hit record and signed a contract to star in a 20th-Century Fox movie.

There was nothing hypocritical about Johnny's attitude toward beer joints and nightclubs. He'd never been a drinker or a drug user or a womanizer. He'd even quit smoking cigarettes several months before his death. In that one respect, at least, he was a whole lot different from Hank Williams.

But when Billie Jean's father broke the news to her about Johnny—just as he had broken the news about Hank—that difference was lost among the similarities of the two biggest tragedies of her life.

"I'm only twenty-eight years old," she said after the funeral, "and now I've buried two legends."

But unlike Hank Williams, who concluded near the end of his life that "there ain't no light," Johnny met his fate armed with a firm belief in the Almighty and the hereafter. When Billie Jean went to the little meditation room Johnny had had built behind their house, she found a Bible lying open to the Ten Commandments. The passage containing the laws handed down by God to Moses was circled, and a note in the margin in Johnny's handwriting said simply: "Billie, teach the children this."

Maybe his faith was one reason that Johnny never seemed to get depressed or down in the dumps the way Hank did, even with those heavy premonitions he was carrying around. As Claude King put it, "Even when things were going bad for him, he'd just laugh it off. He'd say, 'Nothing's worth worrying over, Ace. It'll just give you wrinkles.'"

Johnny's services were held on Tuesday afternoon, November 8, 1960. Billy Franks, Tillman's brother, preached the funeral sermon. Tillman was also there, but he was in a wheelchair and hardly able to sit up. The Plainsmen sang and Johnny Cash, who'd flown in by chartered plane from Nashville, read the twentieth chapter of the Gospel of John, the story of the resurrection. Shreveport Mayor Clyde Fant and Louisiana Governor Jimmie Davis were both among the mourners. So were Merle Kilgore, Columbia Records executive Don Law, and many of Johnny's other friends from his *Hayride* days.

I didn't go. After witnessing the circus that Hank Williams's funeral had turned into, I couldn't bring myself to go. Instead, I chose another way to say good-bye to my old friend.

I drove to Shreveport from Dallas and went to a sporting goods store, where I bought a Shakespeare reel and one of the best casting rods they had in stock. Then I took them out to Caddo Lake, to a quiet spot among the cypress trees where Johnny and I had fished dozens of times.

I don't know how long I just sat there in the boat staring into the dark water and thinking about that unexpected gift of fishing gear Johnny had given me years before. Finally, I unwrapped the new rod and reel I'd just bought. I admired them for a minute, then slipped them into the lake and watched them slowly disappear into the depths.

I closed my eyes, wondering if there were fish in heaven. For Johnny Horton's sake I hoped so. Sitting on a cloud and strumming a harp and singing to the angels might be reward enough for most guys in the music business, but I knew what Johnny's reaction would be.

"I'd rather be fishin'," he'd say.

"So long, Johnny," I said. "Catch a big one for me." I started the motor and turned the nose of the boat back toward shore.

What I'd done probably would've struck a lot of people as a silly, pointless gesture. But I was pretty sure the "Singing Fisherman" would understand.

{ 11 }

Cashing in
With the
"Man in Black"

Out of all the thousands of youngsters who look for a start in show business each year, no more than a tiny handful are destined to achieve sudden stardom. Even fewer have the talent, luck, and perseverance to hang onto that stardom once they get there. Only one in a million manages to do both.

But that's exactly what my friend Johnny Cash is—one in a million. Nobody ever made a faster rise from total obscurity to national fame. And nobody I've ever known has stayed at the top longer. Today, after more than forty years as a superstar, Johnny's not only an entertainment legend but also remains one of the world's most popular artists.

Although Johnny had shown some interest in writing songs when he was just a schoolboy in Arkansas, he had absolutely no track record as a performer when he was discharged from the air force in July 1954 at the age of twenty-two. Nobody who understood the odds of succeeding as a professional singer would've given him a ghost of chance to get a record contract, much less break into the big time. In fact, if Johnny had been a better salesman, he might never have tried for a career playing and singing.

And yet, less than eighteen months later, he was a coast-to-coast sensation. Johnny gave the *Louisiana Hayride* a major share of the credit for his remarkable rise, but his exceptional talent, original style, and deep feeling were the ingredients that made him great and kept him that way.

A month after leaving the service as a staff sergeant, Johnny married a girl named Vivian Liberto. They moved into a rented house on Tutwiler Avenue in Memphis, and, with his brother Roy's help, Johnny found a job selling appliances and home improvements door-to-door. Within a short time, a baby was on the way — the first of four daughters to be born to this marriage — and Johnny knew his first responsibility was supporting his family.

It didn't take long, though, for him to realize he was in the wrong line of work. "I was the world's worst salesman," he said. "I spent more time in my car listening to the radio than I did knocking on [customers'] doors."

After one particularly frustrating day of rejections, Johnny recalled making his last call of the afternoon and greeting the lady of the house by saying, "Good afternoon, ma'am. I don't guess you want to buy anything, either, do you?"

At night, he'd lie awake listening to the Top 40 shows and thinking about some songs he'd written while he was stationed in Germany. That was where he'd bought his first guitar and amused himself by picking out the tunes he'd written, including one called "Folsom Prison Blues." Now that he was back home, he sang the songs for his friends and family, hesitantly at first but then with more confidence.

He was especially interested in knowing what his brother Roy thought about his songs and his singing. Roy had tried to be a musician himself before he gave up and went to work for a Chevrolet dealer. The encouragement Johnny got from Roy and others inspired him to apply for a job on a small radio station in Corinth, Mississippi. He knew he wasn't ready to sing professionally, so he applied to be an announcer.

When he admitted he didn't have any experience, he was turned down cold. But the station manager also gave him a few words of friendly advice. "You're never going to get a radio job on guts alone," he said. "You need some training."

Johnny took the advice. He enrolled in Keegan's School of

Broadcasting in Memphis, taking courses designed to train him as a staff announcer disc jockey, and news broadcaster. He could only go part-time, though, because he still had to earn a living. Meanwhile, Roy introduced him to a couple of mechanic friends, Marshall Grant, a novice bass player, and Luther Perkins, who played electric guitar. The three of them started getting together almost every night to make music, mostly gospel songs. Luther was the son of a Baptist preacher while Johnny's own father had been a deacon in the church, and Johnny himself had strong religious beliefs.

"We got to be friends," Johnny said, "and we were always playing and singing at Roy's house or mine. Friends and neighbors started dropping in to listen, and we'd play till after midnight just for the love of it."

After a few months of this, one of Johnny's neighbors invited him and his friends to play at a church in North Memphis. It was his very first public performance, and when Johnny's singing drew substantial applause and a hearty round of "amens" from the congregation, he was excited by the response. He wrote later that he felt "a door had opened" for him somewhere. He'd already seen what happened to Elvis Presley as the result of a single record on the Memphis-based Sun label, and Johnny decided that "door" he was looking for just might be the one to Sam Phillips's office.

So on the strength of that lone unpaid performance in a church, Johnny called Phillips on the phone and told him about a religious song called "Belshazzar" that he'd written. He asked Sam for an audition, but Sam said no thanks. Sun wasn't interested in recording gospel music by an unknown singer. There just wasn't any market for stuff like that, especially in the midst of Elvis's rockabilly revolution. Phillips told Johnny "good luck" and hung up.

Johnny wasn't very good at taking "no" for an answer, though — when he wasn't trying to sell secondhand refrigerators or televisions, that is. An early life marked by hardship, poverty, and the tragic death of his older brother, Jack, had given Johnny an inner toughness that most people don't have.

A few days after that first phone call, he went to Phillips's office in person to try to tell him that gospel music wasn't the only thing he could sing. Johnny wanted to tell Sam about "Folsom Prison Blues," but he couldn't get in, so he went back to the phone and called again. Once more, Phillips refused to give him an audition. A week later, Johnny called again with the same result. Johnny started dropping by regularly on his way from his sales job to his radio announcing class, but he was always told that Phillips wasn't in.

Finally, though, he managed to get Sam on the phone one more time.

"You don't give up easy, do you, John?" Phillips asked.

"No sir, I don't," Johnny said.

"Well, come on down and let's hear what you've got," Phillips said.

As it turned out, Sam wasn't all that taken with "Folsom Prison Blues" when he heard it. One reason he wasn't is because at the time Johnny was trying to sing it in a high-pitched voice instead of his natural baritone. But Sam did like a couple of the other non-gospel tunes Johnny had written — a train song called "Hey Porter" and a "weeper" that was appropriately titled "Cry, Cry, Cry." By the time Johnny left that afternoon, he had a contract with Sun Records.

When Sun released "Hey Porter" and "Cry, Cry, Cry" on June 21, 1955, Johnny didn't have more than four or five live performances under his belt. As a matter of fact, until that day he didn't even officially have the name by which he'd later become known around the world. Johnny had been named simply "J. R." at birth, and neither of the initials had stood for anything. Names like that were a widespread custom in the South during the thirties. As a teenager, he started calling himself "John," but he'd never used "Johnny" until Sam Phillips decided "Johnny Cash" had a nice ring to it and put it on the label of his first record.

"Who's this guy Johnny Cash?" people said. "I never heard of him before."

It was no wonder they hadn't heard of him. Nobody else had ever heard of Johnny Cash, either—mainly because he hadn't existed until that record was released. Except for a handful of personal appearances in the immediate Memphis area, that craggy face with the deep-set eyes and scarred right cheek was utterly unknown.

Johnny was awed when Sam landed him a guest appearance in Covington, Tennessee, on the same program with Sonny James. He was even more awestruck when he made a guest appearance with Elvis at Overton Park in Memphis. He also met Carl Perkins, another rising star of Sun Records, and they formed a long-term friendship.

The first time I heard the name Johnny Cash was that fall just after "Hey Porter" and "Cry, Cry, Cry" hit number one on the Memphis-area charts, pushing past Elvis's "Baby, Let's Play House" in the process. Johnny's record wasn't doing much anywhere else in the country, but I figured anybody who could outsell Elvis in his hometown was worth checking out. So when Sam Phillips sent me a copy of it in November 1955, I played it right away. I liked the songs and the singer instantly. They were totally different from Elvis and the music he was doing, but they had their own distinctive kind of sound—something I was always looking for.

Sam called a couple of days later and asked me if we could use Sun's newest artist on the *Louisiana Hayride*.

"Sure, Sam," I said. "The way Elvis has gone over on our show, how could I say no? We've got a guest slot open in a couple of weeks. I'll put him on then."

When Johnny and his Tennessee Two made their debut on the *Hayride* on December 10, 1955, he was an instant hit with our audience. I have to admit he was pretty rough around the edges—rougher even than Elvis was when he'd debuted just over a year earlier. But the raw talent was there. So were the sincerity and style that would soon make Johnny famous, and the crowd reacted warmly. After Johnny sang the two songs on his record, he encored with "Folsom Prison Blues," which he'd cut for Sun the previous summer but which hadn't been released yet. It was the first time the song had ever been heard on national radio.

Johnny himself described that first night on the *Hayride* as "in-toxicating." It looked to me like the fans in the Municipal Auditorium shared that feeling. As soon as he came off stage, I asked him to join our cast as a regular, and he eagerly agreed.

In the early going, fans liked Johnny's music for several reasons that seemed to defy musical logic. One reason was a distinctive sound from Marshall Grant's bass that was more of an accident than anything else. Johnny described it as a "boom-chicka-boom" sound, and Marshall freely admitted later on that it was mainly the result of his inexperience with the instrument. "I didn't work for that sound," he said. "It just happened that way."

Audiences also liked the generally lean, no-frills quality of the backup music. This, too, was largely caused by inexperience and lack of confidence. Luther Perkins was a mediocre guitarist, and he knew it. He never did much more than keep time because he was always afraid of messing up, and he dreaded playing solo parts. But this worked to Johnny's advantage because it allowed his voice to come through with a lot of strength and force, and those vocal qualities became his principal trademark.

In short, he was living proof that raw talent can beat out even the most intensely cultivated skills if it's channeled in the right way. What Johnny brought to country music — and later to pop — was an originality that hadn't been seen since Hank Williams. And as he gained confidence and became more relaxed in front of a crowd, his voice grew steadily stronger and more assertive.

Along with his exposure on the *Hayride* came a sudden flood of show dates in the Ark-La-Tex area, where Johnny made his first decent fees for personal appearances. In Texarkana, Johnny and Carl Perkins played in support of George Jones, who was in the spotlight with his first big hit, "Why Baby Why?" It was 350 miles from their home base in Memphis and the furthest either one of them had ever traveled to fill a show date.

From there, they moved on to Tyler, Texas, where the promoter had promised them 100 dollars apiece. It must have sounded like 100,000 dollars to Johnny. Up until then, his biggest payday had been in Parsons, Arkansas, where they divided up the dollar-per-person admissions deposited in a cigar box and ended up with 18 dollars each.

In January 1956, Johnny signed a contract that officially made him an every-Saturday-night regular on the *Hayride*. He had a quiet, low-key, unassuming way about him that quickly established him as a favorite with his fellow artists as well as with the audience. Since he and Elvis were both from Memphis, they and their sidemen formed a sort of car pool and traveled back and forth together many weekends in one or the other of their old cars.

Even with an occasional good paycheck like the one at Tyler, I know Johnny had a helluva hard time financially during those early months. With a wife and baby at home and another baby on the way, he had no choice but to hang onto his sales job for the time being. After pounding the sidewalks and knocking on doors Monday through Friday, he'd make the long haul to Shreveport every Saturday, often getting there with very little time to spare before he had to get behind a microphone and start singing.

I remember one Saturday in particular when he had Elvis stop off in Minden, Louisiana, long enough for Johnny to run into a store and buy a shirt. He hadn't had anything clean to wear when he'd left home that day, and he didn't want to go onstage in a dirty shirt. To me, the most surprising thing about the incident was that Johnny actually had enough money to buy a new shirt in the first place. More often than not, he didn't.

Johnny got along well with everybody, but he developed an especially strong friendship with Johnny Horton. Although they didn't agree on everything, they shared a deep interest in spiritual matters, and they spent hundreds of hours discussing their theories about God, religion, psychic phenomena, and life after death. Both of them were also "straight-arrow" types who didn't like playing honky-tonks, didn't get drunk or stoned and didn't run around on their wives—not even on the road.

In fact, it was Johnny Cash's honorable, moralistic approach to his career, his marriage and life in general—his insistence on walking the line that so many other artists ignored—that became the basis for the hit song that propelled him to the top levels of show business.

Some years later, Johnny recalled how the song and its title—"I Walk the Line"—came into being. After finishing up a show in Texas one night, he was struggling with an idea for a new song and trying to think of a title when he and Carl Perkins got to talking about their wives and the tempting opportunities to be unfaithful that they faced almost daily.

"I had a brand new baby back in Memphis, and I said, 'Not me, buddy. I walk the line,' " Johnny remembered. "Carl said, 'There's your song title right there.' I wrote the whole thing that night in fifteen or twenty minutes."

It was a stroke of pure genius, and it became the biggest-selling single of Johnny's career.

During the weeks and months after Elvis left the show, it was Johnny's rising popularity more than anything else that kept national attention focused on the *Hayride*. He recorded "I Walk the Line" in early April 1956, and when it was released a month later, it shot up the charts like a rocket. Before long, it not only reached the number-two slot on the country charts but was also number nineteen on the pop charts, and for months it held its position against all competition. At the end of 1956, it was still number three on the country charts.

For that whole year, Johnny ranked third among the best-selling country artists in America, right behind Marty Robbins and Ray

Price. Not bad for a guy who'd been known only as J. R. Cash, appliance salesman, just a year and a half earlier. He'd accomplished in eighteen months what many other country artists hadn't been able to achieve in decades of playing cheap nightclubs, American Legion dances, and crossroads schoolhouses.

With the stunning success of "I Walk the Line," I could tell that Johnny was starting to outgrow Shreveport. The more acclaim he earned, the more inevitable it became that he'd be leaving soon, like Elvis and Hank and so many others before him. If we'd started years earlier to install the key publishing, recording, and booking services that were essential to major stars, it might have been a different story. But now it was too late.

Johnny started receiving invitations to the *Grand Ole Opry* as early as the summer of 1956. But being the man of honor that he was, he stayed on to fulfill the terms of his agreement with the *Hayride.* Ironically, he had gotten so big so fast—and so firmly established himself as a crossover artist—that by now he really didn't have to rely on the *Opry* to ensure his success.

I'd never claim that the *Hayride* alone transformed Johnny from a nobody into one of the most celebrated figures in the entertainment industry. Johnny displayed, and continues to display, rare talent and originality. The songs he wrote and recorded would surely have been hits, even if he'd never sung them on the Municipal Auditorium stage. But his rise also might not have been nearly as swift and spectacular without the nationwide exposure he and his Tennessee Two got from the *Hayride.*

I think Johnny realizes this as well as I do. As a perceptive, intelligent person, he knew he'd defied all the odds and logic of the music business, and he knew the *Hayride* was one of the major factors in his success. When he left the show, he told the whole entertainment world about his gratitude in a full-page ad in *Billboard.*

"I want to thank the *Louisiana Hayride* and Horace Logan for everything they've done to further my career," the signed ad said.

It was a dramatic gesture, but one that was also straightforward and heartfelt—two characteristics that are basic Johnny Cash. Nothing that ever happened to me in the music business touched me more deeply.

Even after Johnny left the *Hayride,* he declined to become an *Opry* regular. Because he was in such wide demand from TV shows like *American Bandstand, Ed Sullivan, Jackie Gleason, Lawrence Welk,* and Red Foley's *Ozark Jubilee,* and handling a heavy personal appearance schedule to boot, Johnny did only occasional guest appearances on the *Opry* for the next few years.

I think it's safe to say that the *Opry* needed him a whole lot more at this point than he needed the *Opry.* By mid-1958, when he quit Sun Records and recorded "Don't Take Your Guns to Town" as his first release for Columbia, Johnny was quickly becoming larger than life—a legend in his own time. His fans weren't nearly as loud and demonstrative as Elvis's, but there were just about as many of them, and their loyalty and devotion to the singer who would become the "Man in Black" was absolutely boundless.

Nothing could stop Johnny Cash now except Johnny Cash himself. Unfortunately, that's exactly what almost happened.

I can't remember a single incident during his time on the *Hayride* that would've given any indication of the devastating drug and alcohol problems that loomed ahead for Johnny. As I've said before, he was as straight and moral and clean-living as any guy I'd ever worked with. But as it happened with so many others before him, the pressures and demands of sudden fame were destined to take a heavy toll. Stardom almost killed Johnny Cash, the same way it had killed Hank Williams.

The lightning-bolt suddenness of his success undoubtedly had a lot to do with what started happening to Johnny in the late 1950s. By his own account, his first experience with "bennies" or "uppers" came while he was on a tour in Florida with Ferlin Husky, Faron Young, and several other artists. On a late-night drive from Miami to Jacksonville, Johnny was getting groggy, and someone offered him "a little white pill with a cross on it." Within minutes, he said, he was "refreshed, wide awake, and talkative." He made it through the whole night without sleep, took another pill before the show in Jacksonville and felt great.

That was the beginning — and almost the beginning of the end for Johnny. Constant doses of amphetamines got rid of the butterflies that had always fluttered in his stomach before he went on stage. He thought the pills gave him poise and confidence as well as energy and stamina. He thought they stimulated and sharpened his mind.

What they were actually doing, of course, was burning him up from the inside out. Within a year or two, he was totally addicted and couldn't perform without them. Amphetamines were remarkably easy to get in those days. Doctors called them "diet pills," and they'd prescribe them for almost anybody. Johnny literally started living on them. He went for days without sleeping or eating. Whenever he did "come down" from the pills, he was exhausted, agitated, depressed, and in a mental fog. To relieve these symptoms, he started dosing himself with barbituates. He also drank vodka, beer, and wine to try to relax.

By late 1958, Johnny and I had both left the *Hayride,* and by coincidence both of us had moved to California, where we crossed paths again and discovered that we were practically neighbors. Johnny had moved his wife and daughters into a house in Woodland Hills, a suburb of Los Angeles, and my family and I were living in Canoga Park, another suburb that was no more than three or four miles away.

For a few months, I saw Johnny fairly often, and I was shocked at what was happening to him. He'd lost quite a bit of weight and his eyes were sunken with dark circles under them. He was nervous and twitchy and couldn't seem to keep still. There were times when he didn't act like the person I'd known in Shreveport. Deep down, I knew he was still the same decent, goodhearted guy he'd been when I first met him, but something was bad wrong. Some kind of demon had Johnny by the throat. There was a wild, out-of-control look about him. Vivian and the little girls seemed almost scared of him sometimes.

"Are you okay, John?" I asked him at one point. "I mean, do you feel all right?"

"Sure, I feel great," he assured me. "I'm on top of the world. What makes you ask?"

"I don't know. You just look a little peaked, that's all."

"I'm fine," he said. "I see doctors all the time. They say I'm in great shape."

"Well, that's good," I said. "I'm glad to hear it."

I didn't believe a word that either one of us was saying, of course. I'd seen the same symptoms too many times before. When I looked at Johnny, I could tell he was tearing himself apart. Seeing him abusing himself and wasting all his God-given talent was like watching Hank Williams floundering toward an early grave all over again.

I wanted to yell at him or shake him—or something. But at the same time, I knew there was nothing I could do. I was as powerless to help Johnny as I'd been to help Hank. Johnny was twenty-seven years old at the time, just two years younger than Hank had been when he died. Was I witnessing another tragedy in the making? Was the same insidious thing about to happen all over again? I knew how easily it could. The combination of drugs and booze had a way of making you old long before your time.

There was still a chance for Johnny to turn himself around, but it was all up to him. He was the only one who could stop this free fall he was in. To be brutally honest, I figured the way he was going now he'd be lucky to make it another two years.

The thought made me sick to my stomach.

After I left California and moved to Texas to manage a small Fort Worth radio station and serve as emcee of the *Big D Jamboree* in Dallas, I saw Johnny hit absolute rock bottom. His marriage to Vivian fell apart and he moved to Nashville, leaving his family behind on the West Coast. Eventually, the combined effects of the amphetamines and barbituates he was taking left him with chronic laryngitis and almost totally unable to perform. Sometimes he missed dates altogether, but more often his voice was reduced to a hoarse whisper and he simply couldn't sing.

The sudden death of his friend Johnny Horton in November 1960 plunged him into an even deeper state of depression. Publicly, he's never had much to say about Horton's death, and even today, I don't think he'd really relish talking about it. But I know how close the two of them were, and I know from my own reaction how much that tragedy must have hurt. Johnny's pain was also intensified, I'm sure, by the guilt and regret he felt for refusing to take Horton's last phone call the day before the fatal accident. Knowing what an intense, introspective person Johnny Cash is, I can imagine how many times he must have grieved because of that.

He also felt a lot of guilt over his kids and the fact that he'd become a stranger to them. Part of it was an inevitable result of being on the road so much, but for several years, even when Johnny was home, he was in no condition to play with his children or take part in their lives.

Johnny's actions grew increasingly bizarre and unpredictable. He was arrested in Nashville at two o'clock one morning for trying to break down the door of a nightclub that had already closed. He was arrested by police in Starkville, Mississippi, while picking flowers in someone's yard in the predawn hours. When the cops took him to jail, he kicked the cell door so hard that he broke his big toe.

One night during a guest appearance on the *Opry*, Johnny had trouble getting the microphone off the stand, and it sent him into a sudden rage. He threw down the stand and dragged it along the edge of the stage, breaking several dozen footlights and sending shattered glass flying into the audience. Later that night, after the *Opry* manager told him he wouldn't be welcome there anymore, he drove off in a semi-stupor, totaled his car, and woke up in a hospital emergency room with his nose and jaw both broken.

I'll say this for Johnny, though. Even in the darkest of those dark days, he always tried to satisfy his audiences. I had him on the *Big D Jamboree* several times during this period, and I saw him in as bad a shape as a man could be and still stand upright. But he never tried to back out of a show because of the way he was feeling or because his voice was shot.

I especially remember one night when he was supposed to be flying into Dallas from West Texas. When the show started, he was still nowhere to be seen, but I wasn't too worried at first. Since he was the headliner and closer for the show, he still had enough time to get himself together and get on stage. Two hours later, there was still no Johnny Cash, and the crowd was getting restless. Actually, they were more than restless. They were downright mad.

It was after 11 P.M. when he finally got there, and I was just holding my breath and praying he'd be able to sing. Otherwise, I'm pretty sure the situation would've gotten just plain ugly. As it turned out, though, I had absolutely nothing to worry about. Johnny came out, apologized profusely in that deep, sincere voice of his, then proceeded to put on one of the best shows I've ever seen him do. He stayed on stage for a full two hours, and when he got through, the crowd gave him a standing ovation.

When he was reasonably straight and sober, there wasn't a more likeable guy in the world than Johnny. He had a great sense of humor, too. This was very obvious early in his career when he was always cracking jokes on stage (usually at Luther Perkins's expense), but many people forgot about it after he adopted a more somber, solemn performance style as the "Man in Black."

In one of his *Hayride* appearances before "Don't Take Your Guns to Town" was released, Johnny was previewing the number on our show when we decided to add a little something extra for the audience's amusement. I came onstage with no less than thirteen guns on my person—in two holsters, all around my waist, strapped to my legs and even under my hat. Every time Johnny would sing the line, "Don't take your guns to town," he'd reach over and take a gun out of one of the holsters and lay it on the piano, but I'd immediately replace it with one of the others I was carrying. By the time he got to the last verse, all the guns were piled on top of the piano. It was all Johnny could do to keep a straight face, and the audience was hysterical.

"Doggone it, Logan, that's supposed to be a serious song," he said afterward.

By the mid-1960s, though, Johnny's behavior had become so erratic that even his best friends and closest relatives were starting to give up on him. His life had come to resemble a repetitious horror movie, without much of a plot and certainly with no happy ending.

He bought a huge lakeside house in the Tennessee hills and asked Carl Perkins and another friend to come and stay with him while he tried to straighten up. But after he treated them to the wildest Jeep ride of their lives—running through fences, grazing trees, and chasing cattle—they decided to leave while they were still able. He got into a fistfight with his brother Tommy at the Nashville airport. He was ordered off a commercial flight in Memphis after he passed out cold and fell in the aisle of the plane. He was busted by narcotics agents in El Paso and thrown in jail.

Johnny was half-frozen and probably as close to death as a man could get when June Carter and Dr. Nat Winston, a psychiatrist, pulled him from an icy lake where he'd fallen in a drugged daze. This was in October 1967, and it was the low point of his life. Johnny had fallen as far as he possibly could and still be alive. But luckily there was someone there to catch him when he hit bottom.

The doctor told him he didn't have much of a chance to recover, but if he wanted to try he should get ready for the fight of his life. Johnny said he *was* ready, and this time he meant it.

Johnny won that fight, but he never could've done it without June Carter and her parents, E. J. and Maybelle Carter. All the members of the famous Carter Family had been appearing regularly with Johnny for several years, and they all cared a lot about him. They moved into his house and stayed with him day and night while he endured what he called "my forty days in the wilderness."

He was addicted to both amphetamines and barbituates, and

the withdrawal symptoms were pure hell—nightmares, hallucinations, fits of trembling, cold sweats, pains like slivers of glass slicing through every part of his body—but with his friends' support and constant presence, he came through it.

Almost everybody knows the rest of the story, of course. Johnny and June were married on March 1, 1968, and together they built a wonderful new life—a life free of drugs and alcohol and filled with love and goodness and decency. Johnny would be the first to give June all the credit for that new life, but I know how hard he worked for it, too.

It was during his recovery period that I had a meeting with Johnny that I'll never forget. Johnny was and is as much of a gun lover as I am. Nobody I ever knew, except possibly Hank Williams, has a greater affection for rare or antique pistols than Johnny has.

Before the show on this particular night in Dallas, Johnny was practicing his fast draw—and he really *was* fast—when he showed me the beautiful single-action Colt .45 he was using. The interior parts were all polished as smooth as glass, and the mainspring had been altered for easier fanning.

"This is a really fine piece, John. It looks like an Arvo Ojolla gun," I said, referring to one of Hollywood's best-known trick-shot artists and special-effects men.

"You're right," he said. "You must know a lot about guns yourself if you recognize Arvo's work."

He handed the pistol to me, and when I cocked it, it had an action like oiled silk.

"It sure has a sweet feel to it," I said. "How in the world do you get a gun like this?"

I started to hand it back, but Johnny grinned and shook his head. To my amazement, he unbuckled the holster and held it out to me.

"It's yours," he said simply.

I stared at the Colt, then at him. "But John, I couldn't—"

"Sure you can," he said. "I want you to have it. It's good to see somebody else that appreciates workmanship like this." Then he laughed. "Just don't take it to town—and keep it off the piano, too, okay?"

Over the decades since then, I don't think I've ever run into Johnny that he didn't ask me the same question: "Hey, Logan, you still have that gun?"

And I always assure him that I do.

That Colt's easily worth 4,000 dollars or more at today's prices, but Johnny gave it to me as freely as he would've given an autograph. It was an impulsive act of caring and generosity that, for me, has always symbolized the man who made the gesture. It happened more than thirty years ago, and I've treasured the Colt ever since.

But even more than the gun, I cherish the memory of that day. It was when I knew for sure that the real Johnny Cash was alive and well—and that an old and dear friend had miraculously escaped from the threshold of death.

12

Ringing Down
the Curtain

In January 1952, I told Henry Clay I'd made a firm decision to leave KWKH by early the following year, in effect giving the station twelve months' notice. There were two primary reasons for dragging out my departure this way. In the first place, I thought it would give KWKH time to find and hire a fully qualified program director and producer for the *Hayride*. In the second place, I had no idea what I was going to do or where I was going to go, and it would give me time to explore the market for opportunities.

My announcement came as no great surprise to Henry, I'm sure. For seven or eight months, I'd made no secret of the fact that I felt it was time for a change in my life and that I was considering moving on. In fact, I'd talked about it so often that Henry may not have believed me when I gave him my formal notice. Maybe that's why he made no effort to talk me out of it. On the other hand, maybe he was so tired of my bitching by then that he considered it good riddance.

I didn't want to go. Shreveport had been my home from the time I was in grade school, and except for my stint in the army and about a year spent running a gun shop, I'd worked for KWKH ever since I was sixteen years old. I also had no desire to uproot my family and force my three kids to adjust to a new place and new schools. But I have to admit that leaving the *Hayride* itself was the hardest part of all. Dozens of people had contributed directly to the success of the show since its beginning, but I honestly believed—and still believe to this day—that nobody had played a bigger role in that success than I had.

I felt almost like a parent where the *Hayride* was concerned. Walking off and leaving it would be like abandoning one of my own children.

At the same time, though, equally powerful emotions and motivations were pushing me away. For ten years, I'd done everything in my power to persuade the management and ownership of KWKH to help the *Hayride* hold onto the artists it developed by providing them the services they needed to further their careers. I said if the station itself didn't want to set up these services— which it could clearly have operated at a profit—it could at least encourage other business interests to come in and establish them instead.

But John Ewing not only wasn't interested in funding such businesses himself, he was also afraid that if outside entrepreneurs came in and started them, they'd end up taking revenue away from KWKH. Ewing was so intent on keeping competition out of the area that he couldn't see the broader picture.

So in all this time the only response I'd gotten to my pleas was Henry's halfhearted agreement to pay Tom Parker's expenses to come to Shreveport and tell us what would be needed to start an artists' service bureau. Henry had turned white as a sheet when Parker said it would take 12,000 dollars in startup money, and that had been the end of it. But the truth was, an operation of this type could have returned many times that amount within a couple of years.

Every time I thought about what adequate recording, publishing, and booking enterprises could have meant financially to the station—and to the whole Shreveport economy, for that matter— I got mad all over again. If we'd started to build these services in the late forties when the *Hayride* first began, Shreveport might well have become a major music center in its own right. Nashville hadn't been all that far ahead of us in those days. Before World War II,

Atlanta and even Dallas had had recording facilities that matched or exceeded Nashville's.

The *Opry*, of course, was the center of Nashville's music industry. But the mere fact that it was the home of the *Opry* didn't give Nashville the overwhelming advantage that many people believe it did — not in the beginning, anyway. The emergence of Nashville as "Music City" certainly didn't take place overnight.

What happened was, the Nashville music industry fed off the artists drawn there by the *Opry*. Each time the *Opry* lured another rising star away from Shreveport and the *Hayride*, the Nashville interests that served those stars grew stronger and more profitable. By the time this process had been repeated a couple of dozen times over a period of seven or eight years, Nashville had put together enough music-related companies to become the undisputed capital of country music.

Maybe it's unrealistic of me to think we could actually have competed with the Nashville power structure, but I still believe it was possible, especially if we'd started early. It was obvious to me by 1949 when Hank Williams left Shreveport behind that we absolutely had to set up some booking agencies or artists' service bureaus if we expected to keep the same thing from happening over and over again.

On a small scale, Tillman Franks proved that booking country music acts could be a highly profitable business. But Tillman's contacts were mainly in Texas, Louisiana, and Arkansas. At that time he lacked the connections in major cities outside the region that could get an artist all the way to the top, and the only ones he managed to national prominence were Johnny Horton and David Houston, who finally just got so big the promoters couldn't ignore them.

Webb Pierce and I also proved in 1951 that recording and music publishing operations could work in Shreveport. For a period of several months, Webb and I were partners in two companies — Pacemaker Records and Ark-La-Tex Publishing. We made a significant amount of money, and we could have made much more. But then Webb moved to Nashville (where he promptly went into partnership with Jim Denny in a similar enterprise), and we dissolved the companies.

At the time Webb left, I was already under a lot of pressure from KWKH to get out of these outside operations, and I didn't want to jeopardize my job, so I did. I would've been glad to give the station a share in the businesses or even accept a deal to make them wholly owned subsidiaries of KWKH, but nobody in authority was interested. The only thing they cared about was making money in the short-term and stifling anything that could possibly cut into their total domination of the artists who worked for them. And they couldn't have cared less about planning for the future.

For me, the crowning blow came when we lost Elvis. That's ironic in itself because, on the surface, we looked to have less of a chance to hold onto a crossover star as hot as Elvis was than we'd had with any of the other artists who slipped away. But if KWKH had been willing to bankroll Tom Parker as a booking agent at that very critical stage in Elvis's career in early 1955, it might've turned out to be a whole different story.

Although Parker had handled some big-name stars in the past and was still doing bookings for Hank Snow and his supporting artists, the "Colonel" was actually no more than an arrogant, small-potatoes hustler at that time. His "office" was the lobby of WSM radio, where he used a pay phone to conduct his business. Much as I disliked and distrusted him, and as shabbily as I think he treated Elvis, all it would have taken in 1955 to make Shreveport his headquarters was 12,000 dollars in seed money.

Elvis himself most likely would've chosen to live in his hometown of Memphis regardless of what happened, as his later actions pretty well proved. But sometimes I still catch myself speculating about what it could've meant to the Shreveport-area economy if Elvis had decided to build his mansion there instead. Or if Johnny Cash had chosen to build his lakeside retreat on Cross Lake instead of in the Tennessee hills, and so on.

What if Webb Pierce had stayed in his native north Louisiana and elected to let his own company release his records and publish his music? What if Faron Young had been able to stay right there in Shreveport where he grew up and still book all the high-paying, high-profile shows he could ask for? What if the business leaders of Shreveport had gone after representatives of the music industry as aggressively as those in Nashville did?

What if?

God knows, there were plenty of people in Nashville who looked down their noses at "hillbilly musicians," too. Most likely, some of them still do. But there were plenty of others with enough sense to know a good thing when they saw one. Their foresight and willingness to take a risk has syphoned untold billions of dollars into Nashville over the past fifty years. At least part of those billions could have gone to Shreveport.

It's all water under the bridge now, of course. It was probably water under the bridge back in 1955, too. But I still can't help but wonder about it occasionally.

As 1957 wore on, I gave more and more thought to moving to California. Next to the South and Southwest, country music had its biggest following on the West Coast, and there were plenty of opportunities out there for someone with my experience and background in radio.

Unquestionably, I would've had an easier time getting a job in Dallas or Houston or Memphis or even Nashville — all places where I was known and had solid contacts — than in California. And relocating to another southern city wouldn't have been nearly as big a move, either geographically or culturally, as going all the way to the Pacific. But I kept hearing an insistent little voice inside my head.

"As long as you're pulling up stakes, anyway, you might as well go all the way," it kept telling me. "You need to go someplace where you can really make a fresh start, and there's no place better to do that than California."

In addition to the small voice, two main factors finally made up my mind to heed it. One was a series of two-to-three-week trips I made to California in mid-1957 to appear in a couple of movies. I'll talk more about the movies themselves in the next chapter, but the important thing about those trips, as far as my eventual move was concerned, was that they allowed me to get a feel for the West Coast before I took the big plunge. I really liked it out there. In comparison to the hot, muggy summertime conditions in north Louisiana, the weather in California was almost ideal. There was also an infectious sense of excitement about the place that appealed to me.

The second factor in my decision was Fabor Robison, the owner of the Abbott record label, who spent a lot of time around Shreveport but whose home base was in the Los Angeles area. Fabor and I had been friends for years, and he'd helped launch the careers of many young *Hayride* artists. He told me if I decided to move west, he'd give me a job with his company, either permanently or just until I could find something else.

"I'm going to do it," I told my wife just before Christmas 1957. "It can mean a completely fresh start for us. Maybe it's exactly what we need."

She was far from overjoyed about it, and the kids were naturally pretty apprehensive about traveling all that way into totally unknown territory. But we spent the next few weeks packing our belongings, telling our longtime friends good-bye and winding up our business in Shreveport.

In late January, we set out on the long cross-country jaunt with my wife driving our '55 Mercury and me at the wheel of our old Nash sedan. Several promising regulars from the *Hayride* were planning to join us as soon as we got settled and I was able to line up some work for them. The group included David Houston, Bob

Luman, Fred Carter, Butch White, James Burton, and James Kirkland. All of them were young — several of them still in their teens — and eager for the challenge and opportunity that California represented.

I caught myself wishing they were traveling along with us. I could've used a dose of their youthful enthusiasm to keep my own spirits up. For the moment, though, the five of us Logans were on our own, and it was a pretty lonely feeling. As we headed west on U.S. 80, I knew that a major chapter in my life had ended and another one was about to begin.

I could only guess where the road ahead might lead us, but there was no turning back now.

Despite my determination to focus on the future, my thoughts kept drifting back to the *Hayride* as the miles clicked by on the odometer. When the curtain went up on next Saturday night's show, somebody else would be behind the emcee's microphone. After ten years, it was hard to imagine not having any connection at all with the show anymore, but that was apparently the way KWKH and Henry Clay wanted it.

Right up until my final day on the job, Henry had never once asked me to reconsider. As I prepared to leave the studios for the last time, Henry and I had shaken hands, and he'd wished me good luck, but that was it. If he felt any regret at my leaving, he didn't show it. As far as Henry was concerned, nobody was indispensable, and I was sure he was right.

The show would go on, I told myself. It had suffered much costlier losses than mine and not only survived but continued to prosper. It was the artists that people came to see and tuned in to hear, not the producer or the emcee. With or without Horace Logan, there would always be a *Louisiana Hayride*.

I was wrong, though — dead wrong. I'm not nearly vain enough to think my leaving was the fatal blow that ended the *Hayride*, but the show was destined to live less than ten months after that day. A combination of causes led to its death, and some of them may have been beyond anyone's control.

By the late 1950s, the entertainment industry in America was undergoing vast changes. Television was rapidly replacing radio as the number-one entertainment medium. The nation's musical tastes were changing drastically, too. The basic hillbilly music that had been the *Hayride*'s main stock in trade in the beginning was giving way to rock, "new country," and other popular styles.

And yet it was the *Hayride* itself, more than any other network radio show, that paved the way for these changes and actually set them in motion. It was the *Hayride* that introduced Elvis to America, and nothing was ever the same after that. But the show didn't flounder when Elvis left. Instead, it kept right on creating new stars and showcasing new musical styles. Instead of losing its place as a popular art form, country music has only expanded its share of the market in the years since the *Hayride* folded. Today, you don't need to look any further than the Nashville Network to see how well country music fits into the TV format.

It's not my purpose here to point the finger of blame at anybody for the death of the *Hayride* — most certainly not at Tillman Franks, who took over as producer of the show when I left, or Frank Page, who succeeded me as program director of KWKH. Tillman and Frank did their best to keep the show going and supply it with solid talent.

Along with Henry Clay and Pappy Covington, Tillman even made a belated attempt to set up an artists' service bureau, but the essential contacts in major markets simply weren't there. Besides, Johnny Cash had left the *Hayride* by this time, and David Houston and Bob Luman were in California with me. Except for Johnny Horton and one or two other artists, the *Hayride* didn't have anyone that could be booked successfully on a national scale. If the same effort had been put forth three or four years earlier, the outcome could've been completely different, but as it was, the agency formed by Tillman, Henry, and Pappy never really got off the ground. It was too little too late.

When the artists' service bureau shut down after only a couple of months and rumors started circulating that CBS was thinking of canceling the *Hayride,* I think Henry began to see the handwriting on the wall—or at least convinced himself that he did. In true Ewing style, once a show that had produced a healthy and contin-uous stream of profit for more than a decade started showing signs of needing a little financial pump-priming, KWKH decided to pull the plug instead.

Frank Page has often been quoted as saying that television alone doomed the *Hayride.* With a wide array of Saturday night enter-tainment available on home screens, nobody was interested in coming to the Municipal Auditorium or listening to the show on the radio, according to Frank. But I have to take issue with that kind of reasoning. In the early-to-mid-fifties when the *Hayride* was in its prime, it was widely recognized as superior to the *Big D Jam-boree* in Dallas. Yet the *Big D Jamboree* continued to draw large, profitable crowds on Saturday nights for years after the *Hayride* was allowed to go down the drain (and I'm extremely glad it did, since I ended up being its emcee for a number of those years after my sojourn in California).

It doesn't do much good, of course, to argue these points today. What's done is done, and no amount of discussion can undo it.

When I first arrived on the West Coast, I made a habit of tuning into the *Hayride* just about every week. It was the first time in many years that I hadn't been working behind a microphone on Satur-day evenings, and it was nice just to be able to settle back and lis-ten for a change. KWKH's signal came through loud and clear, and it was like a visit home when I heard those familiar voices coming to me over the air.

Then, just ten months after I left, it all came to a halt. The *Hayride* ceased to be a live, every-Saturday-night show. It struggled along for a while on a monthly basis, then on an occasional basis. Old tapes of the original show continued to be broadcast for years, and in the 1980s, a Shreveport clothing store owner named David Kent bought the *Hayride* name from KWKH. He tried—without long-term success—to revive the idea, using little-known artists in a country supper club setting in Bossier City.

But the original *Hayride* that radio listeners all over America had known and loved ended in November 1958, when it closed a run that spanned more than 550 straight Saturday nights.

For all practical purposes, when the curtain rang down on that final weekly performance, the *Louisiana Hayride* was history. Although I was far away at the time, I mourned its passing along with millions of other country music fans.

One day in the summer of 1959, I happened to be back in Shreveport on business, and I decided to drop by the KWKH studios. It was my one and only return visit to the station after I resigned as program director.

I was visiting with friends and former coworkers when Henry Clay asked me to come down to his office for a few minutes. To be polite, I excused myself from the others and went along.

When we were alone in his office with the door closed, Henry looked me straight in the eye and told me something that I know was very hard for him to say.

"I owe you an apology, Logan," he said. "I didn't treat you right when you were here, and I'm sorry for that. I know now I should've paid more attention to what you kept trying to tell me over the years. The *Hayride* might still be going strong if I had."

I shrugged. "Don't worry about it, Henry. No use crying over spilled milk."

He shook his head. "It took me a long time to realize it, Logan," he said, "but you *were* the *Hayride.*"

It was the nicest thing Henry ever said to me.

{ 13 }

Hillbillies in

Hollywood

California turned out to be more of a false start than the fresh start I'd been hoping for, but that doesn't mean we didn't have some memorable times there. There was no more exciting place in the world in the late 1950s than the Los Angeles area, and all of us got caught up in that excitement to some extent — especially the young guys I was working with.

Before we officially made the move to the West Coast, we'd gotten a fairly generous taste of the free-and-easy California lifestyle during our trips out there in 1957 to take part in the production of two movies.

Neither of the films we worked in was destined to win any Academy Awards. Both, in fact, were totally forgettable — the kind of movies Hollywood was still cranking out by the dozens in those days. But the first of the two gave David Houston a timely boost in his career. It was called *Carnival Rock,* and it at least had some "name" actors in the cast, including Natalie Wood and William Conrad.

I had a bit part in the picture as an emcee at a nightclub, which didn't require much acting talent from me. David did a little singing, along with such well-known groups as the Platters, and Butch White, James Burton, and James Kirkland also had small roles.

We didn't kid ourselves about the quality of the finished product, but it was a new experience for all of us, and it was fun. We were flown from Shreveport to L.A. in a twin-engine Cessna, paid a good wage for not much work, and had all our expenses generously covered. One of the best parts was that the producers put us up at the Knickerbocker Hotel in Hollywood, where Elvis's band stayed when he was in town. It gave me a chance to see Elvis for the first time since his last big concert in Shreveport six months before, and I enjoyed catching up on his latest successes and conquests.

"I sure do like these Hollywood girls, Mr. Logan," he confided. "It's still hard for me to get over how, you know, how fast and loose they are."

"Faster and looser than the ones that used to buzz around you back at the Al-Ida Motel in Bossier City?" I teased.

He grinned at the memory. "I dunno," he said. "They're just different out here, that's all. They're, well, more glamorous, I guess you'd say, and they don't mind a bit lettin' you know what they want, either. Sometimes I do miss those shy little southern girls, though. I really do."

After our small parts in *Carnival Rock,* David and I were signed for minor roles in a low-budget western called *King of the Mountain.* This was one of those class D quickies that took a grand total of about three weeks to shoot. It was produced by a Shreveport businessman named Joy Houck who owned a large chain of drive-in theatres. The film was made exclusively for Houck's drive-ins and was never shown anywhere else. I never even saw the whole thing myself, but I'm sure I didn't miss much.

The main thing I remember about filming the picture was a scene where David sneaks up behind me and gets the drop on me, then jams a pistol barrel into my back. The scene ended in a big shootout, but I can't remember for sure if I was a good guy or a bad guy. Most of the people who saw the movie probably weren't sure, either.

In those days, though, the average ticket buyer at a drive-in movie was more interested in the girl he was with than what was on the screen, anyway. This was why Houck filmed quickies like *King of the Mountain* in the first place. Since the customers were too busy necking to know what they were watching, it was cheaper to produce his own movies than to pay the fat fees the major studios charged for theirs.

Still, this was my one-and-only chance to be a "movie star," and David and I had a great time hamming it up in front of the cameras.

To begin to understand what a big deal this first exposure to California was for Bob Luman and David, you've got to realize that neither of these guys had ever been within a thousand miles of Hollywood—or much of anywhere else, for that matter. They'd each had some success as recording artists and they'd performed for huge radio audiences, but they knew very little about the world outside of Louisiana and East Texas. They might've been as far from home as the Gulf of Mexico, but if they'd ever laid eyes on a real ocean before, you couldn't tell it. The first thing Bob Luman did when he saw the Pacific was run across the beach and straight into the surf, ruining an expensive pair of two-tone shoes in the process.

"The boys," as I called them, had also never brushed elbows with as many nationally famous people, either, as they met within their first few weeks in California. And they'd never encountered so many available girls or been exposed to so many forbidden pleasures.

They were really just kids. Bob and David were both only nineteen years old when we made those first trips to California. As a matter of fact, Bob celebrated his twentieth birthday during one of the trips. I remember him coming up to me that day with a really worried look on his face.

"I wanta ask you a favor, Mr. Logan," he said. There was a dead-serious tone in his voice.

"Okay, Bob," I said. "What's on your mind?"

"I sure would hate for these girls to find out I ain't a teenager anymore," he said. "They might start thinkin' I'm too old for 'em or somethin'."

"Well, don't worry," I assured him. "You're secret's safe with me."

I was close to twice the age of these young guys, but even a mature person like me could get a little carried away in circumstances like this. For a while there, I guess you could say we did a pretty good imitation of the *Beverly Hillbillies.*

I had a feeling we were in for trouble the very day we checked into the Knickerbocker for the first time. Luman and Houston started clowning around out by the swimming pool, which was next to the hotel's main lobby, and they ended up pushing each other into six feet of water with all their clothes on. They were giggling like idiots and looked like a couple of drowned rats when I finally got them on the elevator.

Maybe the most unforgettable thing they did, though, was getting us kicked out of two luxury hotels in the very same night.

Faron Young was visiting with us, and there was quite a party going on in our adjoining rooms at about one in the morning when the Knickerbocker security people and an assistant manager showed up and warned us to quiet down. We were having ourselves one helluva good time, but we were also keeping about a hundred other people awake.

"The other guests on this floor and the one below say it sounds like World War III's breaking out in here," the assistant manager said. "You're going to have to knock it off."

"Sorry," I told him, "we'll try to hold it down."

We had the best of intentions, but somehow it just didn't work out. Within ten or fifteen minutes, everybody was laughing and yelling again, and the music was loud enough to wake the dead. This time the security people practically had to beat the door down before we even heard them knocking.

Their message this time was short and to the point.

"Out," they said. "Get your stuff and get out. Right now."

We were all somewhat plastered, I have to admit, but I felt incredibly stupid, and at first the young guys seemed embarrassed, too. By the time they got downstairs, though, they were stifling their laughter. It was all they could do to keep from breaking up as we left through the deserted hotel lobby. At least I managed to keep everybody out of the swimming pool.

Any misconceptions I might have had about my young friends' willingness to clean up their act were quickly dispelled. We went over to the Hollywood Plaza a block or two away and checked in there. About an hour later, we got kicked out of that hotel, too.

I'm not sure where we spent the rest of that night. Fortunately, the Knickerbocker let us back in the next day after we promised to behave.

The situation was much different when I moved to California with the intention of staying. Accommodations at the Knicker-bocker weren't in the budget this time, and I moved my family — my wife, Mary; my two sons, Lee and Tommy; my daughter, Gale; and a pet parakeet named Toby Bird — into a small apartment in Santa Monica.

Within a few weeks, I was able to find two houses in a new de-velopment in Canoga Park that were available for rent. They were almost next door to each other, and I took one of them for my fam-ily and put the boys from the *Hayride* in the other one. It was a con-venient arrangement. I was close enough to keep an eye on the boys and see that they didn't get into too much trouble, but my family and I were still able to maintain our privacy.

While I appreciated the job that Fabor Robison had let me have with his company, I really didn't find it very satisfying. It was easy enough work, mostly just traveling around the area, talking to disc jockeys and other radio people and trying to promote Abbott records. But I missed being behind a microphone, either in front of a live audience or on the air. I immediately started looking for opportunities.

The boys and I did a number of guest shots on a popular Saturday night dance show called *Town Hall Party,* where we met some other young entertainers who were on their way to superstardom, including Ricky Nelson and Merle Travis. Legendary country singer Tex Ritter was also a regular on *Town Hall Party.*

These turned out to be productive associations for some of our *Hayride* expatriates. For example, our young bass player, James Kirkland, and pianist, James Burton, both joined Ricky Nelson's band later on, and Burton eventually got a job playing with Elvis.

Long Beach was a major center of interest for country music on the West Coast. I did a show for several months on a radio station in Long Beach and also hosted a Sunday afternoon TV show.

It was at the Long Beach Coliseum, incidentally, that Elvis and I appeared together on the same stage for the last time. I was a little surprised—and very flattered, too—when he asked me to emcee his show at the coliseum. At this point Elvis could've gotten any master of ceremonies he wanted, and I was virtually unknown in California, but Elvis invited me for old time's sake.

"I'd sure appreciate it if you could do it, Mr. Logan," he said. "It'll make me feel like I'm back on the *Hayride* again, and those were some of the happiest times of my life."

It was a fantastic experience, one I'll remember the rest of my life. For one thing, it was by far the largest live audience I ever faced in my career. The coliseum seated twenty-three thousand people, and the place was overflowing. If there was an empty seat in the house for that matinee performance, I couldn't see it. And all those seats were filled with girls. I don't remember seeing a single boy in that audience—just twenty-three thousand screaming, glassy-eyed females. It was a sight that defines description.

"Elvismania" was at its peak right then, and as if his fans weren't hysterical enough already, a publicity stunt the day before had them even more stirred up for this concert. As a gag, Elvis had been "arrested" for being too explicit with his body movements during his performances. I think every teenage girl in Long Beach was trying to get into that coliseum to see for herself just how "suggestive" his movements really were.

From my point of view, the whole thing was blown completely out of proportion. On the other hand, I never blamed Elvis for getting all the mileage he could out of the hullaballoo. In the entertainment business, if you've got a gimmick that works as well as this one did, you'd have to be stupid not to take advantage of it.

David Houston had his first serious romance while we were in California, and God only knows how many dogbites he suffered as a result.

I'd known David ever since he was twelve years old. That was when he'd first come to me and asked to audition for the *Hayride*. And behind all the boyish pranks and adolescent silliness, I knew there was genuine talent, keen intelligence, and a sensitive nature. That's why I'd put him on the *Hayride* when he was still in high school and told Tillman Franks I thought he had a solid future as an artist.

David was born and raised near Minden, Louisiana, and both his parents were interested in music. One of his father's closest friends was Gene Austin, the famous pop singer whose records of "My Blue Heaven," "Sleepy Time Gal," and "Five Foot Two, Eyes of Blue" took the nation by storm in the 1920s, and Austin saw talent in David when he was still just a toddler. He encouraged David's parents to start him on singing lessons when the kid was barely four.

In one of those peculiar twists of fate, Gene Austin's daughter, Charlotte, had moved to Hollywood a few years before David arrived on the West Coast. She was a promising young actress with several film roles to her credit when she and David happened to run into each other.

For David, it turned out to be a whole lot more than just the renewal of a childhood friendship. The fact that Charlotte was two or three years older than he was didn't keep him from falling for her, and falling hard.

David and the other boys couldn't afford cars of their own, so they were always bumming rides from me or asking to borrow one of my two vehicles. (At first I couldn't understand why they always seemed to prefer that old Nash of mine to my nicer, later-model Mercury, but then I figured it out. Among the Nash's most widely advertised features were seats that folded down into a double bed. Need I explain further?)

Anyway, David started pestering me almost every evening to take him over to the Hollywood Hills and drop him off at the little hillside bungalow where Charlotte lived.

It was fifty or sixty steep steps up the side of a bluff to the door of Charlotte's house, and David was always so anxious to see her that he'd charge up those steps as fast as he could. Before he was halfway to the top, he'd be met by Charlotte's ornery old German shepherd.

That dog was big and ugly enough to scare most people away at first sight, but David wouldn't ever let on that he was scared of him. The dog would grab hold of David's pants leg with his teeth and hang on for all he was worth. David couldn't shake him loose, so he'd just have to drag him the rest of the way. The boys and I would sit there in the car and laugh until tears came to our eyes at the sight of David pulling that shepherd up those steps. We used to make bets on how many steps David could make before the dog latched onto him.

I guess getting up there to be with Charlotte was worth it to David, but it happened the same way almost every time. You'd have thought the dog would get used to David sooner or later, but as far as I know he never did. There's no telling how many pairs of pants David ruined that way.

We had some laughs along the way, but in the end the California experience turned into a big washout for me. Instead of the new beginning I'd hoped for, it marked the end of the life I'd known up until that time.

It brought an end to my marriage, although that probably would've happened even if we'd never left Shreveport.

The West Coast adventure ended with one of the biggest disappointments — and worst decisions — of my adult life. I still feel like kicking myself when I think about it.

Texas-born singer/guitarist Buck Owens had a radio station in Bakersfield, and he offered me a job as station manager. The salary was excellent, but that was only the beginning. He also offered me a chance to acquire 49 percent of the stock in the station, plus shares in a music publishing company, a record company, and a promising Saturday night show.

"This situation was made for you, Hoss," Buck told me. "You've got the perfect personality and background for it. There's no way you can miss."

I liked Buck a lot — and still do. In addition to being a talented artist, he's also a prince of a guy. Regardless of my personal feelings about Buck, this was the best business opportunity I ever had, before or since. To this day, I firmly believe I'd be a millionaire right now if I'd taken it.

But there was trouble at home — extremely bad trouble.

My relationship with my wife had been deteriorating for quite a while. Even before the move to California, we hadn't been on the best of terms. She'd felt insecure and uncertain about the future, and my bouncing around among three or four different jobs didn't help any.

When I told her about the opportunity in Bakersfield and said I thought I should take it, matters suddenly came to a head. She said she'd had all of California she could stand. She wanted to go back to Louisiana, or at least someplace close to Louisiana, and if I wouldn't go with her, then she'd take the kids and go alone.

I'd seen this happen dozens of times in the past to friends and coworkers of mine — the inevitable clash between career and family. And I'd invariably seen marriages wrecked when guys insisted on putting their careers first. I'd turned down any number of other opportunities, including the chance to manage Elvis, for that very reason.

So I finally told Buck Owens no. It hurt like hell, but I made myself believe I was doing it to save my marriage. I was stupid. The marriage was already dead and just waiting to be buried, but I was too emotionally overwrought to realize it at the time.

In late 1958, I gave up on the California adventure. We loaded up our essential belongings and headed back east, retracing the same path we'd followed about nine months earlier. At the time, I had no job and no prospects. I was full of bitterness and resentment, but I was trying to do what my wife wanted.

I made it as far as Fort Worth, Texas. I decided to stop there overnight and check out the local employment situation. I didn't relish the idea of going all the way back to Shreveport with my tail between my legs.

The very next day I was hired as program director of radio station KCUL. A short time later, I met Ed McLemore, a promoter who owned a five-thousand seat tin barn called the Sportatorium near downtown Dallas. The Sportatorium was primarily a wrestling arena, but on Saturday nights it was also the site of the *Big D Jamboree* country music show. McLemore was looking for an emcee for the show, and he offered me the job.

I'd taken a roundabout route to get there, but I'd finally found another home.

{ 14 }

Casualties,
Survivors,
and Outlaws

What started as a spur-of-the-moment stopover in Fort Worth turned into a ten-year stay in the Dallas/Fort Worth area and one of the busiest, most demanding periods of my career.

My job on the *Big D Jamboree* was a lot different from what I'd been doing at the *Hayride.* My only responsibility was to get behind the mike, introduce the acts, and provide some continuity in between. Producing the show and lining up the talent was somebody else's responsibility, which made my job on the *Jamboree* easier. Part of the time the show was broadcast on KRLD radio, and it was even on TV for a while, but it was never carried by a national network, and that took some of the pressure off, too.

I found other ways to build up the pressure in my life, though— some of them enjoyable and some tormenting. My wife and I separated soon after we arrived, and I moved into an apartment that was close enough to allow me to see my kids regularly. But except for the time I spent with them, I kept myself buried in work. I know now that I did it intentionally, so I wouldn't have time to think about my personal life. Being on my own after so many years of family life was a tough transition for me.

Within a few months, I resigned as program director at KCUL and took a job at KPCN, a little station that broadcast from the suburb of Grand Prairie, Texas, halfway between Dallas and Fort Worth. At just 100 watts—the minimum the FCC allows for a commercial station—KPCN was among the least powerful radio voices in America. But instead of being located in some isolated podunk town like most of the other 100-watters, it was sitting almost exactly in the center of the most populous area in the Southwest and within range of more than a million listeners.

The staff was small but talented and energetic. It included Bill Mack, who went on to become a fixture at 50,000-watt WBAP in Fort Worth and one of the best-known country deejays in America. When Bill and I and the other staffers suddenly discovered that KPCN ranked number two in listeners in the whole Dallas/Fort Worth market, right behind KLIF, the 50,000-watt flagship of Gordon McLendon's broadcasting empire, we started taking ourselves more seriously.

We all worked hard to make KPCN the best country station in the market, and I put in a lot of long hours trying to figure out ways to keep us one step ahead of the competition. In addition to the *Big D Jamboree,* I also took on a couple of other part-time jobs, as the announcer for a motor speedway and a quarter horse racetrack.

With all due respect to Ed McLemore, who was a great guy and a good friend, the *Big D Jamboree* never measured up to the *Louisiana Hayride* in quality. It never created any major stars, and that was never its intention. It was designed to make money, and it did that very well for many years. It copied the idea of the *Hayride* to some extent, but in variety and originality it never compared to the show in Shreveport.

The thing I liked most about the *Jamboree* was that it allowed me to stay in touch with many of the artists I'd helped get established on the *Hayride.* It also gave me a chance to work with some top country stars that had never played the *Hayride* as well as an occasional promising newcomer on the way up.

One of the best of those newcomers wasn't really so new at all. He'd been kicking around the music business for years as a deejay and part-time country singer, then as a bass guitarist in Ray Price's band, then as one of Nashville's most successful songwriters. Several of the songs he'd written had turned into top-ten hits for other artists—like "Crazy" for Patsy Cline and "Hello Walls" for Faron Young.

When I first met him, though, his own singing career was at such a standstill that he was trying to earn some extra money as a carpet installer's helper. As a matter of fact, the first time I ever laid eyes on him, he'd just been fired by the carpet company he was working for. They said he spent more time jotting down the lyrics for country songs than he did nailing down tack strips.

His name, by the way, was Willie Nelson.

By the time he showed up on the *Big D Jamboree* in 1961, Willie had a contract with Liberty Records and a couple of his singles had made the national charts. He was also playing regularly at the Longhorn Ballroom, the biggest country nightclub in Texas at the time. The Longhorn's owner, Dewey Groom, had taken a liking to Willie's singing and given him one of his biggest breaks so far. But Willie still wasn't setting the world on fire as a singer. He had an odd, whispery, irregular singing style that backup musicians had a hard time following until they got used to it.

Willie didn't really become famous until he changed his singing style, but I always thought his early stuff was unique, and I loved it. I would've put him on the *Hayride* in a New York minute if there'd still been a *Hayride*.

Another thing that held Willie back as a performer was his natural shyness. He'd been raised by his grandparents on a farm near the little Central Texas town of Abbott, and he had an inbred love for the peace and quiet of the countryside. He got married when he was about twenty years old and for a while he thought of becoming a farmer himself. He was uncomfortable in crowded cities and the glare of the spotlight, especially when he was just starting out as a musician. But he also had a deep inner strength and lots of faith in his own abilities. Those qualities pulled him through some rough times.

"I always thought I could sing pretty good," Willie recalled after he'd established himself as one of the century's most innovative forces in country music, "and it kinda bothered me that nobody else thought so. I guess I was into a lot of negative thinking back then. I did a lot of bad things, got in fights with people, got divorced, all that stuff. My head was just pointed the wrong way, you know."

Being an intelligent, introspective person, Willie did a lot of reading—much of it deep philosophical stuff. It helped him develop more confidence and a more positive attitude.

In 1962, he scored with two top-ten singles. "Touch Me," his own composition, climbed all the way to number one on the country charts, and he followed it up with "Willingly," a duet with Shirley Collie, which also did very well. These successes brought him his first big flurry of major show dates, including several weeks in Las Vegas, and by late 1964, he was a regular on the *Grand Ole Opry.*

He had several other big hits over the next few years, including "The Party's Over," "Blackjack County Chain," and "Little Things." But it was only after he turned his back on Nashville in disillusionment in 1972 and moved back to Texas that Willie really found himself as an artist. He signed with Columbia records, and they gave him total control over his material. The result was a blockbuster single, "Blue Eyes Cryin' in the Rain." Then, after his first Columbia album, *Red-Headed Stranger,* went platinum, Willie formed his own Lone Star label and just used CBS as his distributor.

But his revolt against the rigid Nashville power structure was even more important than Willie's personal success to the history and direction of country music over the last quarter of the twentieth century. Up until the "outlaw" movement spearheaded by Willie and Waylon Jennings, the big recording studios in Nashville had always been able to dictate the style that every successful country artist followed. Before that, all the big names had to come to Nashville to make their records, and they either conformed to the so-called "Nashville sound," or else.

WSM, the *Opry*, and the recording studios dominated everything. It was one big clique, and unless you were in it, you were out of luck.

Willie had the talent — and the guts — to change all that. He was the first major star to defy this trend. What he and the other "outlaws" staged was a rebellion in the strictest sense of the word. When it was over, Nashville's stranglehold on country music had been broken. For the first time, innovative artists were free to play and sing — and sell — music that didn't fit the narrow Nashville norms.

Without this revolution, the public might never have had a chance to hear today's "new country" sounds and styles. The George Straits, Reba McEntires, and Garth Brookses of this world owe a tremendous debt of gratitude to Willie Nelson.

Speaking of gratitude, Willie never forgot anybody who offered him a boost while he was struggling up the lower rungs on the ladder of success. He's one of the most unselfish guys I've ever known, and thousands of people have benefited in one way or another from Willie's generosity. But if you gave him a helping hand back when he needed it most, Willie always made sure he returned the favor.

I can't tell you how many times over the years Willie asked me to emcee one of his shows when he was appearing in my part of the country. One reason is that we're friends, but I think another reason is that I gave him some warm, sincere introductions on the *Big D Jamboree* in the days when few people had heard of Willie Nelson.

Before the late Dewey Groom retired and sold the Longhorn Ballroom several years ago, the old club that had once been one of the most glamorous nightspots in the Southwest went through some pretty lean times. Dewey could no longer afford to book the big-name acts for his dwindling clientele. On most nights a hundred or two regulars would sit around the big dance floor with their brown bags and setups and listen to Dewey and his house band play. But once every few months, Willie Nelson's name would go up on the marquee outside. When it did, of course, the crowds would once more descend on the nineteen-hundred-seat Longhorn, and Dewey would have himself one helluva payday for a change.

One day in the early eighties, when Willie was getting up to 55,000 dollars for personal appearances, I asked him how Dewey could possibly afford to book someone of his stature.

"Back when I didn't have two coins to rub together and really needed some work, he'd always make a spot for me at the Longhorn — and he always paid me, too," Willie said. "I stay pretty busy these days, but whenever Dewey Groom wants me, I'll be there. And I'll play for whatever he can afford."

Once they get to be headliners, some folks are quick to forget the favors and good turns that came their way when they were only footnotes. Willie's one of the best of the good guys with long memories, but he's not the only one. I've known any number of other performers who kept right on being human beings even after they got rich and famous.

Another one that stands out in my mind is Ernest Tubb. Country music never produced a more enduring star, but as big as Ernest got, he never lost sight of his humble beginnings. He always remembered those who helped him along the way, especially Jimmie Rodgers's widow, Carrie, who opened doors for him that might otherwise have remained closed and locked forever. In later years, Ernest did likewise for dozens of struggling young artists.

He used his *Midnight Jamboree* radio show, which immediately followed the *Opry* on WSM, to promote many a kid who was just starting out — including Elvis Presley. It was Ernest's influence with the *Opry* brass more than anything else that persuaded them to give Elvis his one tryout on the *Opry*.

In his forty-plus years as an *Opry* star, Ernest became as much a permanent fixture as Minnie Pearl or Roy Acuff. Understandably, he never once set foot on the *Hayride* stage, but after I moved to the *Big D Jamboree*, he was on the Dallas show quite a bit. I considered him a prince of a guy and a good friend, but I don't know of anyone who ever came in contact with him that didn't feel the same way about him.

One Saturday night in the early sixties, there were five thousand people packed into the Sportatorium to see Ernest and his Texas Troubadors, and my heart sank when I got a telegram saying that he and several members of his band had come down with the flu in San Antonio and couldn't make it to Dallas.

Everyone in the audience groaned when I read the telegram aloud. I said if any of them didn't want to see anyone but Ernest Tubb that night, we'd gladly refund their money, but I assured them we had other quality acts, including Tony Douglas, coming in to fill in. In the end, only twenty-six out of the crowd of five thousand actually took me up on the refund offer.

About two months later, we booked Ernest on the *Jamboree* again, and this time he showed up bright and early and in good health.

"This one's on the house, Logan," he told me. "I want to make up for that problem I caused you the last time."

"But we couldn't ask you to do that, Ernest," I said. "What happened before was unavoidable — just one of those things. Everybody here that night understood. Nobody was mad at you."

"Doesn't matter," he said. "I wouldn't feel right taking Mr. McLemore's money under the circumstances. Like I said, it's on the house."

After the show, I tried again to get him to reconsider, but he wouldn't accept a cent. To him, it was a matter of personal honor.

In a business often characterized by vicious backstabbing and almost unrealistic jealousy, it's easy to assume that everybody's out for himself and doesn't give a damn about anybody else. But my experiences in the business over more than half a century have proven that isn't true.

Several others stand out in my memory for their generosity and genuine concern for others. As I've mentioned before, Webb Pierce often went out of his way to help youngsters who were just starting out. So did Tex Ritter. While we were in California, Tex took Bob Luman and David Houston under his wing and freely used his influence and contacts to add momentum to their careers.

Merle Kilgore also belongs on my list of good guys. Merle joined the *Hayride* while he was still in high school — Byrd High School, my alma mater in Shreveport, to be exact — and was a regular in our cast for years. Since then, he's not only attained stardom as a singer and written some of the most memorable songs in the history of country music, but he's also lent encouragement to a lot of young artists and helped several superstars over some rough spots, too. Today, as Hank Williams Jr.'s manager, he's helping guide the career of one of the greatest country stars of all time.

All told, I've known at least as many princes as frogs in country music, and I'm sure my good guy list could go on for several more pages. But the point is, some folks never forget a favor while others always seem to be looking for the next one.

It's never been hard for me to decide which one of those two kinds of people I'd rather be around.

Many of the friends and coworkers who shared the *Louisiana Hayride* stage with me forty or fifty years ago have now passed from this earthly scene. It saddens me to think that as many members of the old *Hayride* "family" are dead as alive today. Every loss leaves a void inside that can't be filled.

Bob Luman was only forty-one when he died of pneumonia in December 1978. He'd come down with a throat infection that put him in bed for several days, then insisted on getting up too soon and going out duck hunting. He made his last appearance on the *Opry* on December 16. A week and a half later, he was dead. Johnny Cash sang at his funeral, and Ralph Emery delivered the eulogy.

David Houston was killed by a cerebral hemorrhage that struck him like a bolt out of the blue in November 1993. He was still in his fifties and looked to be in perfect health.

Lefty Frizzell, who was already a well-established artist and songwriter with a string of hit records to his credit when he joined the *Hayride* for several months, died of a massive stroke in Nashville in 1975 at the age of fifty-seven. Lefty wrote or cowrote and recorded many major hits of the fifties including "Always Late," "I Want to Be with You Always," "Look What Thoughts Will Do," and "Mom and Dad's Waltz." But he was most fondly remembered on the *Hayride* for "flubbing" a line in his top-ten 1950 hit, "If You've Got the Money, Honey, I've Got the Time." He was on a portion of the show sponsored by Jax Beer, and we thought it'd be clever if he'd change a line that said "dance, drink beer and wine" to "dance, drink Jax, it's fine." He consistently failed to do it, though, and it frustrated him. Once he stopped right in the middle of the song, turned to me and yelled, "Doggone, it, Hoss, I forgot it again!"

Red Sovine died of a sudden heart attack in 1980, shortly after being honored by *Cash Box* magazine as America's Top Recitation Performer. Webb Pierce died in 1991 after a bout with cancer. Faron Young took his own life in late 1996. Bill Black, whose musical skills played a key—and largely unappreciated—role in Elvis's early success, was still in his thirties when he died in 1965. Drugs and alcohol reportedly were major contributors to his death.

And then, of course, there was the tragedy of Elvis himself.

I saw the "King" in Monroe just over a year before his death in August 1977. Although I spent only a few minutes with him, I remember him being as polite and courteous as ever. But except for that, he bore very little resemblance to the shy, eager kid from Memphis I had introduced to the nation in 1954. He was grossly overweight under his sequined suit. His body was bloated and his face was puffy and pale. There was a tired look in his eyes. He seemed detached and preoccupied.

I thought I detected a tremor in his hand as I shook it, and I couldn't help thinking about how Hank Williams had looked and acted during the last few months of his life. It was almost like see-ing a ghost.

"Y'know, sometimes I wish I could go back to those days on the *Hayride* and do it all over again," Elvis said.

"You think it'd be as much fun the second time around?" I asked.

"Maybe not," he said, "but there's a lotta things I might do dif-ferent if I had a second chance."

No other performer of this century had as great an impact on popular music and the American public in general as Elvis had — at least that's my opinion. But as a human being, he wasn't all that different from countless other performers who let the pressures and frantic pace of show business drag them into a maze of drugs and booze and doom them to an early death.

In Elvis's case, the problem was magnified by the seductive in-fluences of Hollywood and its atmosphere of make believe and un-reality. Elvis made tens of millions of dollars out of the movies, but they exacted a terrible price from him in return. It's easy to see now that Elvis always had latent health problems. Heart disease ran in his family, and he had a tendency toward overweight that was ag-gravated by his addiction to junk food.

But the drug habit that killed him started in Hollywood. I'm convinced of that. As long as he was associated with the *Hayride,* I never saw him take a pill of any kind or give any indication that he was under the influence of drugs. Yet during the last seven months of his life, his habit reportedly led him to swallow nearly fifty-seven hundred pills — uppers, downers, painkillers, and God knows what else. There were also claims that he was addicted to cocaine and heroin.

When I learned Elvis was dead, my reaction was total shock. I'd heard all the rumors about how he was destroying himself, and I'd seen with my own eyes how bad he'd looked some thirteen months earlier. He was forty-two years old, but I could still close my eyes and see him as a nervous nineteen-year-old kid pacing the aisles of the Municipal Auditorium in Shreveport.

Just as he was the ultimate entertainer, Elvis is also the ultimate symbol of all the tragedies that tore so many of the great artists away from us while they were still in the prime of life or at the peak of their careers. I still grieve for the others, too.

Hank Williams always seems to come to mind first. Then Johnny Horton. Then Jim Reeves and Dean Manuel. The list lengthens out from there to take in other lost stars, people who weren't necessarily connected with the *Hayride,* but who were struck down violently and long before their time. Patsy Cline. Buddy Holly. Rick Nelson. The list goes on.

Making music has always been a risky business, but there was a lot more physical danger attached to it in the forties, fifties and sixties than there is today. To make their next show dates, hundreds of dog-tired, bleary-eyed entertainers drove through the wee hours of the morning at high speeds on narrow, two-lane highways. To get where they had to be, they jumped onto small planes and flew off into rain and fog and snow where ordinary people would never have ventured. Day after day, they kept up a furious, relentless pace, grabbing rest and meals when they could, using pills to wake up, pills to go to sleep and alcohol to uncoil the knots inside them.

When you stop to think about the kind of lives they led, the remarkable thing isn't that so many of them died. It's that so many managed to survive.

When I heard about the plane crash that killed Jim Reeves and Dean Manuel, I was doing a two-hour morning show on KPCN, and the next day I devoted the whole time to what I believe was a unique Jim Reeves tribute. I got together as many of his records as I could find, then started with the oldest of them and worked forward to his latest hits.

In between, I talked about my friendship with him and how he developed from just another radio announcer into one of America's great singers, and I let the records themselves illustrate how Jim had perfected his voice and style from year to year and song to song. Out of respect for Jim, there wasn't a single commercial break or interruption during the whole two hours. I think Jim would've been pleased with the presentation.

There've been many times in my life when I've felt a touch of envy for some of the performers I've worked with. Part of me was just enough of an extroverted hambone that I would've loved to be a singing star and recording artist. But I had enough sense to know I didn't have any talent for singing. My talent was mainly in being able to spot other people's talent.

That morning as I sat there playing one Jim Reeves record after another, I had no regrets at all about how my own career had gone. A couple of days earlier, if somebody had offered me a chance to trade lives with Jim, I just might've taken them up on it.

But if I had, I thought, it would've been Jim Reeves, radio announcer, sitting here playing records by Hoss Logan, recording star. And I'd be lying dead out on some mountainside.

It was the kind of thought that makes you realize how fortunate you are when some of your wishes *don't* come true.

Even while I mourn the casualties that have depleted our ranks, I cherish and celebrate the survivors. How much more tragic would the country music story be if Johnny Cash hadn't managed to pull himself back from the brink of death? Or if George Jones hadn't found the courage to confront and defeat the personal demons that tried to end his career and his life?

The living artists whose energy and talents enriched the *Hayride* are now scattered far and wide across the whole continent, and even beyond. I've lost touch with some of them, but I've maintained at least occasional contact with many others, enough to know they're still alive and kicking. I think about them almost every day: Johnny and George. Kitty Wells and Johnny Wright. Billy Walker and Jimmy Newman. Merle Kilgore and Hank Locklin. Scotty

Moore and D. J. Fontana. Floyd Cramer and Slim Whitman. Mac Wiseman and Tibby Edwards. Hoot Raines and Curley Herndon. Goldie Hill and Ginny Wright. Sonny James and the Browns. Claude King and Felton Pruett and Bill Carlisle.

What a gang they were, and what a time we had!

{ 15 }

It Was One

Helluva Ride!

After an absence of more than a dozen years, I came home to Louisiana in the fall of 1971. I was considerably older — and I hope a little wiser — than when I left.

Ed McLemore, the promoter who singlehandedly created the *Big D Jamboree* and had run it since its inception, had died a couple of years earlier, and the *Jamboree* had almost immediately died, too. Life in the big city had lost much of its appeal for me, anyway. My three oldest children were out of school and grown by now, and my fourth child — a daughter named Cassandra — had gone to live in France with her mother, my second wife, following our divorce. I was ready for a change of scene and maybe a little slower pace.

By the time of McLemore's death, changing musical tastes and trends, plus the emergence of the Dallas/Fort Worth Metroplex as one of the nation's largest and fastest-growing urban centers, were already cutting deeply into the *Jamboree*'s popularity and attendance. Top-name country artists were no longer that interested in playing in a drafty old tin barn like the Sportatorium, anyway — not when they could book shows at the new Dallas Convention Center or Six Flags Over Texas or other more comfortable, attractive facilities.

Anyway, in early seventy-one I'd pulled up stakes and headed for Florida, but it didn't take long for me to realize I'd made a mistake, and that's when I heard Louisiana calling me. My father was getting along in years, and his health was starting to fail, so I decided to move back to my hometown of Monroe to take care of him as best I could. As I'd done before, I made the move without any solid prospects of employment, but once again I hit it lucky. Within a few days after I got there, I landed a very good job as station manager of radio station KREB, where the country music format made me feel right at home.

On a smaller scale, I was able to repeat at KREB what my staff and I had done at KPCN in Dallas/Fort Worth. Within a short time, KREB was ranked number-one in the seven-station Monroe market, a position it held onto continuously for years to come.

I got so comfortable in Monroe that I stayed for twenty-four years. I also got married again (I tell my present wife, Linda, that it took me three tries at marriage to find the right woman, and it's true) and my life settled into a pleasant, predictable routine. But finally, in 1995, Linda and I came to the decision that it was time once again to move on. We gave up our spacious home in Monroe and went to live in a small cottage in the little town of Seadrift on the Texas Gulf Coast.

Except for taping occasional commercials, I don't do any radio work to speak of anymore. I spend much of my time engraving fine guns for other people—a long-standing hobby that's become a profitable avocation for me. I also fish a lot (I wish Johnny Horton could see the string of redfish I brought in the other day). Occasionally, we travel a little. Other times, I just loaf.

But regardless of what I'm doing, the *Louisiana Hayride* is never far from my thoughts. I've carried it with me from the Pacific to the Atlantic and to every place I've paused in between.

It's still part of me, even after all these years—and I wouldn't have it any other way.

Part of me realizes it's been fifty years since the *Hayride*'s first performance, but another part of me keeps saying, "How could that be possible? It seems like only yesterday."

When I close my eyes and let my thoughts drift back, a half-century can disappear instantly. I can see Hank Williams puffing a cigarette and strumming his guitar on a bus heading somewhere. I can see Elvis Presley pacing and fidgeting backstage and pausing to comb his oily hair. I can see Johnny Horton sitting still as a ghost in a fishing boat on the glassy surface of Caddo Lake. I can hear Slim Whitman hitting a high note and Johnny Cash hitting a low note. I can hear Red Sovine doing a recitation and Kitty Wells laughing at something Johnny Wright just said. I can hear the roar of the crowd as the house band breaks into the *Hayride* theme song.

It's all there, locked in my head. I know it'll be there as long as I keep breathing. To me, the *Louisiana Hayride* is still very much alive, and I'm sure tens of thousands of other folks feel the same way. The *Hayride* entertained millions of Americans and helped brighten and enrich their lives. Its memory deserves to survive forever, or at least as long as people continue to sing and listen to country songs.

That's why it's been exciting and gratifying to hear about recent efforts being made in Shreveport by several of my old friends and associates to establish a permanent *Louisiana Hayride* museum in the Municipal Auditorium. In my opinion, this is something that should have been done years ago. Back in the mid-1980s, while I was still living in Monroe, I tried very hard to interest Shreveport community leaders in this same idea. At the time, I didn't have much success, but with 1998 marking the fiftieth anniversary of the *Hayride*'s birth, maybe it's finally the right moment for a fitting, lasting tribute to the show and the people who made it possible. I hope so.

Tillman Franks and Frank Page are both actively involved in this effort, and I wish them all the luck in the world. Both of them still live in Shreveport, and, in fact, Frank still works for KWKH, which dropped its country music format years ago and is now an all-talk station.

Setting up a *Louisiana Hayride* museum won't be an easy task. It's been nearly forty years since the show ended its run of every-Saturday-night performances, and a lot of irreplaceable memorabilia has been lost in the meantime. But I know that many of the surviving members of the cast would gladly contribute to the effort. I certainly would. The *Hayride*'s contribution to American music is simply too vital to let it be forgotten.

On a more practical note, a *Hayride* museum could be an important tourist attraction and a major economic asset for Shreveport. I can even envision an annual *Louisiana Hayride* festival that would bring big-name performers and thousands of country music fans to the city each spring. The new hotels and casinos would benefit tremendously from this type of event, and I think they'd support it wholeheartedly.

If it happens, you can be sure I'll be there—and I'll bring my memories with me.

Over the years, I've been asked more times than I can count to pick out the *Hayride*'s single "greatest moment," but I've never been able to do it. Elvis's debut and Hank Williams's seven-encore farewell performance both come to mind, of course, but there were countless other moments of greatness, too.

In my judgment, what really made the *Hayride* great—and made the whole experience a priceless treasure for me—can't be measured in moments or brief flashes. It was a long, involved process that stretched over months and years. It was finding and presenting one new talent after another, followed by the honing and polishing of that talent. It was the steady, ongoing effort of hungry young artists that carried them from nowhere to the top of the charts. Sometimes it happened in a matter of weeks. Other times it took years.

This was the essence of the *Hayride*'s greatness, and I was fortunate enough to be there to see it and be part of it.

It awes me to think of the talent the *Hayride* introduced and the trends in modern music that it launched. It amazes me to remember standing on the same stage—only a few feet away—when Hank, Elvis, Johnny Cash, Johnny Horton, Jim Reeves, Webb Pierce,

Slim Whitman, Faron Young, and so many others made themselves known to America for the first time.

The parallels between Hank and Elvis are incredible. Both grew up dirt-poor and deprived. Both became stars with shocking suddenness. Both found far more misery than fulfillment in success. Both were idolized by millions. Both died of their own self-inflicted excesses. And both left a permanent mark on popular music.

I don't mean to imply that they were the only *Hayride* stars who left that kind of mark. In his own way, Johnny Cash has had as much influence on musical styles as either Hank or Elvis. The difference is, Johnny's still alive and still performing. The fact that both Elvis and Hank died young and tragically undoubtedly added to their status as cult heroes and tended to transform their fans into worshippers. But a hundred years from now, I firmly believe that their contributions to our musical culture will still be recognized as fully and widely as they are today—maybe even more so.

Fate allowed me to be in the right place at the right time to be a friend, advisor, and confidant to both of these larger-than-life individuals. I consider it an overwhelming honor, as well as a distinction that nobody else in the world shares, at least to my knowledge. I'll always be grateful for that unique opportunity, although it still makes me shake my head in wonder sometimes.

The *Louisiana Hayride*—the "Cradle of the Stars"—was the magic vehicle that made it all possible. Without the *Hayride* and all the hundreds of people who worked so hard to keep making it special and different, none of it would've ever happened.

It was, indeed, one helluva ride—and I thank everyone who helped keep the wheels turning. God bless you all.

Artists and Bands

That Appeared on the

Louisiana Hayride

Note: This list does not include musicians who performed as sidemen in the various bands.

Betty Amos and the Lump Boys
Buddy Attaway
Gene Autry
Bailes Brothers
Benny Barnes
Sammy Barnhart
Clyde Baum and the Bayou Boys
Tom Beardon and the Rhythm Harmoneers
Carl Belew
Eddie Bond
Gene Bradley
Carolyn Bradshaw
Douglas Bragg
Elton Britt
Blondie Brooks
The Browns
Gary Bryant
Aunt Bunie
Smiley Burnette
James Burton

Buzz Busby
The Carlisles
Kitty Carson
Fred Carter
Johnny Cash
Chelette Sisters
Circle 6 Ranch Boys
Zeke Clements
Pappy Covington
Riley Crabtree
Floyd Cramer
Blackie Crawford
T. Tommy Cutrer
Don Davis
Jimmie Davis
Link Davis
Davis Sisters
Jimmy Day
Deep South Quartet
The Delta Boys
Dub Dickerson
Tony Douglas
Arlie Duff
Buddy and Marian Durham
Bob Eaton
Tibby Edwards
Cousin Emmy
Melvin Endsley
Werly Fairburn
D. J. Fontana
Jack Ford
Four Deacons
The Four Diamonds
Curly Fox

Artists and Bands that Appeared on the Louisana Hayride

Lefty Frizzell
Bobby Gallion
The Geezinslaw Brothers
Barney Grant
Marshall Grant
Rudy Grayzel
Tex Grimsley and the Texas Playboys
Preacher Harkness
Dale Hawkins
Jeanette Hicks
Goldie Hill
Tommy Hill
The Hired Hands
Hoot & Curley
Johnny Horton
David Houston
Van Howard
Jack Hunt and the Rhythm Ranchhands
Autry Inman
Shot Jackson
Sonny James
Johnny and Jack
Dobber Johnson
Johnny Johnson and the Carolina Sunshine Girls
George Jones
Oakie Jones
Jerry Kennedy
Doug Kershaw
Rusty Kershaw
Merle Kilgore
Claude King
Curley Kinsey and the Tennessee Ridge Runners
James Kirkland
Sleepy La Beef

Artists and Bands that Appeared on the <u>Louisana</u> <u>Hayride</u>

Martha Lawson
Jimmy Lee
Hank Locklin
Bob Luman
Martha and Lucy Lynn
Maddox Brothers & Rose
Johnny Mathis
Clayton McMitchum and his band
Mercer Brothers
Charlie Monroe
Ken Montana
Patsy Montana
Clyde Moody
Scotty Moore
Moon Mullican
Jimmy Newman
James O'Gwynne
Leon Payne
Carl Perkins
Luther Perkins
Webb Pierce
Elvis Presley
Felton Pruett
Wayne Rainey
Rangers Quartet
Jim Reeves
Tex Ritter
Rowley Trio
Tommy Sands
Bob and Joe Shelton and the Sunshine Boys
Jean Shepard
Harmie Smith
Warren Smith
Eddie Snell

Artists and Bands that Appeared on the Louisana Hayride

Socko Sokolosky
Southern Valley Boys
Red Sovine
Stanley Brothers
Texas Bill Strength
King Sterling
Al Terry
Texas Lil
Texas Ruby
Rufus Thibodeaux
Buddy Thompson
Hank Thompson and his Brazos Valley Boys
Mel Tillis
Floyd Tillman
Tommy Tomlinson
Mitchell Torok
Sonny Trammel
Tommy Trent
Zeb Turner
T. Texas Tyler
Billy Walker
Billy Wallace
Kitty Wells
Butch White
Slim Whitman
Cousin Wilbur
Wilburn Brothers
Slim Willett
Curley Williams and Georgia Peach Pickers
Hank Williams
Willis Brothers
Smiley Wilson
Mac Wiseman
Boots Woodall and His Band

Artists and Bands that Appeared on the Louisana Hayride

Sheb Wooley
Ginny Wright
Faron Young
York Brothers

Index

Index